THE
GREATEST
STORY
EVER SOLD

THE PENGUIN PRESS

New York · 2006

THE

GREATEST

STORY

EVER SOLD

THE DECLINE AND FALL OF TRUTH

FROM 9/11 TO KATRINA

FRANK RICH

THE PENGUIN PRESS
Published by the Penguin Group
Penguin Group (USA) Inc., 375 Hudson Street, New York, New York 10014,
U.S.A. • Penguin Group (Canada), 90 Eglinton Avenue East, Suite 700,
Toronto, Ontario, Canada M4P 2Y3 (a division of Pearson Penguin Canada
Inc.) • Penguin Books Ltd, 80 Strand, London WC2R 0RL, England •
Penguin Ireland, 25 St. Stephen's Green, Dublin 2, Ireland (a division of
Penguin Books Ltd) • Penguin Books Australia Ltd, 250 Camberwell Road,
Camberwell, Victoria 3124, Australia (a division of Pearson Australia Group
Pty Ltd) • Penguin Books India Pvt Ltd, 11 Community Centre,
Panchsheel Park, New Delhi–110 017, India • Penguin Group (NZ),
Cnr Airborne and Rosedale Roads, Albany, Auckland 1310, New Zealand
(a division of Pearson New Zealand Ltd) • Penguin Books (South Africa)
(Pty) Ltd, 24 Sturdee Avenue, Rosebank, Johannesburg 2196, South Africa

Penguin Books Ltd, Registered Offices:
80 Strand, London WC2R 0RL, England

First published in 2006 by The Penguin Press,
a member of Penguin Group (USA) Inc.

Copyright © Frank Rich, 2006
All rights reserved

ISBN 1-59420-098-X

Printed in the United States of America

1   3   5   7   9   10   8   6   4   2

DESIGNED BY AMANDA DEWEY

*With love and gratitude
to the strongest alliance of all,
my axis of family—
Alex, Nathaniel, and Simon*

CONTENTS

INTRODUCTION

O N THAT CRISP blue Tuesday morning I got the news, as most did, by phone. It was my sister-in-law calling from her office in midtown Manhattan. She and her husband lived a block from the World Trade Center. "We're okay," she said. "What are you talking about?" I asked. "Turn on the television," she said.

Thus began a day unlike any other that Americans of post–Pearl Harbor generations had seen. In my shock, the only analogue I could summon was the assassination of President Kennedy, which happened on a similarly placid day, a Friday afternoon, when I was a junior high school student in Washington, D.C. Then, as on September 11, 2001, we knew we were experiencing some great yet, at some fundamental level, incomprehensible national trauma. Then, too, you could pick up the phone and not get a dial tone. Then, too, life in the foreground shifted into slow motion—if it was stirring at all—while the grave murmur of the network anchors continued without pause in the background. Then, too, we had to awaken to the reality that our country and our lives were in the hands of a Texas politician who up to that moment had not been counted among the more inspiring or impressive American leaders.

But there were some differences. We'd never before seen colossal towers with thousands of people in them—perhaps people we knew—collapse into dust in real time before our eyes. When my wife and I briefly turned away from the TV screen to look out of our window, we saw the chilling sight of military aircraft hovering over the Hudson River. That was something else we hadn't seen before. We didn't have to be told we were at war.

The enemy, though long hiding in plain sight, was one about which we knew scarcely more than we did about Lee Harvey Oswald. We knew just enough to be afraid.

Although 9/11 was not yet known by that linguistic shorthand, it was a new morning in America—a wake-up call, you'd think, for a country that had become habituated to peace and prosperity and had had the luxury of devoting several years to obsessing about a president's seamy sex life. But whatever else 9/11 was, we can see now that it was the beginning of a new national narrative—a compelling and often persuasive story that was told by the president of the United States and his administration to mobilize a shell-shocked country desperate to be led. The story was often at variance with the facts that were known at the time, let alone with the facts that have come to light since. But it did have a slick patina of plausibility—the element that the satirical television talking head Stephen Colbert would later label "truthiness." The story was effective enough to take America into a war against a nation that did not attack it on 9/11.

This book is not intended to be a harangue about George W. Bush or the war in Iraq, though my views will certainly be evident. What it is instead is a critical retracing of the sophisticated steps by which some clever people in the White House, handed an opportunity and a mandate by the shocking events of 9/11, unfurled a brilliantly produced scenario to accomplish a variety of ends, the most unambiguous of which was to amass power and hold on to it. While the controversial policy choices made by the Bush administration are well known, equally important is the way it dramatized its fable to the nation and made it credible to so many, even when it wasn't remotely true. The chronicle of how a government told and sold its story is also, inevitably, a chronicle of an American culture that was an all-too-easy mark for the flimflam.

The synergistic intersection between that culture and the Bush administration's narrative is a significant piece of the puzzle. Only an overheated 24/7 infotainment culture that had trivialized the very idea of reality (and with it, what once was known as "news") could be so successfully manipulated by those in power. In an earlier America, it would have been far harder for a White House to get away with so many hollow spectacles and misleading public statements for as long as it did. When future Americans look back on this period and ask, "How did this happen?" the cultural context of the early twenty-first century may explain at least as much as the characters and official actions that played out against that backdrop.

The scenario unfolds in two acts. Part I, "Making the Sale," retraces the elaborate propagandistic stagecraft with which the Bush administration rolled out and prosecuted the war in Iraq, and which reached its crescendo with the president's triumphant declaration that "major combat operations" had ended on May 1, 2003. Though the events recounted are of recent vintage, looking back on them even at this early date sometimes resembles a stop-action replay of a train wreck. Yet that wreck might have been averted: it's striking how many clues to the administration's subterfuge were plainly visible in the months before the war. Part II, "Buyer's Remorse," tells how that story literally and figuratively sprang leaks, culminating in the catastrophe of Hurricane Katrina, which, four years after 9/11, wreaked havoc on what was left of the Bush administration's credibility following the calamity of Iraq. It was then that Bush's approval ratings fell into the 30s, never, as of this writing, to rise out of them for any sustained period of time. In the appendix, readers will find two time lines of the central dates in this tale: crucial events and public remarks leading up to and through the war in Iraq are presented in juxtaposition to relevant events that were taking place behind the scenes in Washington but would be illuminated only much later, by journalistic enterprise, official inquiries, and the special counsel Patrick Fitzgerald's investigation into the leaked identity of the CIA officer Valerie Plame Wilson.

In what may have been the single most revealing paragraph anyone has reported about the Bush administration, the author Ron Suskind, writing in *The New York Times Magazine* two weeks before the 2004 election, recounted a conversation with a presidential aide who spoke sarcastically of journalists and their "reality-based community." The aide, who sounded uncannily like Karl Rove, informed Suskind with great condescension that a "judicious study of discernible reality" is "not the way the world really works anymore." The aide explained: "We're an empire now, and when we act, we create our own reality.

And while you're studying that reality—judiciously, as you will—we'll act again, creating other new realities, which you can study too, and that's how things will sort out. We're history's actors . . . and you, all of you, will be left to just study what we do."

What follows is one reality-based observer's study—judicious, I hope—of how those fictional realities were created and how they came undone when actual reality, whether in Iraq or at home, became just too blatant to be ignored.

PART ONE

MAKING THE SALE

ONE

"HOME TO THE HEARTLAND"

T HE SUMMER OF 2001 had been one of national torpor, with some cheap entertainment for spice. The still-novice president was vacationing in Crawford, Texas, but he was hardly the only American gone fishing. In New York, the tabloids whipped up a frenzy about the legal travails of a marginal but conspicuously wealthy thirty-year-old show-business publicist, Lizzie Grubman, who in an apparent fit of impatience had plowed her SUV into a crowd outside a nightclub in the Hamptons and then fled. The rest of the country, having quickly determined that the murder of the wife of the actor Robert Blake was too B-list to qualify as an O. J. Simpson rerun, feasted instead on Gary Condit.

A back-bencher congressman from Modesto, California, Condit could not explain the abrupt disappearance of a twenty-four-year-old Washington intern, Chandra Levy, with whom he may or may not have had an extramarital affair. In retrospect, the Condit affair (or nonaffair—we never did find out) was the last gasp of the fin-de-siècle Clinton culture and its bread and circuses of sex scandals. With Bill Clinton gone from center stage, the country had to settle for a dim-witted Price Club surrogate—and did. Desperate pundits worked overtime to turn a pale understudy into a star.

The Condit-Levy soap opera was a snapshot of a waning era. It quickly mushroomed into a classic 24/7 cable TV mediathon in the O.J.-pioneered format. A nugget of salacious news was rapidly inflated with acres of speculation, a large cast of supporting players, and teams of bloviating "experts"—the familiar set of ingredients that has become electronic journalism's equivalent of Hamburger Helper. The circus provided continuous infotainment for a nation with time on its hands.

The moralists and publicity seekers (often one and the same) turned out in full force. "Condit makes our former president look like the model of monogamy," observed Jonathan Turley, one of the many Monica-era talking heads who seized an opportunity for renewed television face time.[1] But while Condit was a Democrat, he was a conservative Democrat who had once co-sponsored a bill calling for the display of the Ten Commandments in public places. In the end, about the only person in America to stand up for the guy was the virtuecrat William Bennett, who entered the fray to argue that Condit belonged on a higher moral plane than the philandering president whom Bennett had spent the past decade vilifying. "Hypocrisy is better than no standards at all,"[2] Bennett explained, coining a maxim that would come in handy two years later, when he was exposed as a gambling addict with losses of at least eight million dollars.[3]

If there was a real moral to Condit's tale, however, it had nothing to do with sex; it was that the culture valued a politician's performance above all else. And Condit had steadfastly refused to perform. He didn't apologize for anything. He didn't express sorrow for the Levy family. He didn't cry. Other politicians, pundits, and citizens faulted him for not being phony enough—for not being as good an actor as Bill Clinton. As the self-appointed voice of the masses, Bill O'Reilly of Fox News Channel's *O'Reilly Factor,* elaborated after Condit gave a TV interview to ABC's Connie Chung in August, "This guy doesn't look like he's broken up about this at all. . . . If I were Condit, I would have cried. He could have done the lip thing." The conservative commentator William Kristol astutely observed that politicians of all stripes were most likely to "condemn Condit for terrible P.R. judgment—not for being a terrible human being."

Though Americans were fond of saying that they valued authenticity in their politicians above all else, they didn't really mean it. Condit's sleaziness was authentic; what they wanted from him was fake contrition. In 1961, the year after John F. Kennedy won a crucial campaign debate with the charisma-challenged Richard Nixon because of his telegenic charm rather than the substance of what he said, the historian Daniel Boorstin canonized this sea change in American public life with his classic book *The Image: A Guide to Pseudo-Events in America.* Four decades later this cultural strain had metastasized. As Condit learned the hard way, the performance of a politician, the image, was sometimes the only thing that mattered.

Along with Condit, another heavily hyped product from California provided escapist entertainment for a bored country in a sleepy summer—*Pearl Harbor,* a Jerry Bruckheimer extravaganza from Disney. With a 95 percent awareness factor (according to Hollywood tracking polls), *Pearl Harbor,* the movie, was better known to most Americans than Pearl Harbor, the historical event. The peacetime navy had cooperated with the making of the film, and it donated the aircraft carrier *John C. Stennis* as a stage for revelers at the gala premiere in Hawaii. That night the movie's star, Ben Affleck, told reporters that the film's "message is not one about the United States or Japan or the Second World War, right or wrong" but just about how "terrible" war is in general.[4] To have raised matters of right and wrong might have depressed ticket sales in Tokyo. *Pearl Harbor* is so scrupulously nonpartisan that it never explains Japan's motives for its attack—or, for that matter, why anyone fought in Asia or Europe during World War II.

The vapid *Pearl Harbor* was an essential historical artifact anyway—not of its ostensible subject but of the tranquil American summer of 2001. The forty-minute bombing sequence looked like a state-of-the-art digital video game, with even the bloodshed sanitized to preserve the financially desirable PG-13 rating. The flyboy fashions, complete with product placements for Ray-Ban, were as pristine as those in the Abercrombie & Fitch catalogue. The war itself was transformed into a content-free but vaguely uplifting exercise in team gamesmanship whose main purpose was to put randy pilots in proximity to bodacious nurses. America is invincible; any and every battle can be won without working up a sweat. Even medical miracles are effortlessly within reach: in one scene of high drama, FDR, trying to rally his Cabinet, miraculously rises from his wheelchair to stand on his own two feet, polio be damned.

Pearl Harbor was at once the peak and the reductio ad absurdum of the World War II nostalgia boom that had preoccupied America for several years. That craze had produced so many movies, books, and TV series that the greatest generation was less an idea than a brand, useful for selling anything. (Amazon opened up a Pearl Harbor Store in tandem with Disney's film.) What was it all about? Tom Brokaw, whose bestselling book had helped kick off the phenomenon, noted that only a decade earlier the fiftieth-anniversary ceremonies at Pearl Harbor received scant attention; he was the only TV anchor on hand. But that was in 1991, when a World War II vet was still president. Now the boomers had ascended to power. Just as *Pearl Harbor* was more about the present than the past, so the overall World War II obsession said more about the generation born after the war than the generation who fought the war. After all, it was mainly boomers—and others too young to remember Pearl Harbor firsthand—who created the idea of the greatest generation and its sundry product lines, not the reticent and dwindling ranks of World War II veterans.

The motivation, in part, was overcompensation for what was missing in our national life: some cause larger than ourselves, whatever it might be. So debased was the notion of sacrifice by the summer of 2001 that when the White House press secretary, Ari Fleischer, was asked if Americans should think about altering their lifestyles to conserve energy, he declared that the president believed that the current gas-guzzling lifestyle was "the American way of life" and that "it should be the goal of policy makers to protect the American way of life—the American way of life is a blessed one." The Democrats' idea of sacrifice was scarcely different. The opposition party's leadership had unveiled a so-called alternative energy plan that also swore off "reductions in our standard of living" and featured on its cover a photo of a family polishing its SUV.[5]

For all the differences between the Clinton-Gore and Bush-Cheney administrations, together they formed a boomer continuum. Each was ruled by narcissists who wanted what they wanted when they wanted it and were convinced of their own righteousness. Clinton and Bush were masters at using the sweet-talking language of "compassion," "feeling your pain," and "faith" as a rhetorical substitute for, say, expending political capital to bring medical insurance to poor children. If the Republicans offered greater tax cuts instead of more New Deal–Great Society entitlement programs, neither political party wanted voters to give up anything for any common good larger than feathering their own immediate nests. "Both parties have reversed J.F.K. Their mantra is 'Ask not what you can do for your country, but rather what your country can do for your stock portfolio/benefit package,'" said Marshall Wittmann, then of Washington's conservative Hudson Institute.

And so the Clinton-Bush boomer generation turned a nominally selfless tribute to its fathers' generation not only into a lucrative branch of show business but also into an implicit, cost-free celebration of its own worthiness. By exulting in our parents' wartime service, we could practice what the writer John Gregory Dunne labeled a "virtual patriotism"[6] that made us look noble by association. Seeing *Pearl Harbor* or giving *The Greatest Generation* as a Father's Day present could become the cost-free moral equivalent of going to war. We never imagined that America might actually have to go fight another real one.

Our virtual patriotism also helped us repress more recent memories of the war our generation was asked to fight, Vietnam—a debacle that, not so incidentally, was cooked up by dogtag-wearing members of the greatest generation, including JFK, and that both boomer presidents had ducked. No matter how much Americans doted on World War II, it was still the Vietnam ghosts who lurked in the shadows. They leapt out again during the spring of 2001, when *The New York Times* published revelations about Bob Kerrey's anguish over the women and children who died in a 1969 SEAL raid he led on a peasant village in Vietnam.[7] But hardly did the Kerrey story emerge than boomer politicians and journalists rushed to lock it up again—by throwing up our hands and saying, "Who are we to judge?" and "War is war."

We didn't want to go there if we could help it. *Newsweek*, which had had the Kerrey scoop before the *Times* but dropped it, ran a twelve-page cover story promoting *Pearl Harbor*. At the movie's five-million-dollar Hawaiian premiere, Kerrey's old outfit, the Navy SEALs, parachuted down from the skies to entertain the celebrity guests—a cheerful, Disneyfied inversion of the Playboy Bunnies' USO show in *Apocalypse Now*. The new president, whose political supporters had tried to smear John McCain as a crazed vet during the 2000 primaries, returned to his alma mater, Yale, to deliver a jokey commencement address to the class of 2001. Though Bush's class was riven by Vietnam, and Yale lost a few men there, his reminiscences included no mention of that war or any other.

BY THEN, a half year into his term, George W. Bush was on his way to becoming a forgettable chief executive with no driving agenda beyond traditional Republican tax cuts and a Reagan-bequeathed defense-spending boondoggle (the "Star Wars" missile shield). Unlike his father, a bona fide greatest-generation hero, the forty-third president had ridden out his own war by obtaining a hard-to-secure slot in the Texas Air National Guard, aka the "champagne unit," a well-known parking place for well-heeled and well-connected Texans who wanted to make certain their Vietnam War service was spent safely stateside. Bush was at best a profile in peacetime courage: as a politician, he was determined to say and do nothing that might disturb the country during one of its longest-running naps. He was so unexceptional that *That's My Bush!*, a satirical series on the cable channel Comedy Central, created by the scabrous and highly popular team behind *South Park*, expired at the start of September after a brief run that incited neither laughter nor the expected controversy.

The standard rap on Bush from Democrats in the 2000 campaign deemed him an airhead—or, more commonly, an idiot, a moron, a monkey. Asked by a South Carolina elementary school kid at a campaign photo op to name his favorite book as a child, Bush responded, "I can't remember any specific books."[8] When he seemed to stand up bravely to his party's right flank with a speech referring damningly to the title of Robert Bork's bestselling screed *Slouching Towards Gomorrah*, his spokesman said that the allusion was inadvertent. ("He may not even have realized he was referring to a book," cracked Bork.)[9] *Slate* magazine fastidiously collected the many Bushisms of the malaprop-prone Republican standard-bearer. In March 2000 David Letterman summed up the prevailing bottom line: "This guy, to me, looks like he could be a colossal boob."

That indictment had only gained in vociferousness and decibel level after the bitter battle of Florida, during which James Baker's legal shock troops outwitted their Al Gore counterparts, tossing the recount into its foregone conclusion before a partisan Supreme Court. But there was plenty of evidence to suggest that Bush was no dunce. His mediocre grades at Yale—which he tried to keep private—were indistinguishable from those of the showily wonky Gore at Harvard. The problem with Bush was not that he was stupid but that he thought everyone else was stupid.

He believed he could sell anything if he repeated the pitch often enough (and often verbatim). Like other entitled boomers utterly blind to their own faults, he narcissistically assumed things to be so (and his intentions pure) because he said they were. Thus he could refer to himself incessantly as a "uniter, not a divider" and a practitioner of "compassionate conservatism" even as he made a campaign stop at Bob Jones University, a school notorious for its antediluvian prohibition of interracial dating (a policy abandoned soon after the Bush visit cast it in a harsh national spotlight). How dare anyone question him?

His arrogance and certitude were less a reflection of hard-right ideology than of his soft character, which was in turn the product of a biography full of easy landings. A man who had never faced adversity—who had finessed Andover, Yale, Harvard Business School, Vietnam, and brief careers in business and politics with well-placed cronies and sweetheart deals—was not conversant with reality as most Americans had experienced it. FDR and Ronald Reagan entered the White House as wealthy men, too, but their hard knocks before their arrival gave them empathy for their fellow citizens. Bush was out of touch. He didn't know how much he didn't know about those not of his privileged background, and he was in no rush to find out. His attitude toward his fellow citizens was all too consistent with his attitude toward the world beyond his native shores. He must have been one of the very few Americans of his generation and social class who had never been tempted to bum around Europe on a Eurailpass some summer during his college years, if only to score dope and girls. That he flunked a Boston television interviewer's pop quiz during the 2000 campaign, proving himself unable to identify foreign leaders (among them, Pervez Musharraf, whom he could identify only as "the new Pakistani general"),[10] was revealing of his incuriosity and intellectual laziness, not of his lack of brain power. Some family retainer—Brent, Condi, Colin, whoever—could handle those niggling details.

His sense of entitlement was always visible. At one downturn in the 2000 race, he announced that he would start campaigning more with "real people," in such real places as coffee shops and cafeterias.[11] By "real people" he presumably meant those who hadn't had his easeful career path and hadn't been bailed out by family friends when they fell into financial or personal trouble. This sudden embrace of reality didn't last long. To make the case that his tax cut did not benefit just the wealthy, Bush took to handing out dollar bills[12] to the real people—unaware, apparently, of the gesture's echo of John D. Rockefeller's condescending stunt of handing out dimes to the destitute during the Great Depression. Similarly, Bush's petulance about appearing in presidential debates wasn't merely, as most of his critics felt, a function of his inability to do his homework and his fear of tripping into linguistic disaster. His absurd debate-negotiation demands—among them his brief insistence that one debate be held in the friendly confines of *Larry King Live*—seemed to be those of a spoiled brat who wanted to play by his own rules or else take his feather pillow and go home.

It was to counteract this image that his handlers labored hard to create a more dramatic biography. It wasn't easy. Bush hadn't risen from modest beginnings and a broken family in a town called Hope. He hadn't been a World War II pilot or a PT boat commander. He hadn't coped with polio. He hadn't made his fortune the hard, old-fashioned way, by earning it. His name and family connections had always opened doors for him—not just to elite schools but also to backing in the oil business and to participation (with relatively piddling capital) in the sweetheart partnership that bought and then sold the Texas Rangers for an eye-popping profit. In his largely uneventful single term as governor of Texas, he had not faced even one, let alone six, Nixonian crises—unless you count the pleas for clemency that he routinely ignored in capital punishment cases. "He'll come to the presidency with a lighter resume than anybody has in at least a hundred years," Nicholas Lemann wrote in a *New Yorker* profile, observing that even twentieth-century presidents-come-lately such as Warren Harding and John Kennedy had previously served in public office twenty-one and thirteen years, respectively, next to Bush's six.[13]

A dramatic biography imbuing him with the presidential-caliber hard knocks and tough challenges missing from his bland résumé had to be created by rubbing together what few usable sticks there were and praying they'd create sparks. The key event picked for this purpose was Bush's decision to swear off alcohol after his wife, Laura, gave him an ultimatum at his fortieth-birthday celebration at the Broadmoor resort in Colorado. This tale was especially saleable in a culture where recovery-movement reminiscences were a craze on daytime television and the bestseller lists. It also paid two other political dividends: it inoculated Bush against rumors floating around about Clintonian behavior in his self-confessed "irresponsible" youth and it emphasized his faith; his tutor in finding both sobriety and Jesus was Billy Graham (another useful family connection). Slender as the anecdote was, it was elevated by Bush and his retinue into a George-Washington-and-the-cherry-tree parable, the moral equivalent of wartime derring-do. But like that cherry-tree legend, it didn't necessarily stand up to close scrutiny. By both Bush's own account and those of neutral witnesses, he was never a clinical alcoholic, never drank during the day (or every day), never needed to seek out A.A. or any other treatment. In other words, he was an occasionally out-of-control country-club drinker who quit cold turkey after a bad hangover—a far cry from those who face the far harsher challenge of conquering the crippling disease of alcoholism. All it took for him to bounce back was some can-do entrepreneurial spirit and trust in God—the old-time Dale Carnegie religion. The details of this tale seemed almost as potted as James Frey's subsequently notorious bestselling memoir of substance abuse and rehab, *A Million Little Pieces*.

The one fearless political confrontation in Bush's professional past was also embellished: he did not, as legend had it, undertake the Herculean management feat of slaying the formidable chief of staff in his father's administration, John Sununu; in his capacity as First Son, he only gave Sununu a stiff reprimand in the days before the axe fell.[14] It was enough to make you wonder if all those campaign rumors about Bush's alleged cocaine use were floated by his allies rather than his enemies, just to give him an aura of true grit. That theoretical crime aside, the only really daring move in Bush's entire adult life was to fire Bobby Valentine as manager of the Texas Rangers—though Valentine said that the dismissal took the form of an hour-long love tap rather than a boot administered by a decisive leader.[15]

Bush's fans, both during the campaign and after 9/11, were fond of likening him to Reagan, though Reagan's son would have none of it: well before he turned on Bush for good after his father's death, Ron Reagan scoffed to Lloyd Grove of *The Washington Post*, "What is [Bush's] accomplishment? That he's no longer an obnoxious drunk?"[16] Still, there were superficial similarities to spare: the self-deprecating humor, the delegation of details to subordinates, the return to serene Western colors in Oval Office décor. Bush also owned a Western

White House not unlike Reagan's rustic getaway in the hills above the posh California coastal redoubt of Santa Barbara. In Bush's case, the spread in Crawford had been purchased just before he announced his presidential run. It was routinely labeled a "ranch" by the Eastern press. But the "ranch," with its few head of cattle, was not a working ranch at all; it was more like a stage set. Bush had "reinvented himself as a retro-Texan, a throwback to a place that never existed beyond the Potemkin-village facade of *Giant*'s Reata," wrote Michael Ennis in *Texas Monthly*. It was White House "spin and the media's credulity about all things mythically Texan" that transformed the ranch into "George W. Bush's ancestral domain, the wellspring of those sound bite values that inspire his supporters and inflame his foes."[17] Among the credulous was Bob Woodward, who interviewed Bush in Crawford and who apotheosized the setting as a poetic incarnation of the president's straight-shooting image in the final pages of his post-9/11 hagiography *Bush at War*.

For all Bush's tireless brush-clearing in Crawford, he was at best a digital facsimile of his presidential antecedent. Reagan's steelier character reflected his own un-Bush background: the product of an alcoholic father and modest financial circumstances, he had to work his way through college, where he was elected student body president. (Bush was president of DEKE.) Reagan ran the Screen Actors Guild during tumultuous times and knew his share of career reversals. Though no less a friend to business than Bush, he had deep-seated convictions about a range of issues and thought them through in hundreds of self-written radio scripts during his years in the political wilderness. "Reagan had climbed the ladder of success from the lower rungs, demonstrating a combination of persistence and humility rare among either politicians or actors," writes his biographer Lou Cannon.[18]

Persistence and humility were not words that came to mind when thinking of Bush. Nor was it possible to imagine him leaving behind a cache of handwritten policy musings. The passion that Reagan brought to his crusade against the evil empire surfaced in the pre-9/11 Bush only when Bush was championing baseball. In one manic fortnight early in his presidency, he found the time to throw out the traditional first pitch (albeit into the dirt) at the Milwaukee Brewers' home opener and to preside over two White House baseball events: a tribute to Hall of Famers, to herald the introduction of T-ball to the

South Lawn, and a screening of a new HBO movie about Mickey Mantle and Roger Maris.

These activities were in keeping with Bush's greatest pre–White House successes—as a cheerleader. His cheerleading didn't end with his official role in that capacity at Andover. Both in his oil and baseball careers, he served the same function: he was the glad-handing salesman, the schmoozer, the PR front man who hit up investors for money and roused the fans while other executives actually made the crucial business decisions and ran the companies. For that matter, the less-than-powerful job of Texas governor was primarily to serve as "the head cheerleader or the public relations person," according to Paul Rea, a Texas oilman and Bush pal.[19]

In the untroubled time of pre-9/11 America, a professional cheerleader was not necessarily miscast as president. For every civic problem, Bush could offer cheery bromides such as "leadership" and "vision" and a laissez-faire, let-the-other-guy-do-it solution. Let "our friends" shoulder problems abroad or indulge in the costly folly of nation-building. Let a tax cut and "faith-based charities" lift up the poor. Let industry regulate its own pollution. Declare a "new era of personal responsibility" that requires no individual or national sacrifice. Bush didn't resemble Reagan, who had a firm international worldview, as much as he did the Republicans who presided over the 1920s boom and were gone by the crash: Warren Harding, a likably lightweight senator drafted by his party's powers-that-be as their genial front man, and Calvin Coolidge, Harding's successor. Coolidge's sole credo, like Bush's, was the rock-ribbed Republicanism of huge tax cuts (the estate tax included) that largely benefited the wealthy, and minimalist government.

To THIS UNEXCEPTIONAL Republicanism, Bush brought his particular zest for public relations. Though he wasn't a practiced actor like Reagan, his cheerleading past had its uses. Bush was more than willing to act out scenarios that could help sell him or whatever product (or policy) he was pushing. In his longtime political guru, Karl Rove, he had a producer-director-screenwriter who had brought the photo-op techniques pioneered by Reagan's image maven, Michael Deaver, to a whole new level of sophistication and expertise.

Deaver knew that if Reagan cut any federal subsidy for the elderly, it was a cue for him to be televised surrounded by flags cutting the ribbon at a new nursing home. The pictures could be counted on to carry the day and to drown out any discouraging words from Reagan critics on the evening news. Bush and Rove took this playbook as a starting point and then upped the ante. Though Bush lacked Reagan's experience in the Hollywood studio system, he was not as hostile to show-business make-believe as he let on. In the 1980s he had joined his Yale pal and classmate Roland Betts on the board of Silver Screen Management, a principal investor in the lucrative movies Disney produced under its Touchstone rubric.

Bush had first gotten the hang of doing his own playacting back when the Texas Rangers were struggling as a major-league franchise. To ensure favorable press coverage, he flattered reporters and sweetened the amenities in the press box. When catering to the rich by adding a profusion of luxury boxes to his new stadium, he hired an architect to camouflage the class distinctions from the hoi polloi. "I'm not so sure you can segue from baseball to a presidency," Bush said modestly to *The Washington Post* in 2000, but he did take away "some lessons about management, about developing a strategy." Baseball, he explained, "is a marketing business."[20]

In his first presidential campaign, Bush had some photo-op missteps. The Bob Jones University appearance, besides being damaging in principle, was poisonous as imagery: TV constantly replayed the video of the candidate striding across a vast red carpet that reeked of creepy totalitarian kitsch and unreconstructed Dixie. To make up for it, Bush hastily arranged a visit to the Simon Wiesenthal Center, in Los Angeles, where he donned a yarmulke and paid homage to the Holocaust.[21] The Bush cheerleaders at *The Wall Street Journal* proposed further remedies. Perhaps Colin Powell could be recruited as a running mate or Bush could show his affinity for Latinos by forsaking Hiltons and Four Seasons when in California to stay instead in "little hotels in the barrio."[22] Even for the Rove operation, these suggestions were a bit much.

The "inclusive" 2000 Republican National Convention in Philadelphia brought the most elaborate stunt of all. A nearly all-minority cast of gospel singers and break dancers played to a nearly all-white hall of delegates during the interludes separating the bouts of official business. The only black Republican in Congress, J. C. Watts (who would later retire from the House), was the emcee. Given that only 4 percent of the delegates were black, the convention was actually whiter than the notoriously right-wing Houston convention of 1992, where Pat Robertson and Pat Buchanan set the unreconstructed neo-Dixiecrat tone.[23] The minstrel show in Philadelphia was, in Riefenstahl aesthetics, the Triumph of Compassionate Conservatism, the perfect payoff to the relentless primary-campaign photo ops in which Bush posed with smiling African American children to plug his No Child Left Behind education program.

Once in office, Bush turned the presidency into an ongoing festival of audiovisual cognitive dissonance. The succession of misleading propaganda ploys had an almost farcical quality. In a single week, the president appeared at two national parks, Sequoia and the Everglades, dressed in more earth tones than Gore at his most craven. The message was that Bush liked hugging trees almost as much as he did African American kids, but in reality his environmental record in the White House remained as un-green as ever. The National Parks Conservation Association had given him a D rating, observing that his modest increase in the parks budget was more for buildings and roads than for preserving nature. Bush also posed in front of a sea of police officers in Philadelphia just as the administration was submitting a budget calling for a 17 percent decrease in COPS, the federal program that provides money for police salaries.[24] His repeated presidential visits to various Boys and Girls Clubs, touting them as an example of how the government can "facilitate programs" for children and promote "the universal concept of loving a neighbor," occurred as his budget slashed the clubs' federal appropriation.[25] Even the First Lady enlisted in these bait-and-switch shenanigans, appearing at a Washington public library in April 2001 to kick off a "Campaign for America's Libraries," just one week before her husband's budget cut the federal outlay for libraries by thirty-nine million dollars.[26] While photo ops were nothing new in the modern American presidency, there had been a time when they were at least occasionally used to dramatize a president's policies rather than almost exclusively to disguise them. Now a smiling Bush appearance to bless any cause, program, or habitat was tantamount to a visit from the angel of death.

Though he had accomplished little in his young presidency by the time he reached his first summer vacation, Bush did run into a sort-of crisis, a growing debate over the ethics of medical stem-cell research. He was caught between his conservative religious base, which makes no distinction between a discarded cluster of cells in a laboratory and infanticide, and a large national majority desperate for potential cures for diseases such as Alzheimer's and diabetes. Bush's polls were mediocre, and finding himself denigrated as something of a summer slacker, he seized on the stem-cell debate to transform his image into that of a hardworking philosopher king—grappling mightily with the science and ethics of an issue his handlers advertised as "one of the most profound of our time." To this end, in the dog days of August, he gave a presidential address from Crawford announcing a "compromise" that allowed federal research to continue on only sixty-four already extant stem-cell lines (the majority of which would soon turn out not to be viable).[27]

This was the final presidential performance in an uneventful vacation of brush-clearing and siestas that the White House screenwriters had tried to dress up as a "Home to the Heartland" tour, in the alliterative style favored by the longtime Bush message molder Karen Hughes ("Reformer with Results," "compassionate conservatism"). The gist of the scenario had it that the president was just another "real American," hanging out in jeans, shopping at Target, and chopping wood, not some fancy-pants multimillionaire educated at elite universities and habituated to such fashionable vacation enclaves as, say, Kennebunkport.

All was tranquil in the heartland apparently as the real American who happened to be president made his unhurried way back to Washington in September 2001.

TWO

"DEAD OR ALIVE"

SHARK ATTACKS had been one of the more entertaining diversions of the summer of 2001. When cable news got bored with Gary and Chandra, there was always some sighting of teeth somewhere, replete with *Jaws* footage and the accompanying John Williams thump-thump-thump horror music, even though, in reality, the rate of shark attacks had been routine that year, and sharks were a statistically minuscule cause of mortality at any time. (There had been at most two U.S. shark deaths in any year since 1990.) But by the afternoon of 9/11, the great shark scare of 2001 was officially consigned to the dustbin of history when *People* scrapped its shark cover to make way for the thousands dead. Al Qaeda's attack on America was a genuine apocalypse, not a soap opera that could be turned into a 24/7 cable news miniseries or tabloid fare. It was one tragedy that could not be safely guided to that satisfying denouement that had been in vogue ever since the 1999 shootings at Columbine High School in Colorado: "closure."

Signs of a new realism abounded, at least at first. On television we were told hourly that we had lost the untroubled freedom of movement that Amer-

icans consider a birthright. It was self-evident that our illusion of impregnabil-
ity had been smashed, too. Confronted with catastrophic news and the need
for reliable information about it, TV viewers of 9/11 largely deserted the cable
news networks for the Big Three, as embodied by the supposedly obsolescent
Tom Brokaw, Peter Jennings, and Dan Rather. Americans wanted the authority
of the anchors, and the anchors upheld their part of the bargain, sticking to
pre–Drudge Report, pre-cable journalistic standards and offering reportage
rather than blather and rumor. They didn't make any of the errors that had
pumped up the hysteria of the O.J. and Monica mediathons—and that on 9/11
could have spread wholesale panic across a jittery nation instead of the usual
prurient fun. The anchors, however anachronistic their declining evening newscasts, knew they had to do their part to steady a country that still gathered at
the tube, not the computer screen, during a crisis like this.

In 9/11's immediate aftermath, it even seemed possible that words such as
survivor and *fear factor* would be reunited with their original meanings. Of late
they had been held captive by television's so-called reality programs, which
had turned *Survivor* and *Fear Factor* into brands standing for fantasy entertainment in which nothing really fearful ever happened and every imperiled contestant was certain to survive.

A decade of dreaming was coming to an end. The dream had been simple—
that Americans could have it all without having to pay any price, and that national suffering of almost any kind could be domesticated into an experience
of virtual terror akin to a theme park ride or a Hollywood blockbuster. Even
before 9/11, the mass escapism that defined the 1990s had started to collapse
with the puncturing of the stock bubble and the economic aftershocks. Now
terrorists had achieved the literal annihilation of the most commanding twin
edifices of American capitalism.

Overnight, World War II fetishism was almost ludicrously obsolete. The
lavish promotion of HBO's new series *Band of Brothers* during the days before
9/11 rang hollow in the days after. The HBO posters had to share Manhattan's
signage with the ubiquitous faces smiling out expectantly from the new quilt of
mass death, the vast patchwork of fliers headlined MISSING. "There was a time
when the world asked ordinary men to do extraordinary things," went the *Band
of Brothers* ad copy, which took pains to remind us that the miniseries was
"based on the true story." As of 9/11, the prospect that civilians might have to

make an extraordinary effort for the national good was no longer an arcane fantasy as far-fetched as the knights of the round table.

Most important, 9/11 might just shock the don't-worry-be-happy presidency of George W. Bush into growing up. Perhaps he might tell us that it was not possible to have big tax cuts (for some of us, anyway) along with spending increases for better schools and defense—all without having to dip into the Social Security stash. Maybe we would even be told that it was impossible to lick an energy crisis or navigate the politics of the Middle East while continuing to burn gas as if there were no tomorrow. Perhaps the president would ask for a new generation to sacrifice, as he, his vice president, and the boomer elite running both political parties by and large had not done during Vietnam.

Perhaps irony was dead. Perhaps there was a New Normal. Perhaps 9/11 was the day that changed everything.

Then again, perhaps not.

AT HEART Americans are eternal innocents, and 9/11 did not change that. The question ricocheting throughout the media past the point of absurdity—"Why do they hate us?"—was a sincere one. Few Americans had a clue about who "they" were, let alone why they hated us. Radical Islam was as mysterious to most as quantum physics. In the summer of 2001, there had been far more news coverage of domestic sharks, Condit included, than of the foreign threat of Al Qaeda. Now that the worst had happened, the country wanted desperately to rally around a leader—any leader. We needed someone to root for. We needed someone to take charge. We needed someone to protect us. We needed someone to strike back. The president, hardly visible in the first forty-eight hours after the attacks, left a vacuum in that role, and into the vacuum stepped the unlikely figure of Rudolph Giuliani. New York's mayor was said to be of a type that doesn't play nationally—ethnic, authoritarian, a liberal Republican way to the left of his party's base on culture-war issues such as abortion and gay civil rights. But he was immediately embraced by one and all. His televised omnipresence amid the ruins of Lower Manhattan was seen as fearlessness.

Where was George Bush? The country saw the pictures of him that morning at Emma E. Booker Elementary School in Sarasota, where he was once again posing with schoolchildren to advertise his compassion. He visibly flinched when his chief of staff, Andrew Card, interrupted his reading of "The Pet Goat" to second-graders to whisper into his ear that a second plane had crashed into the South Tower. Some twenty minutes later, at 9:30, the president stood in front of a READ TO SUCCEED banner and appeared on television, declaring that "terrorism against our nation will not stand." What exactly happened in the eleven hours that followed was destined to remain a mystery.

When the president next popped up, it was midday, in a taped appearance from an air force base in Louisiana; in some of the networks' initial airings, the video and audio were disconcertingly subpar. Bush promised that America would "hunt down and punish those responsible for these cowardly acts," but he was the one who seemed on the run, like a panicked fugitive trying to elude authorities. Once more disappearing from view, he skedaddled by a round-about route to another military base, in Omaha, where, the nation was informed, he led a National Security Council meeting by videophone from a bunker. He didn't resurface publicly again until 8:30 that night, when he materialized in the Oval Office to address the nation with pretty words composed by the same glib Hallmark-style poets who fashioned his alliterative campaign locutions. "These acts shattered steel, but they cannot dent the steel of American resolve," he said, sounding every bit as fake as Rudy sounded real.

During the course of the speech, he said, "Immediately following the first attack, I implemented our government's emergency response plans." But Bush's behavior that morning at the Florida school, in which he seemed in no rush to end his visit, belied his claim, which proved false.[1] He remained at the school altogether nearly an hour after the bulletins of the first jet hitting the World Trade Center. Months after 9/11, Bush would directly contradict his assertion that he had instantly implemented emergency plans after the first attack, telling interviewers that he had initially thought, as many Americans did, that the crash into the first tower was "pilot error," not an attack at all.[2]

September 11 was the first time since the British set fire to the White House in 1814 that a president abandoned the capital for security reasons. "Frankly, President Bush made an initial mistake," Boston University historian Robert Dallek told *USA Today*. "The president's place is back in Washington."[3] On the day the quote ran, September 12, Karl Rove took time out from his other pressing duties to call Dallek, whom he'd never met, to tell him that Bush did not return home right away because of threats to the White House and Air Force One.[4] But the White House did not provide any information to substantiate this claim, and, as Eric Alterman would later ask in *The Nation:* "If you think Air Force One is to be attacked, why go up in Air Force One?"[5]

Still, the administration had its 9/11 story and was sticking to it—with Rove making the same unsubstantiated claim to *The New Yorker* and Dick Cheney doing likewise with Tim Russert on *Meet the Press.* CBS News and the Associated Press would soon report that there had been no such threat. No matter. History would record the White House's account, whatever the facts. In Woodward's *Bush at War,* a year later, the scenario of an Air Force One threat surfaced again, once more on the authority of Cheney. In 2003, the scenario became a full-fledged Hollywood screenplay, for the first docudrama about 9/11. Many of the subsequent 9/11 movies would focus on the heroism of the passengers on Flight 93, who revolted against the hijackers and precipitated the plane's crash in Pennsylvania before it reached its Washington target. But not the first out of the box, Showtime's *DC 9/11: Time of Crisis.* It concentrated on the heroism of George W. Bush on Air Force One. The star was Timothy Bottoms—the same actor who less than two years earlier had been playing a cartoon version of the president in the short-lived Comedy Central satire *That's My Bush!* The new screen Bush was an unironic action-movie superhero.

There were no laughs in *DC 9/11,* or at least no intentional ones. Instead, the president could be found overruling his Secret Service detail and ordering his plane back to Washington on the fateful day when many Americans found him harder to find than Waldo. "If some tinhorn terrorist wants me, tell him to come and get me!" the on-screen Bush says. "I'll be at home, waiting for the bastard!" Lest the audience miss the point, he is also given lines like "The American people want to know where their damn president is!" and "People can't have an AWOL president!" Meanwhile, the rest of the White House team was portrayed as the very model of efficiency and derring-do, a tack also taken by Woodward's *Bush at War.* Even a nonentity like the transportation secretary, Norman Mineta (played by the actor best known as Sulu on *Star Trek*), came across so decisively he might be mistaken for Patton.

Unsurprisingly, *DC 9/11* was produced by Lionel Chetwynd, long known as the go-to conservative in B-list Hollywood. Somewhat more surprising was the ease with which official Washington and bona fide journalists were enlisted for this fictionalized effort. *The Washington Post* reported in a feature on the making of the film that Chetwynd had access to top White House officials, Bush included, and also to "a group of conservative Washington pundits, including Fred Barnes, Charles Krauthammer and Morton Kondracke," who vetted the script.[6] In their non-Hollywood day jobs, these same pundits covered the administration for Fox News, *The Weekly Standard*, and, in Krauthammer's case, as a *Post* columnist. It was not disclosed if they were paid for their participation in what was unmistakably a propaganda effort on behalf of a sitting administration.

Three days after 9/11, Bush at last made his way to the smoking ruins of the Twin Towers. In the view of most, he found his voice the moment he picked up a bullhorn and promised the rescue workers at the site in blunt language that the terrorists would soon hear from America. The gesture seemed spontaneous in a way that Bush's controlled public appearances rarely were. He started to resemble the leader the nation was yearning for.

What wasn't clear was where he would lead the country. He wanted "evildoers" brought to justice. Invoking the parlance of a Steve McQueen TV Western of his adolescence, he wanted to hunt down and nab Osama bin Laden "dead or alive." But while polls showed that Americans overwhelmingly supported the idea of going to war, they didn't indicate whether Americans understood that idea. Who would fight and where? Would any kind of sacrifice be required?

On September 20, Bush addressed a joint session of Congress, in a speech that forsook his previous pulp-fiction bravado for substance. He started to make a case for what a war on terrorists might mean. He drew essential distinctions between "Islamic extremism" and Islam, between the Taliban and "Afghanistan's people," between a TV-ready war of "instant retaliation and isolated strikes" and "a lengthy campaign" whose clandestine operations might be "secret even in success."

BUT ALREADY the audience was drifting away. In the country beyond the stunned attack sites of New York and Washington, the old normal was quickly reasserting itself. So was the old culture. By late September, CNN's ratings had dropped 70 percent from their post-attack peak. The prohibition on humor was ceremonially lifted when Giuliani participated in a gag that opened the September 29 edition of *Saturday Night Live*. Flanked by police officers and firemen, the show's producer, Lorne Michaels, asked the mayor, "Can we be funny?" With perfect timing and a Buster Keaton–esque poker face, Giuliani responded, "Why start now?" He brought down the house. The late-night talk shows, which had at first been shocked into playing host to pundits and Middle East experts, brought back their regular guests and opening monologues. It was safe for Jay Leno to deliver a joke linking Osama bin Laden to Anna Nicole Smith.

The time had come for the great commercial engine of the country to rev up again. Interspersed among television's dire reports of Wall Street bloodletting and widespread layoffs in 9/11-affected industries were immaculately produced black-and-white commercials in which corporations asserted their solidarity with the American spirit. In soulless emulation of the countless Americans who had raised a flag after the attacks, TV news stars also started marketing their patriotism: they kept sprouting more and more elaborate lapel effusions, some of them large enough to dwarf that of the country's commander in chief. At ABC News, where the thorny spirit of Peter Jennings prevailed, the lapel pins were soon forbidden. But when the news director at KOMU, an NBC affiliate run by faculty and students at the University of Missouri, announced a similar prohibition on journalistic grounds, a state legislator threatened to have lawmakers scrutinize the school's future budget requests. (The Missouri House voted to cut the station's budget by five hundred thousand dollars in April 2002.)[7] At the network level, NBC was particularly obsessive in its flag-waving. It outfitted its promotional peacock logo in stars and stripes and then affixed it with abandon to virtually every frame of its prime-time schedule, assuring that even a doomed sitcom starring the celebrity chef Emeril Lagasse would be patriotically correct during its brief unhappy life. Rarely had there been such a persuasive argument for a constitutional amendment banning flag desecration.

A vocal but powerless antiwar left notwithstanding, nearly all Americans, liberals included, wanted to go after those who had perpetrated the 9/11 attacks. And in keeping with the president's September 20 speech warning against ill-planned "instant retaliation," much of the country was patient while the administration got its act together. During the 1990s boom, the citizenry had become addicted to instant gratification—and to a post–Gulf War military policy predicated on the slam-dunk idea of a silver bullet fired safely (and often indiscriminately) from on high, as if in a video game. Now it was willing to let the president take his time and choose his means of battle. Bush's poll numbers were in the stratosphere. Ryan Clark, a nineteen-year-old firefighter in Lewiston, Idaho, summed up the mood to a *New York Times*/CBS News pollster: "I would like to see quick justice, but if you jump the gun and attack the wrong person, it's not going to accomplish anything."[8]

If anyone was restless for action, it was Bush's own right flank. *National Review*'s Web edition disseminated a call from the professional provocateur Ann Coulter to invade the hijackers' countries, "kill their leaders and convert them to Christianity."[9] On the same day as the president's measured speech before Congress, a saber-rattling "open letter" signed by William Bennett, Richard Perle, Gary Bauer, and editors of *The New Republic* and *The Weekly Standard* threatened to brand the president a wimp—guilty of "surrender in the war on international terrorism"—should he buck their demand to make "a determined effort" to oust Saddam Hussein "even if evidence does not link Iraq directly to the attack."[10] These signatories and others on the right were so busy accusing Colin Powell of appeasement, because of his known reluctance to wage a new war against Saddam, that they failed to acknowledge that the Democratic leaders, Tom Daschle and Richard Gephardt, as well as Gore, were proving fiercely loyal to the administration.

Other conservatives wanted to make domestic political hay out of 9/11 while the ashes at Ground Zero were still hot. On Pat Robertson's daily television show, *The 700 Club,* Jerry Falwell said, "I really believe that the pagans, and the abortionists, and the feminists, and the gays and the lesbians who are actively trying to make that an alternative lifestyle, the ACLU, People for the American Way—all of them who have tried to secularize America—I point the finger in their face and say, 'You helped this happen.'" Robertson concurred, adding that "the problem is we have adopted that agenda at the highest levels of our government."[11]

These views, though disowned by some other conservative evangelical Christian leaders, were not out of step with the evangelicals' reading of the Bible; it was their deeply held belief that God would withdraw protection from nations that didn't honor His word. In its own pandering to this constituency, *The Wall Street Journal*'s editorial page suggested just eight days after 9/11 that the president use his high poll ratings to push conservative judicial nominees of the Robertson-Falwell stripe through the Senate.[12]

That America's own homegrown admixture of fundamentalism and political paranoia could be Taliban-esque at its extremes was a point fundamentalist fellow travelers such as the Republican hierarchy, the Bush administration, and its press claque at Fox News and the *Journal* largely chose to ignore, if they noticed it at all. The philosophical similarities were not superficial. Sayyid Qutb, the Egyptian intellectual (1906–1966) whose writings were instrumental in formulating the radical, fundamentalist Islamism championed by Al Qaeda, had lived in the United States from 1948 to 1950, when he studied American education on a scholarship at what was then known as the Colorado State College of Education. His ruminations on his time in the town of Greeley were very much in the spirit of the Robertson-Falwell post-9/11 condemnation of American wantonness. Qutb condemned the open sexuality of "the American girl" and decried even a church-sponsored teenage dance for its atmosphere of "desire" as teenagers gyrated "to the tunes of the gramophone."[13]

But as powerful as Bush's own fundamentalist base could be, he put a distance between himself and the homegrown ayatollahs after 9/11 as he had not done in his Bob Jones excursion during the 2000 campaign. Almost immediately, the White House released a statement rejecting the Robertson-Falwell take on 9/11. Falwell had no choice but to beat a hasty and humiliating retreat, trying to eradicate evidence seen by the world on videotape by lamely accusing "news reports" of taking his words "out of their context." Similarly, Bush quickly disowned his early and inflammatory call for a "crusade" against terrorists and was almost slavishly PC in paying public respect to American Muslims. He ignored the *Journal*'s demand that he force right-wing judicial nominations through the Senate.

The White House jumped on its very few liberal critics at least as hard as it did on Falwell and Robertson. Dissent, it made plain, was a synonym for disloyalty. The first administration target was, of all people, a stand-up comic, Bill Maher, the host of the ABC late-night show *Politically Incorrect*. Maher had not directly criticized the government but had made the politically incorrect observation that the hijackers, who committed suicide while committing mass murder, were not cowardly compared with an America that thought it could strike back by launching cruise missiles at targets thousands of miles away. Ari Fleischer, the White House press secretary, denounced Maher, issuing a general warning that in times like these "people need to watch what they say, watch what they do." An uproar ensued, and perhaps more intriguing than Fleischer's statement itself was the revelation that his veiled threat was mysteriously missing from the official transcript the White House later posted of his briefing. A Fleischer deputy explained that this strange elision had been an innocent mistake—"a transcription error." But it remained uncorrected for days.[14] *Politically Incorrect* was soon canceled by ABC.

The White House expected obedience not merely from entertainers but from the press—and mostly it got it. The post-9/11 presidential address to Congress was all it took for Washington to uncork a Hollywood fairy tale, or perhaps a Shakespearean one, in which the immature leader of September 10 was transformed overnight into a giant by a single scripted speech. (Cheney played Falstaff to Bush's Prince Hal.) The awestruck tone was set by David Broder of *The Washington Post,* the so-called dean of the capital press corps and the pacesetter for the city's conventional wisdom. His column was titled "Echoes of Lincoln."[15]

Press adulation was not all the White House wanted; it also wanted control. When the United States made its first strikes in Afghanistan in October, there were no pictures available—except from Aljazeera, the Arab network based in Qatar, whose live shots of nighttime antiaircraft fire around Kabul were conveyed on the American cable-news networks. It was also Aljazeera that, on the very first day of U.S. military action, broadcast a video in which Osama bin Laden threatened further terrorism. Bin Laden was preceded on-screen by his deputy, Ayman al-Zawahiri, who asked, "American people, can you ask yourselves why there is so much hate against America?"

To counteract this propaganda, America fashioned some of its own, even as it experimented with restricting information by canceling a routine daily Pentagon press briefing. The Defense Department's footage to networks included a hokey shot of the launch of a Tomahawk missile set against the backdrop of the American flag. Pilots from the first Afghanistan missions were made available to a pool of reporters. All their news from the front was good news. There were few means for verifying it. Once the bombing of Afghanistan began, press access to U.S. troops was restricted for months, so that Americans learned about even the war's red-letter events, like the fall of Mazar-i-Sharif, only secondhand. At first no American reporter or anchor questioned the spoon-fed government handouts, though a Canadian Broadcasting Corporation reporter, speaking on his own network, was allowed a skeptical observation: "We've heard the Americans describe their missions before as a well-oiled machine and it turned out not to be the case."[16]

Having yet to bring bin Laden to justice either dead or alive, the White House tried another countermove: the president and other administration officials simply stopped mentioning the chief evildoer by name in all public statements. This lasted for all of three days in October, after which the White House slapped bin Laden with that most American form of capital punishment—kicking him off network television. Condoleezza Rice, the national security adviser, held a conference call with the top American network and cable news executives to ask that they no longer broadcast unedited bin Laden rants. She was worried that coded messages would reach Qaeda cells in the United States and incite Muslims to attack Americans in countries where the international incarnations of CNN and NBC were available. But what Rice mainly accomplished was inadvertently to send three not too successfully coded messages of her own: (1) that the administration entertained at least a passing fantasy that Al Qaeda, despite its access both to the Internet and to the Arabic superstation Aljazeera (then with 35 million viewers worldwide, 150,000 by dish and cable in the United States), could be disrupted by having its video kept off the likes of Fox; (2) that the administration's ambitions to manage the news knew no bounds; and (3) that the White House, like the rest of America, had been spooked by bin Laden and Zawahiri's almost instant rebuttal to President Bush as the war in Afghanistan began. Undaunted, the White House asked the same self-censorship of newspapers, requesting that they not publish transcripts of bin Laden's proclamations, for fear they might, in Ari Fleischer's words, find their way "into the hands of people who can read it and see something in it."

The same strictures applied abroad: Richard Boucher, a State Department spokesman, publicly chastised Voice of America for defying the department's request that it not broadcast a rare interview it had obtained with the Taliban leader, mullah Mohammad Omar. Though the mission of Voice of America is in part to demonstrate the value of a free press to societies that don't have one, State was more interested in dumbed-down propaganda with minimal journalistic content. To serve as undersecretary for public diplomacy, it recruited Charlotte Beers, a former chairwoman of the Madison Avenue giants Ogilvy & Mather and J. Walter Thompson, whose career triumphs included campaigns for Uncle Ben's rice and Head & Shoulders shampoo. In her government job, Beers eventually created a "Shared Values" campaign—slick videos featuring American Muslims talking about how wonderful their life in the United States was. The warm multicultural tableaux were reminiscent of testimonial commercials for new household cleaning products—or of the Bush presidential campaign's spots for No Child Left Behind. Many Arab nations refused to show the spots, complaining that they didn't address the most serious problem for America among Muslims—its policies in the Middle East.

Behind the scenes, even more ambitious efforts to manipulate public opinion both at home and abroad were quietly being set in motion. At the Pentagon, a covert Office of Strategic Influence (OSI), with a staff of fifteen, was established to plant helpful "news," some of it phony, with foreign media. The office was headed by Brigadier General Simon Worden of the air force, who reported to Douglas Feith, the undersecretary of defense for policy. Some of the operation's multimillion-dollar budget was going to outside contractors such as the Rendon Group, an international consulting firm in Washington whose clients had included the Central Intelligence Agency, the Kuwaiti royals, and the Iraqi National Congress, the anti-Hussein exile group headed by Ahmad Chalabi.[17]

The existence of the OSI became public just a few months later—in February 2002, when it was reported by *The New York Times*.[18] The *Times* learned that one military unit assigned to carry out the office's programs was the army's Psychological Operations command. In the ensuing debate, some of it taking place within the Pentagon, critics wondered if an American attempt to psych out foreign media with fake press releases and e-mails might backfire and antagonize U.S. allies. A week after the *Times* report on the office ran, Bush distanced himself from the OSI, and a day after that Rumsfeld said it was being "closed down," not so much as a matter of principle but because its clandestine work had been "damaged" by the revelation of its existence. Reports that its activities had merely been rerouted to other parts of the Pentagon bureaucracy persisted after its demise.

More blatant was the administration's plan to turn the war in Afghanistan into a reality TV series. It gave the green light to Jerry Bruckheimer, the producer of the reality hit *The Amazing Race* and the movie blockbusters *Top Gun*, *Black Hawk Down*, and *Pearl Harbor*, to pursue an ABC prime-time series about the "compelling personal stories of the U.S. military men and women who bear the burden of the fighting."[19] Torie Clarke, the Defense Department PR chief, and Rear Admiral Craig Quigley, the chief flack with Central Command, promised Bruckheimer and his colleagues access to the troops, technical advice, and the use of aircraft carriers in exchange for the Pentagon's retention of the right to review all footage (exclusively for catching any security breaches, they said). This proximity to the war was a privilege generally denied to the news media. Just before the series was announced, one *Washington Post* reporter in Afghanistan wrote of having been held at gunpoint by American soldiers when he tried to get to the scene of a missile strike on suspected Qaeda fighters; he was told he would be shot if he pursued the story further.[20] The Pentagon tried to discredit the reporter's account, but the *Post* correspondent, Doug Struck, stood firm, saying that the Pentagon version of what went on (that he was being curtailed only for his own safety) was "an amazing lie" that "shows the extremes the military is going to to keep this war secret, to keep reporters from finding out what's going on."[21]

Understandably, given such restrictions on reporters, ABC's news division complained to its parent company, Disney, that it was unfair for an outside entertainment producer like Bruckheimer to be permitted to create a documentary about the war while actual correspondents were being shut out. But Disney stiffed its own journalists, much to the delight of the military. "There's a lot of other ways to convey information to the American people than through news organizations," Admiral Quigley said in defending his end-run around the press. Bruckheimer had far more clout with this Pentagon than Peter Jennings, though not so much that he could save *Profiles from the Front Line* from almost instant oblivion in the Nielsen ratings when it finally aired a year later on the eve of another war, in February 2003. By then, the war in Afghanistan, forgotten though not gone, was yesterday's news.

THE AFGHANISTAN WAR was branded "America's New War" by CNN, and Americans were on board. Polls showed that 94 percent of Americans supported the war, with even a presumed bastion of leftism like the Harvard student body proving pro-war by more than two to one. The very few who had anything critical to say on the subject were greeted with such a disproportionate avalanche of invective that you would hardly guess that Susan Sontag, Bill Maher, and Noam Chomsky were a writer, a late-night comic, and a linguistics professor—Americans with less clout and a smaller following than a substitute weatherman on the *Today* show. The similarly overheated rage from the angry right about pacifists on and off college campuses suggested that there was a large and serious antiwar movement afoot to rival that of the Vietnam sixties. There wasn't, not even remotely.

You had to wonder if those in and around the administration who protested the minuscule protests against the war were protesting too much. They sometimes sounded as if they had something to cover up. And maybe they did. Giving a first progress report on the war at a press conference in the early going, Bush found solid advances on every single front, without a single setback, not even a minor one, of any kind.

But there were already glitches too visible to ignore in the sweeping war on terror. The first sign was the anthrax scare. It had begun on October 4, when news broke that a Florida man had contracted pulmonary anthrax, which Tommy Thompson, the secretary of health and human services, instantly dismissed as "an isolated case" that was "not contagious" and was most likely environmental in origin. "We do know that he drank water out of a stream when he was traveling to North Carolina last week," the secretary said during a White House briefing. The victim died the following day, but it wasn't for another week, as anthrax proliferated at the Boca Raton offices of American Media, a tabloid publisher, on its way north to congressional offices on Capitol Hill and high-powered media towers in New York, that it dawned on the White House that the crisis had nothing to do with streams in North Carolina. Once it belatedly realized that, in essence, another terrorist attack was under way, the administration's first impulse was not to secure as much Cipro as speedily as possible to protect Americans, but to protect the right of pharmaceutical companies to profiteer by refusing to break Bayer AG's patent and authorize other drug companies to produce generic versions of the drug.[22] Even as Washington fell into panic after anthrax turned up in the office of the Democratic leader

Tom Daschle, Bush said little about it, delegating the problem to ineffectual Cabinet members like Thompson and the attorney general, John Ashcroft.

The rank incompetence of these two Cabinet secretaries, at most thinly disguised by a veneer of supercilious officiousness, was farcical. They were Keystone Kops in the costumes of bureaucrats, ready at any time to slip on a banana peel. Thompson came across as a chamber of commerce glad-hander who didn't know his pants were on fire, and Ashcroft often shook as if he'd just seen not only great Caesar's ghost but perhaps John Mitchell's as well. In his disregard for the law, Ashcroft often did seem determined to emulate the Watergate-era attorney general, though on a grander scale. It wasn't enough for Congress to enhance his antiterrorist legal arsenal legitimately by passing the USA Patriot Act before most of those on the Hill had taken the time or the trouble to read it; the attorney general changed other rules without consulting senators or congressmen of either party at all. He abridged by decree the Freedom of Information Act, an essential check on government misbehavior during peace and war alike, and discreetly slipped into the Federal Register a new directive allowing eavesdropping on conversations between some lawyers and clients.[23] If the administration was really proud of grabbing "emergency" powers at wartime, why was it doing so in the dead of night? Ashcroft refused repeated requests to explain himself before congressional committees. At one House briefing where he did show up, he told congressmen they could call an 800 number if they had any questions about what his department was up to.[24]

What was known was far from encouraging. Eight former FBI officials, including a former director, William Webster, went on the record to criticize Ashcroft's post-9/11 blanket arrests—not because they violated civil liberties but because they violated law-enforcement common sense. By nabbing possible terrorists prematurely, the government may have lost the ability to track them as they implicated the rest of their cells. Of the nine hundred known suspects rounded up since 9/11, none had been criminally charged in the World Trade Center attack. Another Ashcroft brainstorm—an attempt to interview five thousand Middle Eastern men around the United States—was widely ridiculed by FBI veterans, too. (Not one of them would ever be convicted of a terrorist offense.)[25] Kenneth Walton, who established the Bureau's first Joint Terrorism Task Force in New York, said, "It's the Perry Mason school of law enforcement, where you get them in there and they confess. . . . It is ridiculous."[26] Most of the invited interviewees were not turning up anyway, and those who did needed only reply by rote to yes or no questions from a four-page script.

Ashcroft's Justice Department seemed to be squandering time and resources on wild-goose chases that pumped up arrest numbers without making any progress on tracking down terrorists, including those who had so effectively peppered scattered high-profile sites with anthrax. A month after the first anthrax case, the FBI still hadn't located all the American labs that legally handled anthrax, let alone any suspects in the anthrax attacks.[27]

But Ashcroft had been zealous and then some about warning of other terrorism attacks while the anthrax threat was proceeding under his nose. The first alert of a probable new attack was issued two weeks after 9/11. On the first-month anniversary of 9/11, the attorney general and the FBI warned again that new attacks by terrorists either in America or overseas might happen in the "next several days." Bush endorsed this alert, but neither he nor anyone else in the government explained how serious the threat was or what form it might take or where it might happen. The president told Americans "to go about their lives, to fly on airplanes, to travel, to go to work" regardless. On October 29, there was yet another grave alert from Ashcroft, who said that there were terrorist attacks planned against the United States in the next week, though the intelligence did "not contain specific information as to the type of attack or specific targets."

When no attacks occurred, Ashcroft was eager to pat himself on the back for combating them. On November 8, he announced that "the home front has witnessed the opening battle in the war against terrorism, and America has emerged victorious." His evidence for this victory was that "two periods of extremely high threat have passed" without anything happening—though both these periods of high threat were entirely on his say-so. But his boss knew that America needed a pep talk from a leader who inspired more confidence than his attorney general, who seemed to regard battling terrorism as a part-time job. (He was simultaneously freelancing another initiative, the prosecution of doctors assisting the suicides of the terminally ill in Oregon.) So, on the same night that Ashcroft declared victory in the war against terrorism in the capital, the president gave a prime-time speech in Atlanta, calling for the creation of a volunteer civil-defense service and a larger National Guard presence at airports.

Bush stood before a backdrop emblazoned with the slogan UNITED WE STAND and with pictures of America's new heroes, police officers and rescue workers. His speech ended with the exhortation "Let's roll!"—then thought to be the final words of Todd Beamer, a passenger who helped lead the revolt against the 9/11 hijackers on Flight 93.

Eventually the 9/11 Commission would discover that the actual words spoken (not necessarily Beamer's) were "roll it"—perhaps referring to an airplane service cart that the passengers hoped they might use to smash their way into the cockpit. But the number of Americans who heard Bush appropriate "Let's roll!" as an applause line was diminished anyway; only one of the four networks, the one with ratings in the toilet (ABC), interrupted regular programming for his speech. The other three reverted instead to the old normal: *Family Guy, Friends,* and *Survivor 3.* Later that night, CBS at last aired an episode of its CIA drama *The Agency,* which had twice been postponed that fall for fear it would upset the audience. In the can well before 9/11, it predicted an anthrax attack on Washington well before anyone in the government had awakened to that possibility.

BY THEN the Taliban government of Afghanistan had collapsed—a cause for thanksgiving as Thanksgiving approached. Though some skeptical journalists had seen some early signs of a Vietnam-like quagmire, the American public had remained united and resolute. A *Los Angeles Times* poll found that even Democrats supported Bush by a four-to-one margin, as if bitter memories of the Florida recount and its aftermath had been eviscerated. Yet for a country incessantly declaring itself to be at war, the country often didn't seem to be at war. Asked if the American people had to make any sacrifices to defeat terrorism, the only one the president could come up with was longer lines at the airport. His most frequent peroration to the home front was to take more vacations, a cause he believed in so fervently that he lent his image to a TV ad sponsored by the Travel Industry Association of America.[28] As long as we took time off to spend more money, all would be well. No higher calling was necessary.

It was a lost opportunity. After 9/11, the many Americans not in uniform came together, eager to be part of a national mobilization even if they weren't about to enlist themselves. But because there was a vacuum of leadership in defining what form that patriotism might take, the initial national impulse started to diminish. The farther away Americans were from 9/11, both in time and geography, the faster it faded. Or became a brand, ready to do its American duty and move product. Ground Zero soon had its own viewing stand, with vendors selling souvenirs and long lines like those for Space Mountain at Disneyland. When TV correspondents came down to sample the bustling scene, visitors waved and smiled at the camera just as they did uptown at the *Today* show. For the Christmas season, Barnes & Noble offered competing coffee-table books handsomely packaging the carnage of just months before. On Gary Condit's Web site, a snapshot of the congressman's own visit to Ground Zero was posted to help sell his (doomed) reelection campaign. "Portraits of Grief," a popular daily feature in which *The New York Times* profiled the dead of 9/11, was retired at the New Year. In almost a gesture of nostalgia, *Time* magazine picked not George W. Bush or Osama bin Laden as its Person of the Year but Rudy Giuliani, already moving out of the spotlight along with the day that won him American hearts.

The new patriotism boosting America's waning new war often proved to be little more than vicarious patriotism reminiscent of the pre-9/11 fetishism of the greatest generation. While Americans applauded the selfless men and women in uniform, whether at Ground Zero or in battle, we could rest assured that the all-volunteer army would take care of everything. We didn't have to do our part, whatever that part was. There was no incentive to reduce the nation's dependence on the oil from the country that had nurtured most of the hijackers, Saudi Arabia, no interest in Washington in revisiting a $1.35 trillion, ten-year tax cut to find the serious money needed to underwrite a long-term war effort. Supporting the war by plastering flags on a gas-guzzling foreign car, Bill Maher observed, was "literally the least you can do." And we leapt at that option.

While the administration hadn't harnessed the post-9/11 outpouring of national unity to a war effort, it nonetheless wanted the country's war mood to remain at full throttle. As long as terror still lurked, the White House argued, legal superpowers would be required to vanquish the shadowy enemy. To the White House, the other two branches of government, the judicial and the legislative, were just too feckless and untrustworthy to do their part in the battle between good and evil. And so, even as we were tracking down a heinous enemy, Osama bin Laden, who operated out of a cave, our government started moving our own legal system into a cave of sorts.

Bush issued an executive order to set up military tribunals in which neither the verdicts, evidence, nor punishments ever had to be revealed to the public. Ashcroft refused to identify detainees or explain why they were being held or even to provide an accurate count of the detainee population. The attorney general's stated motive for this secrecy was to prevent Al Qaeda from learning if any of its operatives might be locked up, as if the enemy were not cunning enough to figure out on its own which members might have been apprehended (if any). Ashcroft's legal argument was that existing law prevented him from giving out this information, but then his own deputy pointed out that the detainees had the right to publicize their names on their own, through their family or counsel. After much public criticism, Ashcroft relented and released some of the names he had so strenuously withheld. In keeping with his less-than-inspiring public image, he seemed to lack even the courage of his own wrong convictions.

Testifying before the Senate in December, Ashcroft grew defensive. He unveiled a new strategy to deflect critics of his high-handed legal actions—and by implication laid out a way to ward off critics of the administration in general. Those who challenged his policies, he declared, would "only aid terrorists" and "give ammunition to America's enemies." It was hard to know whom he was talking about. The only prominent traitors in sight were the usual civil-liberties watchdogs and a milquetoast legislator or two barely known beyond the Beltway or their own constituencies. Polls found the public squarely on the attorney general's side, and even the few pundits who dared knock him were ridiculed by their journalistic colleagues as hysterics so busy fussing about civil liberties that they had forgotten that "there's a war going on." But a line had been drawn: Americans who were not "with" the administration might just be "with" the terrorists. When Tom Daschle had opposed oil drilling in the Arctic National Wildlife Refuge that fall, an administration ally, the Family Research Council, ran ads in Daschle's home state of South Dakota likening him to Saddam Hussein.[29] The Republican leader Trent Lott would later codify this genre of attack: "How dare Senator Daschle criticize President Bush while we are fighting our war on terrorism?"[30] The new year would soon bring negative TV and radio ads in which firefighters and flags were used as props and incumbent Senate Democrats were demonized as partisans who would "put their interests ahead of national interests."

THE THRUST of a war against terrorism going forward was becoming blurry, however, now that the Taliban had been routed. But shortly after the early-November fall of Kabul a new definition started to come hazily into view. Appearing in the White House Rose Garden for a brief post-Thanksgiving ceremony featuring two American aid workers who had been rescued in Afghanistan, Bush said that "Afghanistan is still just the beginning" of the war, and that if leaders in Iraq developed "weapons of mass destruction that will be used to terrorize nations, they will be held accountable." Hardly had the event ended than the press noted that the president's words were his first direct mention that Iraq might be a new battleground. Ari Fleischer quickly put out the fire. "It's nothing new," the White House press secretary said. "The president is focusing on Afghanistan."

Two weeks later Cheney picked up the subject of Iraq again, this time on *Meet the Press,* where he revised comments he had made to Tim Russert on the subject the first weekend after 9/11. Back then, Russert had asked the vice president about the 9/11 attacks: "Do we have any evidence linking Saddam Hussein or Iraqis to this operation?" The answer was a flat no. Now, on December 9, Cheney spoke of a new development "since you and I last talked, Tim." The vice president said that "it's been pretty well confirmed" that one of the 9/11 hijackers, Mohamed Atta, went to Prague and met "with a senior official of the Iraqi intelligence service in Czechoslovakia last April, several months before the attack."

Soon after Cheney asserted this 9/11-Iraq connection, *The New York Times* ran a front-page article by Judith Miller under the headline "SECRET SITES; Iraqi Tells of Renovations at Sites for Chemical and Nuclear Arms." The December 20, 2001, story began: "An Iraqi defector who described himself as a civil engineer said he personally worked on renovations of secret facilities for biological, chemical and nuclear weapons in underground wells, private villas and under the Saddam Hussein Hospital in Baghdad as recently as a year ago." The defector, Adnan Ihsan Saeed al-Haideri, spoke to Miller in an interview arranged in Bangkok by the Iraqi National Congress, the Iraqi opposition group headed by Ahmad Chalabi and funded by the Rendon Group.[31]

Once the American invasion of Iraq began in 2003, other journalists, including Seymour Hersh of *The New Yorker*, would raise serious doubts about this defector's claims. But in truth the CIA had known that al-Haideri was suspect from the start—he had flunked a CIA lie-detector test three days before the Miller article appeared. Or so it would be reported by Jonathan S. Landay of Knight Ridder,[32] some two and a half years after Miller's front-page scoop gave such scary evidence of the threat posed by Saddam Hussein's weapons of mass destruction as Christmas approached in 2001.

THREE

"I DON'T THINK ANYBODY COULD HAVE PREDICTED..."

On Christmas Day, 2001, Karl Rove, Bush's longtime political guru, told Richard L. Berke of *The New York Times* about a conversation he'd had with the president just after 9/11. In Rove's recollection, Bush set the bipartisan tone for political behavior during a national emergency: "He just said, 'Politics has no role in this. Don't anybody talk to me about politics for a while.'" But that—if it ever happened—was then, and this was now. The New Normal was kaput. The new year—a midterm election year—was at hand. So was the annual State of the Union address. This would be Bush's first speech to the nation since his appearance before a joint session of Congress on the eve of the war in Afghanistan. Now that the war was fast receding in the public consciousness, Berke reported, the White House was having "extensive discussions about how long Mr. Bush can sustain his impressive popularity ratings." One strategist working with the administration explained the game plan: "They're not manipulating the military operations. But there's a manipulation of the environment. They take advantage of the situation to achieve some political objectives."[1]

But to get to the State of the Union at the end of January, the White House had to first run the gauntlet of Enron. The Houston energy giant, the greatest single financial patron of Bush's political career, was imploding under the weight of scandalous revelations. At the end of 2001, it had filed for bankruptcy protection, laid off four thousand employees, and left its stockholders and pensioners with shares plunging toward penny-stock trading levels. News of Enron–White House ties proliferated daily; the Bush administration had been something of a full-employment service for past Enron consultants and executives, from Lawrence Lindsey, the chief economic adviser, to Thomas White, secretary of the army, to the White House counsel, Alberto Gonzales, who had had an attorney-client relationship with Enron while a partner at Vinson & Elkins, in Houston. Enron brass had participated in a secret Dick Cheney energy task force that wrote the administration's energy policy. Even the sole medical heavyweight the White House could produce to endorse its stem-cell "compromise" the preceding August, John Mendelsohn, was tainted by Enron: the MD Anderson Cancer Center in Houston, which he ran, received six hundred thousand dollars in Enron lucre while he was a member of its board, serving on its notorious see-no-evil audit committee.[2] No wonder the number of available stem-cell lines under the Bush plan had turned out to be as inflated as Enron profits.

After New Year's, the Justice Department confirmed that an inevitable criminal investigation of the company was under way–albeit one without the department's chief, John Ashcroft, who recused himself from the case because of his own past political contributions from Enron. The next day, the president addressed the growing fury, telling reporters that Enron's CEO, Kenneth Lay, who had contributed hundreds of thousands of dollars both to the Republicans' post-election legal fight in Florida and to the subsequent presidential inaugural in Washington, was in fact a supporter of Ann Richards, the Democratic governor of Texas whom Bush had defeated in 1994. "And she had named him the head of the Governor's Business Council," Bush said. "And I decided to leave him in place, just for the sake of continuity. And that's when I first got to know Ken and worked with Ken." Bush was either suffering from memory loss or lying outright. The president who said he "got to know" Lay only in 1994 had actually known him since at least 1992, and Lay himself had said in a PBS *Frontline* documentary from early 2001 that he "did support" Bush over Richards in the Texas gubernatorial race.[3]

For a leader who had promised to usher America into a "new era of personal responsibility" after the Clinton years, it was a poor performance; the whole country knew that he had bestowed a nickname, "Kenny Boy," on the man he now publicly referred to at times as "Mr. Lay." But it was nothing Bush couldn't ride out, over the short term at least, thanks to the halo effect of war. The country would cut him some slack, especially if the subject of the national conversation could be moved away from Enron and its implications for an ailing post-9/11 economy and back to the imperatives of terrorism. That war would be the theme of that year's political campaign was laid out explicitly by Rove in a speech in Austin on January 18 as the State of the Union approached. "Americans trust the Republicans to do a better job of keeping our communities and our families safe," Rove told the winter meeting of the Republican National Committee. "We can also go to the country on this issue because they trust the Republican Party to do a better job of protecting and strengthening America's military might and thereby protecting America."[4] The president's post 9/11 directive—"Don't anybody talk to me about politics for a while"—was from that moment defunct. "For a while" had turned out to mean all of four months.

The State of the Union, presented to a cheering Congress still aglow with the post-9/11 bipartisanship that had uncharacteristically suffused the capital, was more explicit about how Rove's "issue" might be sustained. The president larded the audience with heroes and widows from 9/11. "Our war against terror is only beginning," he declared. He made a rare, explicit, if nonbinding, appeal for sacrifice, asking Americans to devote two years (or four thousand hours) to a new and vaguely defined USA Freedom Corps and proposing an expanded Peace Corps. But what most grabbed the world's attention was Bush's vow to take on any "regimes that sponsor terror"—specifically, Iraq, Iran, and North Korea, which he collectively branded the "axis of evil." This embryonic statement of Bush's novel doctrine of preemptive war would be remembered long after the call for volunteerism was completely forgotten (as it was by the following morning).

There was, of course, no mention of Enron in the State of the Union. But rather pointedly, for a speech that was going to sustain the idea of a nation at war, there was also no mention of Public Enemy No. 1, the man wanted dead or alive, the one we were at war with—Osama bin Laden.

———

THOUGH THE ADMINISTRATION had had an on-again, off-again strategy about whether to vilify or ignore bin Laden, it had dramatically pushed him center stage only a month before the State of the Union speech by releasing a video in which the Qaeda leader boasted about his 9/11 handiwork. "We calculated in advance the number of casualties from the enemy, who would be killed based on the position of the tower," bin Laden said, according to the American government translation. "We calculated that the floors that would be hit would be three or four floors. I was the most optimistic of them all." The exact circumstances of how this tape, said to be found in Afghanistan, ended up in the hands of the CIA were not divulged.

What was certain was the White House's confidence that the tape was a coup in the propaganda war. Bush publicized the bin Laden video himself, saying that it depicted "a man who is so devious and so cold-hearted that he laughs about the suicide, so-called suicide bombers that lost their lives." The government sent copies to every American embassy, along with talking points that it hoped would impress Muslims and Muslim governments that bin Laden was a "coward" who defamed Islam. The usual concern that the dissemination of such a tape might upset families of the 9/11 dead—a constituency to which Bush, following Rudy Giuliani's lead, was slavishly deferential—was pushed aside this time. "I was hesitant to allow there to be a vivid reminder of their loss and tragedy displayed on our TVs," the president said, before adding that "on the other hand" the tape "would be a devastating declaration of guilt for this evil person." Also forgotten was the fear, so paramount to the administration only months earlier, that any broadcast or publication of a bin Laden message might impart coded messages to awaken plotting sleeper cells.

Dan Bartlett, a White House flack, told *The New York Times* that he wished "we could take credit for the buildup" to the video's release, so successful had its rollout been in terms of public relations.[5] All of which made it odd that bin Laden would be eighty-sixed just a month later in the State of the Union speech. A possible explanation for the omission emerged three months after that, in April, when *The Washington Post* broke the first account of how the man wanted "dead or alive" had definitively eluded American capture. According to civilian and military officials, the Bush administration had lost its prey in the battle for Tora Bora in the first ten days of December 2001—during the exact period when the White House was so assiduously hawking its bin Laden tape. Rear Admiral Craig Quigley, the Centcom spokesman who had joyously welcomed a Jerry Bruckheimer–ABC spinoff of the Afghanistan war as a helpful alternative to actual war reportage by journalists, now tried his own hand at creating a fictionalized scenario: "We have never seen anything that was convincing to us at all that Osama bin Laden was present at any stage of Tora Bora—before, during or after."[6] But he and his immediate bosses, the Centcom commander Tommy Franks and Defense Secretary Donald Rumsfeld, were the only people in the know who subscribed to that fantasy version of events and continued to push it after the *Post* published its much different account. In the coming months and years, other sources would repeatedly corroborate the newspaper's initial report on the disastrous failure to nab bin Laden in Tora Bora that December, culminating with Gary Berntsen, a top CIA commander on the ground at the time and a leader in the brilliant campaign that undid the Taliban in Afghanistan. In his memoir *Jawbreaker,* published in 2005, Berntsen, a Bush loyalist, tells of how his teams found bin Laden and his remaining entourage in the mountains on the Afghan-Pakinstani border and begged Centcom for eight hundred U.S. Army Rangers to "block a possible Al-Qaeda escape into Pakistan." But instead he was ignored by Franks and the Pentagon, who inexplicably entrusted the job instead to Afghan warlords with agendas of their own. Bin Laden effortlessly slipped away while Berntsen fumed.

That the White House would keep bin Laden out of the first post-9/11 State of the Union address was itself a tacit admission that it knew it had lost him in Tora Bora through carelessness or incompetence. Perhaps if bin Laden's name were kept out of the speech no one would ask too many questions. From then on, the president continued to downplay bin Laden, at one point maintaining that anyone who brought him up did not "understand the scope of the mission" to go after a multitude of terrorists. "Terror is bigger than one person," Bush said in March. "He's a person that's now been marginalized" or "may even be dead." But even if bin Laden were still alive, Bush added, "I truly am not that concerned about him."

The news of bin Laden's easy escape was only the first of a series of embarrassing 9/11-related revelations that spring of 2002. In mid-May the news broke that a photo of Bush staring out the window of Air Force One while talking on the phone to Cheney on the day of the attack was being used to drum up business for the president's first political fund-raiser since the attacks. The pitch hawked a "specially commissioned, individually numbered and matted" reproduction of this "defining moment" for any donor who gave $150 or more, though it declined to untangle the riddle of exactly what Bush was doing posing for pictures on Air Force One while hopscotching around the country on 9/11.[7]

The day after this story came to light, CBS News had a far bigger bombshell, reporting that in early August of 2001 American intelligence agencies had warned the vacationing president that bin Laden was trying to hijack airplanes. Almost simultaneously with the CBS report came the news that an FBI agent in Phoenix had sent a memo to headquarters that summer urging an investigation of Middle Eastern men enrolled in American flight schools and speculating that bin Laden followers might exploit this training in terrorist activities. Ari Fleischer responded to these revelations by saying that the president had put law enforcement agencies on alert at the time, but it was hard to see what Fleischer meant. Contemporaneous reports on the day that Bush received the intelligence report, August 6, indicated that he had broken off from work early and gone fishing. Given the ease with which all nineteen hijackers slipped through airport security on 9/11, it was hard to buy the notion that any meaningful presidential alert had been in place. Nor did the White House press secretary explain why it took eight months for the White House to acknowledge that it had received warnings about bin Laden's hijacking ambitions during the president's vacation—a bit of information that would seem to contradict the long-held official stance that no one in the government had any "specific information" about a possible terrorist plot in the summer of 2001.

When Fleischer's statements failed to put the many questions to rest, Condoleezza Rice stepped into the fray. She spoke of how she had consulted with Richard Clarke, a White House counterterrorism official, in July, when "there was a lot of chatter in the system" about potential terrorist threats. She said that neither she nor the president knew anything about the FBI Phoenix memo but she acknowledged that the August 6 intelligence briefing had said that Islamic militants in bin Laden's camp might hijack American airliners. She added, "I don't think anybody could have predicted that these people would take an airplane and slam it into the World Trade Center" or use "a hijacked airplane as a missile."

For a moment Washington's bipartisan honeymoon was over; the House minority leader, Dick Gephardt, wanted to know more about what the White House had known about the events leading up to 9/11 and when it knew it. He and other critics, among them the Republican senator Richard Shelby, were immediately accused by Dick Cheney of violating patriotic etiquette. Labeling any suggestion that the White House had advance knowledge about the attacks as "incendiary," Cheney stated that merely to raise such questions was "thoroughly irresponsible and totally unworthy of national leaders in a time of war." But the revelations of pre-9/11 failures kept tumbling out anyway.

Hardly had the debate about the president's Crawford intelligence briefing subsided when Coleen Rowley, a senior agent in the FBI's Minneapolis office, sought whistle-blower status and sent a scathing thirteen-page letter to the congressional committee investigating pre-9/11 governmental preparedness. Rowley wrote that the FBI bureaucrats in Washington had prevented agents in her office from aggressively investigating Zacarias Moussaoui, a flight-school trainee arrested on immigration violations three weeks before 9/11; Washington repeatedly rejected the agents' pleas to obtain a search warrant that would allow them to look at Moussaoui's computer and search his belongings. Though the current FBI director, Robert Mueller III, was not in charge of the FBI at the time, Rowley accused him of trying to cover up the agency's blunders by publicly downplaying the value of the pre-9/11 warning signs it had ignored. The clues reported by agents in Minneapolis and Phoenix, Rowley contended, could have tipped off the government to an impending Qaeda strike in the United States.[8]

In direct counterpoint to these horror tales of sloppiness and screwups, the administration sent forth some horror tales of its own—a steady, distracting drumbeat of ominous security alerts not unlike those that had been ignored before 9/11. The week of the Rowley accusations began with Cheney saying on Sunday, May 19, that he was "almost certain" more attacks were on the way. Monday was Mueller's turn; the FBI director declared suicide bombings in the United States to be "inevitable," and his agency reported that New York landmarks such as the Statue of Liberty and the Brooklyn Bridge could be in the terrorists' sights. Rumsfeld followed, warning that terrorists would "inevitably" obtain weapons of mass destruction from sympathizers in various rogue nations, most prominently Iraq. Cheney, speaking midweek on *Larry King Live,* denied that there was any connection between this accelerating pile-up of terror alerts and the accelerating profusion of reports of pre-9/11 governmental ill-preparedness. But for all the warnings of new terror to come, the new homeland-security color-coded alert system didn't budge from its less-than-alarming level of yellow. Meanwhile, Cheney shot down the idea of an independent investigatory commission, first proposed by John McCain and Joe Lieberman, to look into the pre-9/11 mishaps. He instead favored the ongoing congressional inquiry that had already been hobbled and delayed by political squabbling, false starts, and Justice Department and CIA foot-dragging in producing relevant documents.

As more and more information dribbled out, filling in the damning narrative of what the government had been up to (or not) during that sleepy summer of 2001, a climactic TV event loomed: Coleen Rowley was invited to recount her firsthand chronicle of FBI incompetence in person before the Senate Judiciary Committee as part of its ongoing hearings. Curiosity was high. As if to drive up anticipation the day before her scheduled appearance, a Republican on the committee, Arlen Specter, previewed his conclusion: the government had possessed not just unconnected dots before 9/11 but a "veritable blueprint" for impending terrorist operations. The Rowley testimony threatened to create a crisis for this Bush presidency, as Anita Hill's testimony had for the first.

Only a bold PR move could upstage it, and the White House rose brilliantly to the challenge. The very morning of Rowley's Senate appearance came the abrupt and unexpected announcement that the president was now in favor of the creation of the new federal Department of Homeland Security that the Democrats had proposed and that he had heretofore vehemently opposed. As if to rub in the White House's ability to upstage its critics, Bush decided to deliver a national address to announce the new department that night, thereby assuring that Rowley's whistle-blowing would be knocked out of the lead position on the next day's morning shows and newspapers. Four days later would come another PR coup to push Rowley's revelations into the memory hole: commandeering television cameras during a routine trip to Moscow, Ashcroft announced that FBI agents had captured "a known terrorist" planning to explode a "dirty bomb" in the United States—Jose Padilla, a former Chicago gang member who in fact had been in custody since May 8, more than a month before Ashcroft interrupted his trip for his urgent televised bulletin.

This gambit didn't come a moment too soon. A Memorial Day weekend *USA Today*/CNN/Gallup poll the week before these PR stunts found that the spring revelations of pre-9/11 bungling had taken their toll. Only four in ten Americans now believed that America and its allies were winning the war on terrorism, down from two thirds in January, when the Taliban was on the run in Afghanistan.[9]

THAT BUSH had initially disdained the Homeland Security Department made far more ideological sense than his change of heart. This new governmental behemoth would be a Rube Goldberg contraption and a classic New Deal–Great Society bureaucracy with 169,000 employees. It would throw together agencies as far-flung as the Immigration and Naturalization Service and FEMA, the emergency-management office charged with responding to terrorist attacks and natural disasters such as hurricanes. In principle, Homeland Security's unwieldy size and likely inefficiency were an instant repudiation of the lean-government corporate Republicanism that Bush championed.

The first president with an MBA, Bush had billed his administration at the start as a model of CEO discipline. His cabinet was stuffed with CEOs, from Halliburton (Cheney), Searle (Rumsfeld), and Alcoa (the treasury secretary, Paul O'Neill). Two weeks before his inauguration, Bush invited Jack Welch, Ken Lay, and a bevy of CEOs down to Texas, to wave the flag of big-business hardheadedness and efficiency. After Clinton slovenliness, the new White House would be run like a Fortune 500 corporation by a steely, no-nonsense team of razor-sharp executives. This hoopla was reminiscent of that surrounding President-elect John F. Kennedy's nomination of Robert McNamara as secretary of defense in 1960. McNamara was apotheosized as the very model of the modern star business executive, the first non-Ford to be president of Ford Motor Company and the first MBA from Harvard to ascend so high in government. Or so he was lionized until his management genius (and its accompanying arrogance) proved to be worthless, if not counterproductive, to managing an intractable guerrilla war in Vietnam.

Like Kennedy, Bush had never run a successful business; his greatest management experience had been as governor in a state where the governor's powers were tightly limited. The inexperience showed. The image of CEO competence his handlers worked so hard to create during the campaign and at the inception of his presidency didn't square with the administration's early history. What the Princeton economist and *New York Times* columnist Paul Krugman labeled the "fuzzy math" of the Bush economic program—in which the inherited budget surplus would somehow remain intact despite the handing out of enormous tax cuts to those in CEO brackets—was only one aspect of the competence shortfall. Well before the missed Qaeda signals of the summer of 2001, there were signs of laxity in national-security management at the very top of the administration.

Back in May 2001, Bush had with great fanfare charged Cheney with overseeing a "national effort" to coordinate all federal programs for responding to domestic attacks in league with a new Office of National Preparedness at FEMA (even as FEMA was being downsized with a two-hundred-million-dollar budget cut).[10] The vice president had publicized his assignment from the president at the time, going on CNN to say that "one of our biggest threats as a nation" may include "a terrorist organization overseas." Cheney vowed "to take on the responsibility of overseeing all of that, reviewing the plans that are out there today," and Bush himself said he would "periodically chair a meeting of the National Security Council to review these efforts." But when Ari Fleischer was asked to list the vice president's policy portfolio at a press briefing on June 29, 2001, he made no mention of this task. When a reporter then specifically asked him if he could recall what task force Cheney had been appointed to head besides Energy, Fleischer answered, "No." Months later, after the attacks of 9/11, the new Homeland Security impresario, Tom Ridge, went on the *Today* show to reassure America that he would "continue the work the vice president started back in May of 2001." But no such work had been done in the first place by the vice president, and no National Security Council meetings chaired by the president had ever reviewed these nonexistent efforts.[11]

If this was a business culture, it was less like that of Jack Welch's General Electric than that of the smoke-and-mirror companies, many of them with swaggering CEOs and little accountability or board supervision, that had been laid bare by the dot-com crash. From the start, the administration was in the habit of cooking the books, even regarding the government's allegedly empirical scientific data on public health. The annual federal report on air pollution trends simply eliminated its usual (and no doubt troubling) section on global warming,[12] much as accountants at Arthur Andersen might have cleaned up an Enron balance sheet by hiding an unprofitable division. At the Department of Health and Human Services, expert advisory committees were being "retired" before they could present data that might contradict the president's policies on medical matters[13]–much as nay-saying Wall Street analysts of the 1990s were sidelined in favor of boosters who could be counted on to flog dogs like WorldCom or Pets.com right until they cratered.

As if to emphasize unwanted comparisons between the administration's conduct of official business and the sleazy ethos of the boom, Enron would just not go away. Its horrors were rapidly being echoed by bad corporate actors taking their own turn in the spotlight, including WorldCom and Tyco. Cheney's former company offered the makings of another scandal. Don Van Natta, Jr., and Jeff Gerth of *The New York Times* reported that the Kellogg Brown & Root unit of Halliburton had received a sweetheart deal with the army three months after 9/11, despite being the target of a criminal investigation for reputed bill-padding.[14] The contract, which called for KBR to take on such tasks as building cells for detainees at Guantánamo Bay in Cuba and feeding American troops in Uzbekistan, was for a ten-year term and was unique among comparable army contracts because it put no ceiling on costs. Soon Bush's own checkered history as a corporate officer and Texas oilman in the 1980s returned to the news, forcing him once again to defend his own prescient sale of stock as a Harken Energy insider before the company announced big losses. The scenario echoed executive stock sales at Enron that had been exquisitely timed to precede the company's collapse.

Faced with a growing crisis in capitalist confidence, Bush reverted to his old calling of cheerleader, hyping the prospects for the economy and demonizing corporate "wrongdoers" (not to be confused with jihadist "evildoers"). He announced a "financial crimes SWAT team" on July 9, 2002, but it curiously resembled one of Enron's phantom Cayman Island shell subsidiaries. It existed mainly on paper, as a coyly named entity with no real assets. There was no provision for new employees or funds or for FBI agents to replace those whom the Bureau had reassigned from white-collar crime to counterterrorism after 9/11.[15]

Such rhetorical quick fixes had zero effect. The markets soon hit their worst half-year finish since 1970, the Nasdaq was at a five-year low, the dollar was on the skids, and a majority of Americans told pollsters that the country was in a recession. The normally circumspect chief of Goldman Sachs, Henry M. Paulson, Jr., concluded, "I cannot think of a time when business over all has been held in less repute."[16] (Four years later, the White House would turn to Paulson to be its third secretary of the treasury.)

As the summer of 2002 wore on, nothing could knock Wall Street from the top of the evening news. Not a White House lawn presentation of the Homeland Security master plan. Not the sentencing of John Walker Lindh, the Marin County "Taliban" who had once been a national obsession. Not Ashcroft, in full quiver, telling Congress that the country was dotted with Qaeda sleeper cells "waiting to strike again." Not the resolution of the battle among Ted Williams's relatives over the fate of his corpse.

A worried president gave two more cheerleading speeches in July reassuring worried Americans that help was on the way. For his first pitch, he appeared against a blue background emblazoned with the repeated legend CORPORATE RESPONSIBILITY. Next came a red backdrop, with STRENGTHENING OUR ECONOMY as the double vision–inducing slogan. When the market failed to respond, Bush waxed philosophical, professing shock that his fellow citizens would care about something as base as money. Invoking 9/11, he said, "I believe people have taken a step back and asked, 'What's important in life?' You know, the bottom line and this corporate America stuff, is that important? Or is serving your neighbor, loving your neighbor like you'd like to be loved yourself?" It was the first and last time he sounded as if he came of age in the era of Flower Power.

By August, Bush was back on vacation in Crawford, though now chastened by the legacy of the previous summer's indolence. This was therefore to be a "working vacation." He would decisively deal with the problem at hand, convening a "forum" on the economy, conveniently situated in Waco, a half-hour drive from his ranch. The initially announced speakers were almost exclusively major corporate donors to the Republican Party, but after a barrage of criticism, other participants were added, including what the White House chief of staff, Andrew Card, referred to on CNN as "so-called real Americans." The so-called real Americans just happened to be enthusiasts for the administration's fiscal policies. Typical was Phyllis Hill Slater, an entrepreneur from Floral Park, New York, who echoed Bush's message that his tax cuts should be permanent. "I'm so glad to see you're on track," she told the president. The resulting evening-news video clips, not any changes in policy or debate, were the real point of the event; all eight panels in the forum were convened simultaneously on a Tuesday morning, ensuring that they would get at most fragmentary television coverage everywhere except on C-SPAN. The president pronounced the forum a "great show," and so it was. Every participant sounded scripted. The new backdrops carried soothing legends like SMALL INVESTORS/RETIREMENT SECURITY. Afterward, Karl Rove said that he was "not aware" that the White House had handed out talking points to the speakers, but added, "That's not to say there weren't any."[17]

DURING AND AFTER the Waco show, there continued to be reports of homeland security breakdowns that a new federal department would not be able to remedy anytime soon. At the FBI, a *Los Angeles Times* investigation revealed, the prehistoric computer system remained in disarray even as the agency's top executives were either being pushed out or fleeing for private employment (among them the counterterrorism chief).[18] *The Wall Street Journal* discovered that when the federal government issued a terrorist warning to shopping centers four months earlier, the Mall of America learned about it only by watching CNN.[19] Air marshals told *USA Today* that the undercover skycop program that was to be strengthened on commercial flights after 9/11 was in disarray, "a laughingstock."[20]

Ashcroft's managerial follies continued to abound. The attorney general announced a plan for the Immigration and Naturalization Service to fingerprint one hundred thousand largely Middle Eastern foreign visa holders the day before his own department's inspector general testified before Congress that the INS and FBI were still "years away" from absorbing into their records the fingerprint files already in their possession.[21] Responding to the cable-TV craze of that summer, recurrent horror tales of abducted girls, he went on the CBS *Early Show* to announce what he called the "first ever White House conference on missing and exploited children." (FBI figures actually showed a decline in the kidnapping of children—this new "crisis" had been manufactured for the nation's entertainment much as shark attacks had been the summer before.) Perhaps most farcically of all, the attorney general held a press conference to boast that a thirteen-month investigation into prostitution in New Orleans had yielded twelve arrests—not exactly the law-enforcement coup to inspire confidence in his ability to track down less conspicuous miscreants, such as terrorists.

These failures challenged a hagiographic story line of administration invincibility that had been codified everywhere from Annie Leibovitz's triumphalist photos of the White House honchos in *Vanity Fair* to a multipart series co-written by Bob Woodward for *The Washington Post*. But Karl Rove was hardly deterred from his continuing plans to capitalize on the president's image as a decisive wartime leader. In a news story that was little noticed at the end of the spring of 2002, a computer disk with a PowerPoint presentation by Rove and Ken Mehlman, the White House political director, strategizing that fall's coming elections mysteriously turned up in Lafayette Park, across from the White House. The disk ended up in the hands of a Democratic staff member, who passed it on to the Hill newspaper *Roll Call*.[22] There was much Washington fuss over the candid inside skinny the PowerPoint presentation revealed about which Republican senators and governors were and weren't vulnerable in various local races that year. But the most significant words of the whole purloined presentation, echoing those of Rove's speech to the Republican National Committee at the start of 2002, were the first three: "Focus on war."

FOUR

"YOU DON'T INTRODUCE NEW PRODUCTS IN AUGUST"

AYS AFTER Karl Rove and Ken Mehlman's PowerPoint disk fell into *Roll Call*'s lap, the Washington press was taking a curtain call. It was the thirtieth anniversary of the break-in by Nixon operatives to Democratic Party headquarters at the Watergate complex, and an occasion to celebrate once more the dogged investigative reporting by Bob Woodward and Carl Bernstein that had covered *The Washington Post* in glory and led to the unraveling of a criminal presidency. The contrast between that halcyon achievement and the present could not have been more pronounced. With a few notable exceptions—including, most famously, the congenitally skeptical Seymour Hersh of *The New Yorker*, who had made his own reputation as an investigative reporter in 1969, even earlier than Woodward and Bernstein, uncovering the My Lai massacre—there was only sporadic digging into the war-ennobled administration by mainstream journalists. Network television journalists, the primary source of news for most Americans, barely raised questions at all.

The White House was so accomplished at managing the press that it couldn't resist boasting about its own slick moves in much the way a Hollywood producer might brag about his cynical marketing plans for a can't-miss summer blockbuster. Thus, as the summer of 2002 ended, the president's handlers laid out their merchandising campaign for a war in Iraq. The kickoff event would be a short prime-time speech delivered by Bush from New York to commemorate the first anniversary of 9/11–the day before he was to make a longer address to the United Nations General Assembly.

Much deliberation went into choosing the setting. The winning site, Ellis Island in New York Harbor, beat out the competing alternative of Governors Island because from Ellis Island the camera angle could include the Statue of Liberty ablaze with light in the background behind Bush. "We had made a decision that this would be a compelling story either place," Dan Bartlett, the White House communications director, told Elisabeth Bumiller of *The New York Times*.[1] "We sent a team out to go and look and they said, 'This is a better shot,' and we said OK." Leading that team were Scott Sforza, a former ABC producer and the creator of message-laden White House backdrops such as those used at the Waco economic "forum"; Greg Jenkins, a former Fox News producer; and Bob DeServi, a former NBC cameraman. DeServi, a lighting maven, rented three barges' worth of giant Musco lights, like those used to bathe sports stadiums in a twinkling glow for prime-time television, and put them at the base of the statue, pointed upward to illuminate its entire height.[2] This stunt was a grander version of one from the summer, when television crews were carefully positioned at an angle to shoot Bush in profile during a speech at Mount Rushmore, thereby superimposing his face into the monument alongside those of George Washington, Thomas Jefferson, Theodore Roosevelt, and Abraham Lincoln.[3] No less an authority than Michael Deaver, the impresario of Ronald Reagan's 1980 presidential announcement speech, with its own Statue of Liberty backdrop, was impressed by how the Bush administration updated his playbook. "They understand the visual as well as anybody ever has," he later observed. "They watched what we did, they watched the mistakes of Bush I, they watched how Clinton kind of stumbled into it, and they've taken it to an art form. . . . They understand that what's around the head is just as important as the head."[4]

Timing, being everything, was at least as important as the visuals. For Americans in 2002, no date could lend more emotional weight to a speech about war than the first anniversary of 9/11. And besides, the country was just back from vacation, ready to focus on big-ticket items. "From a marketing point of view, you don't introduce new products in August,"[5] explained Andrew Card, the White House chief of staff, who, after a gig in the first Bush White House, had headed the trade association for the Big Three automakers in Detroit. The looming midterm election figured in the calendar calculus as well. The White House goal was to rush a resolution approving the use of force in Iraq in four to five weeks, a senior administration official told the *Times*'s Bumiller—in other words, when the pressure on congressmen facing reelection to prove their war-waging machismo would be at its nastiest. Any weak sisters could expect a thrashing much like that Republicans inflicted on Democrats who had failed to vote for the "use of force" resolution sought by the first President Bush before the Persian Gulf War in 1991. "In the end it will be difficult for someone to vote against it," the official said of the Iraq rerun.[6]

But in reality the rollout of the product had begun, if somewhat subliminally, just two months after 9/11, in November 2001. That was when Bush first specifically said that Iraq would be held responsible for harboring any "weapons of mass destruction"—a declaration followed up by Cheney's assertion on *Meet the Press* that it was "pretty well confirmed" that there was a pre-9/11 meeting between the hijacker Mohamed Atta and a Saddam intelligence operative in Prague. The message was steadily stepped up thereafter, reaching a crescendo just before the Bush oration from Ellis Island began the official introduction of the product. As early as March 2002, Cheney said of Saddam Hussein on CNN that "he is actively pursuing nuclear weapons at this time," and the vice president reiterated on *Meet the Press* in May that "we know he's working on nuclear." In August, as the president juggled a Crawford vacation and his Waco show on the economy, the vice president kept providing previews of coming attractions for the next show, just audibly enough to leave an impression on the vacationing American psyche. "What we know now, from various sources," he told the Commonwealth Club in San Francisco during a Q&A session on August 7, is that Saddam "continues to pursue a nuclear weapon." On August 26, in Nashville, he addressed the Veterans of Foreign Wars: "There is no doubt that Saddam Hussein now has weapons of mass destruction. There is no doubt that he is amassing them to use against our friends, against our allies and against us." He added that a return of United Nations weapons inspectors would lead to pointless delay in the face of imminent peril. "Time is not on our side," he said.

On September 8, 2002, just three days before Bush's Ellis Island appearance, Cheney was again on *Meet the Press,* this time to offer one-stop shopping for both his Iraq themes—the pre-9/11 connection between Saddam and Al Qaeda and the zeal of Saddam to acquire not just chemical and biological weapons of mass destruction but in particular the scariest of them all, nuclear weapons. "I'm not here today to make a specific allegation that Iraq was somehow responsible for 9/11," Cheney said. "I can't say that." Then he made unspecific allegations suggesting exactly that. "On the other hand," he continued, "new information has come to light" revealing that the lead 9/11 hijacker, Mohamed Atta, "did apparently travel to Prague on a number of occasions. And on at least one occasion, we have reporting that places him in Prague with a senior Iraqi intelligence official a few months before the attack on the World Trade Center." Was there a direct link between Saddam and Al Qaeda? Tim Russert asked after the vice president ran through a list of other possible links between the two "going back many years." Cheney replied, "I'll leave it right where it's at. I don't want to go beyond that. I've tried to be cautious and restrained in my comments, and I hope that everybody will recognize that." Few did.

As for Saddam going nuclear, the vice president walked through three requirements needed for Iraq to build a weapon: technical expertise, a weapons design, and, last but not least, "fissile material, weapons-grade material" in the form of "either plutonium or highly enriched uranium." Saddam, he said, had all three. To prove the most speculative, the third, Cheney pointed to "a story in *The New York Times* this morning"—the byline was shared by Michael R. Gordon and Judith Miller—indicating that Saddam was "seeking to acquire" the "kinds of [aluminum] tubes that are necessary to build a centrifuge."[7] That centrifuge, Cheney explained, was capable of enhancing low-grade uranium "into highly enriched uranium, which is what you have to have in order to build a bomb." After a brief disclaimer—"what we know is just bits and pieces we gather through the intelligence system"—Cheney concluded that "we do know, with absolute certainty, that he is using his procurement system to acquire the equipment he needs in order to enrich uranium to build a nuclear weapon."

The vice president was one of four top administration officials introducing the new product on the network shows that back-to-school Sunday after Labor Day. Condoleezza Rice appeared on CNN's *Late Edition.* "We don't want the smoking gun to be a mushroom cloud," she said—a nearly exact reiteration of a sentence in the *Times*'s front-page story, in which unnamed "hardliners" told Gordon and Miller that "the first sign of a 'smoking gun' . . . may be a mushroom cloud." Donald Rumsfeld was on CBS's *Face the Nation* and Colin Powell on *Fox News Sunday,* both delivering the same message, with Powell also citing the "reporting just this morning" on aluminum tubes that Sunday as evidence for the Saddam nuclear threat.

The unofficial motto of the 9/11 anniversary may have been "Never forget," but the war on Al Qaeda was already fading from memory as the world was invited to test-drive a new war in Iraq. A year after that idle August of 2001 when Bush failed to heed the intelligence warnings of a possible Qaeda attack, there was new evidence that the war against Al Qaeda was still being left unfulfilled in the wake of the early and successful routing of the Taliban. The *Los Angeles Times* reported that the nearly six hundred prisoners from forty-three countries being held in U.S. military custody at Guantánamo Bay had yielded no senior Qaeda leaders whatsoever.[8] *The Washington Post* found that two of the senior Qaeda leaders we hadn't captured were operating at full tilt out of Iran, where they were directly involved in planning terrorist operations, despite the Pentagon's announcement that one of the pair (Mahfouz Ould Walid) had been killed in Afghanistan in January.[9] A leaked draft version of a UN report on the failure to shut down terrorists' cash flow said that "Al Qaeda is by all accounts 'fit and well' and poised to strike again at its leisure."[10] (It had already struck at least a half-dozen times around the world since January.) As the satirist Harry Shearer said in his radio program, *Le Show,* 9/11 is "the event that changed everything except terrorism." But the mission to track down Osama bin Laden and Al Qaeda, dead or alive, was rapidly blurring into the new war that had been grandfathered into "the war on terror." Any news of glitches in the war against the enemy who had attacked America a year earlier was inexorably drowned out by the masterly selling of the new product by marketers with the biggest megaphone in the land.

Public opinion was consistently ambivalent about the wisdom of fighting a war in Iraq, so the sales pitch became more fevered, with Bush himself leading the charge. The day after his Ellis Island speech, he told the UN that Iraq had made "several attempts to buy high-strength aluminum tubes used to enrich uranium for a nuclear weapon" and that "should Iraq acquire fissile material, it would be able to build a nuclear weapon within a year." In a weekly radio address in late September, Bush warned that Qaeda terrorists were "inside Iraq." On October 7, he addressed a cheering crowd in Cincinnati, joining the others in his administration in recycling the image that had first been floated on the front page of *The New York Times* a month earlier: "Facing clear evidence of peril, we cannot wait for the final proof—the smoking gun—that could come in the form of a mushroom cloud." The president also fine-tuned the specificity about the Saddam-Qaeda bond: "We know that Iraq and al Qaeda have had high-level contacts that go back a decade. Some al Qaeda leaders who fled Afghanistan went to Iraq. These include one very senior al Qaeda leader who received medical treatment in Baghdad this year, and who has been associated with planning for chemical and biological attacks. We've learned that Iraq has trained al Qaeda members in bomb-making and poisons and deadly gases."

Within the next week, both the House and Senate passed a resolution authorizing the use of force in Iraq. The victory for the administration was huge. In 1991 the resolution authorizing George H. W. Bush to use "all necessary means" to drive the Iraqi army out of Kuwait passed by 52 to 47 in the Senate and 250 to 183 in the House.[11] In 2002, with the Iraqi army invading no one, the margins were 77 to 23 in the Senate and 296 to 133 in the House.[12] The midterm election was but three weeks away.

Throughout the selling of the Iraq War, there were questions raised by some leaders—most pointedly so by Republicans. Foreign-policy realists from the first Bush administration, such as Brent Scowcroft[13] and James Baker, had their strong doubts, with Baker warning that the war "cannot be done on the cheap."[14] The former Reagan speechwriter Peggy Noonan, the most faithful Bush partisan imaginable, implored the president to provide facts instead of sermons in making his case. "'Saddam is evil' is not enough," she wrote. "A number of people are evil, and some are even our friends. 'Saddam has weapons of mass destruction' is not enough. A number of countries do. What the people need now is hard data that demonstrate conclusively that Saddam has weapons of mass destruction which he is readying to use on the people of the U.S. or the people of the West."[15] Though some Democrats in the House were outspoken critics of a war in Iraq, Senate Democrats were mostly obedient. It was left to the Republican Chuck Hagel, a Vietnam War hero, to say, "If you think you're going to drop the 82nd Airborne in Baghdad and finish the job, I think you've been watching too many John Wayne movies."[16] As the vote neared in the Senate, Hagel, who would vote yea, became almost mournful in his pro forma support of his party's president on the Senate floor: "We should not be seduced by the expectations of 'dancing in the streets' after Saddam's regime has fallen."

The White House kept saying that no decision had been made about Iraq, but only the blind or the deaf could fail to see that a decision had long ago been made. Richard Perle, a neoconservative Iraq hawk on the administration's Defense Policy Board, gave away the game eight months before the invasion of Iraq began: "The failure to take on Saddam after what the president said" would lead to "a collapse of confidence."[17] Translation: If Bush didn't get rid of Saddam after all this saber rattling, he will look like the biggest wimp since— well, his father. If he didn't do it soon, after all these months of swagger, he would destroy his own credibility and hurt the country's. To no small extent, Bush was in a box of his own making. Writing in *National Review,* William F. Buckley, Jr., suggested, not entirely in jest, that "the American people should now be told that we are at war against Saddam Hussein."

Democrats, as ineffectual and timid in challenging a popular president on Iraq as they were in preventing his tax cuts from speeding through Congress, kept calling for a "debate" on the war. Ari Fleischer responded by saying the debate was already going on and the president was "listening to all sides," even though it was evident from the get-go that Bush would do pretty much what he always intended after a few weeks of ostentatious "listening." This drill was a re- peat of Bush's highly publicized weeks of listening to the debate over stem-cell research in the summer of 2001, before he went ahead and did what he'd wanted to do in the first place. In the case of Iraq the "debate" was largely a parochial Washington affair about process anyway: first, about the timing and wording of whatever rubber-stamp approval Congress was inevitably to deliver and, once that was done with, about whether the president would consult the UN Security Council. To question Bush on anything more substantive was an invitation to have one's patriotism besmirched. The invective aimed at those with the toughest questions, almost all of them pillars of the Republican or military establishments, was borderline ugly, complete with the requisite allu- sions to Neville Chamberlain. (Hagel, Scowcroft, and Colin Powell were cited as fellow travelers with Howell Raines, the purportedly antiwar editor of *The New York Times,* in a *Weekly Standard* editorial titled "The Axis of Appeasement.")[18] But there were few, if any, Washington doubters of the war who wanted to appease Saddam or defend his criminal regime. What most critics were asking was why he had jumped to the head of the Most Wanted list when the war on Al Qaeda remained unfinished and American resources were finite.

That Democratic leaders added so little to the discussion was attributed to their intimidation by the president's poll numbers, their fear of being branded unpatriotic, and their eagerness to clear the decks (whatever the price) to focus on the supposedly winning issue of the economy before Election Day. (They were still fighting the last political war: "It's the economy, stupid" had worked for Clinton against a Bush, hadn't it?) Al Gore did speak out about Iraq in late September, then dropped the subject altogether. Agree with the president or not, at least Bush stood for something. He led, and the Democrats followed. The polls, far from rationalizing the Democrats' timidity, suggested that they might have won a real debate had they staged one. Support for an Iraq war was falling, with a CNN/*USA Today* survey predicting a Vietnam-like 33 percent support level if there were five thousand casualties, as well there could be. But even so, the Democratic leaders never united around a coherent alternative vision to the administration's preemptive war against the thug of Baghdad. Perhaps through their loyalty they hoped to aspire to post-9/11 patriotism, but in practice their stance was more like an abdication.

Once the war resolution passed, the Senate leader, Tom Daschle, summed up the feeble thrust of the opposition when he said he hoped to "get this question of Iraq behind us." He later told NBC's Tim Russert, "The bottom line is . . . we want to move on." But move on to what? The dirty secret of the Democrats was that they had no more of an economic plan than they had an Iraq plan, even were the country in the mood to listen to one.

Whatever scant hope the Democrats had of changing the subject to the economy evaporated overnight when snipers started striking in the Washington, D.C., area in October 2002, killing random citizens without rhyme or visible reason. It was the second most highly watched TV news story in a decade, second only to 9/11, no doubt because it was a proxy illustration of how vulnerable the nation's capital was to a terrorist attack. In the three weeks before anyone was apprehended for the murders, the city was paralyzed. As with the still-unsolved anthrax attacks of 2001, there were failures of cooperation between federal and local law enforcement. In one careless moment, the Pentagon inadvertently tipped off the snipers of its air-surveillance plans for the D.C. area.

To confirm what was visible to anyone watching this police drama, the Council on Foreign Relations happened to simultaneously release an alarming report titled "America—Still Unprepared, Still in Danger," written by a bipartisan task force headed by Gary Hart and Warren Rudman and stocked with intelligence, military, and foreign-policy heavies as various as the former FBI superagent James Kallstrom, the Iraq hawk George Shultz, and the former National Institutes of Health head Harold Varmus. "The next attack will result in even greater casualties and widespread disruption to American lives and the economy," they wrote. The facts backed up their fears. They found that the nation's 650,000 local and state police still had no access to federal terrorist watch lists. They found minimal surveillance of the potentially explosive cargo containers transported to and within the United States by ship, truck, and train. While Bush was warning the nation that a single "Iraqi intelligence operative" could with one "small container" wreak havoc with chemical and biological weapons, America was largely defenseless against just such an attack: "[E]mergency first responders—police, firefighters, and emergency medical personnel—in most of the nation's cities and counties are no better prepared to react now than they were prior to September 11."[19]

The Washington snipers—a drifter and his teenage accomplice—were arrested on October 24. The midterm election some ten days later was an unambiguous Bush victory. In a rare coup for a party holding the White House, Republicans expanded their majority in the House and regained control of the Senate. As the reigning cliché had it, 2002 was the *Seinfeld* election—an election about nothing. But how could an election in the midst of one war and on the eve of another be about nothing? To make it so was the Democrats' sole significant, if self-annihilating, achievement of the entire campaign.

ALL THAT WAS LEFT now was a completion of the niceties needed to pave the way to America's inevitable new war. The only mystery was the exact timing of D-day—still another four months hence, it would turn out. As little scrutiny of the Iraq product as there was—by much of the press, most politicians, or the public—there was nonetheless a steady drip of information in plain sight casting doubt on the two most persistent and explosive premises of the White House's merchandising campaign: Saddam's nuclear capabilities and an Iraq-Qaeda connection. Yet little of this gap between the known facts and administration assertions had any impact on the rush to war.

On the day before Cheney and company talked about Saddam's aluminum tubes on the Sunday chat shows, for instance, the president had been caught retailing a fiction. Appearing at Camp David with the British prime minister, Tony Blair, he told the press that "when the inspectors first went into Iraq" and were denied access, the International Atomic Energy Agency of the UN had concluded "that they were six months away" from producing a weapon. "I don't know what more evidence we need," Bush said. NBC News, which took the trouble of actually contacting the IAEA to check this out, discovered that Bush was citing a report issued in 1998 about Iraq before the 1991 Gulf War. Since then, UN weapons inspectors had destroyed Iraq's nuclear weapons sites. Both an IAEA spokesman and unnamed American officials told NBC that "there is no conclusive proof that Iraq has restarted its nuclear weapons program."[20]

At the height of the Washington sniper frenzy a few weeks later, James Risen of The New York Times reported that the Czech president Václav Havel had told the White House that there was no evidence to support the story that Mohamed Atta and an Iraqi intelligence officer had met in Prague in the months before 9/11.[21] Risen added that "for months, American intelligence and law enforcement officials have cast doubt on the reports of the Prague meeting, which proved to be based on the statements of a single informant, and last week the director of central intelligence, George J. Tenet, told Congress that his agency could find no evidence to confirm that the meeting took place." Czech officials had no evidence that Atta was even in their country in April 2001, when the meeting purportedly took place, and American records put him in Virginia Beach, Virginia, then. Yet not only did this refutation of the Atta-Saddam link gain no traction with the public; it also failed to deter Cheney from continuing to make the claim, as he would do repeatedly until 2004, the year when the 9/11 Commission would also conclude that the Prague meeting never took place.

The administration's excuses about its laxity before 9/11 also started showing holes, raising questions about its overall credibility. Even with little White

House cooperation in its inquiry, far-from-thorough congressional intelligence hearings presented a chilling portrait of the administration's efforts to cover up its pre-9/11 lassitude about terrorist threats. Exhibit A was Condoleezza Rice's pronouncement of months earlier: "I don't think anybody could have predicted that these people would take an airplane and slam it into the World Trade Center . . . that they would try to use an airplane as a missile, a hijacked airplane as a missile." In fact, the 9/11 Commission reported, U.S. intelligence had picked up a dozen plots of a similar sort, over a period from 1994 to pre-9/11 2001, with some of them specifically mentioning the World Trade Center and the White House as potential targets. In the weeks before 9/11, the CIA had learned that in Afghanistan "everyone is talking about an impending attack."[22]

Vietnam analogies, which had proved wildly premature when applied to the discouraging early stages of the successful war in Afghanistan, were not entirely out of bounds now. The White House's high-handedness echoed the run-up to Vietnam, at least for those with memories of the Gulf of Tonkin incidents that sped LBJ's prosecution of that war. The Vietnam analogy could be overdone, certainly, because American armed forces of the twenty-first century were unlikely to find Iraq a military quagmire, and no one could try to make a case for the legitimacy of Saddam's regime as many did for that of North Vietnam. But the arrogance of the CEO administration, which gave citizens no better information than companies such as Enron had given to their stockholders, recalled the hubris of those Ivy League and corporate "whiz kids" on Robert McNamara's Pentagon team who had seen themselves as better and brighter than the rest of us.

Instead of writing a probing book like David Halberstam's *The Best and the Brightest* or his own *All the President's Men,* the country's premiere investigative reporter, Bob Woodward, produced *Bush at War,* just in time for Americans' 2002 Christmas lists. It is a revealing document in its way. The same secretive administration that was fighting in the courts to keep Americans from finding out who the oilmen were on Cheney's secret energy-policy task force handed Woodward the notes from "more than 50 National Security Council and other meetings." (Even Newt Gingrich found this odd, observing that "it makes no sense for an administration that has jealously guarded its executive privilege to allow a reporter the access it denies to members of Congress.")[23] The president himself was interviewed by Woodward—against the hagiographic backdrop of his nonworking "ranch" in Crawford—and was "quite open," the author said. And why not? The man had a story to sell.

Woodward described his book as "a neutral, non-judgmental account,"[24] but that is not the same as an objective account. When he quotes Bush calling Seymour Hersh, the Woodward rival who has reported on wartime military failures, "a liar," Woodward lets the charge sit there unanswered, without comment from Hersh or anyone else. Sensitive issues for the Bush administration are given short shrift or omitted entirely—another form of "non-judgmental" journalism. There are no inside accounts of the administration's failure to track down the anthrax terrorists. Ashcroft's inability to arrest a single terrorist during his post-9/11 mass roundups goes unremarked. The pivotal battle of Tora Bora receives only two paragraphs, though it was the Waterloo that allowed more than a thousand Qaeda operatives (bin Laden among them) to escape. A "non-judgmental" account meant that there would be no notice paid to the possibility that the same war planners who had bungled a serious opportunity to get bin Laden dead or alive and the same officials still bungling homeland security might be similarly fallible in plotting the presumed cakewalk in Iraq.

Still, Woodward offered some useful, if unexamined, nuggets on the coming war. He wrote that Rumsfeld's influential deputy, Paul Wolfowitz, wanted to target Iraq right after 9/11—not because of any certainty of a connection between Saddam and Al Qaeda, but because "war against Iraq might be easier than against Afghanistan." But back then, at least, Bush had vetoed the idea of going to war simultaneously with Al Qaeda and Saddam after 9/11. The president explained: "If we tried to do too many things—two things, for example, or three things—militarily, then . . . the lack of focus would have been a huge risk."[25] The follow-up question that was not to be found in *Bush at War* was simple enough: If it was a huge risk to split our focus between Saddam and Al Qaeda then, why wasn't it now?

As Christmas 2002 approached, the president met with great fanfare with General Tommy Franks, the commander of American forces in the Middle East, to plan moving more troops to the Persian Gulf. Colin Powell witheringly attacked the documents that Iraq tardily provided to the United Nations about its weapons capabilities. "The [Iraqi] declaration ignores efforts to procure uranium from Niger," read the official State Department response to the Iraqi documents. "Why is the Iraqi regime hiding their uranium procurement?" It was the first time the United States highlighted uranium as a component of Saddam's nuclear arsenal—and uranium obtained from a specific source, Niger. The aluminum tubes discovered the previous fall, Powell explained, would be used to enrich this uranium and produce nuclear weapons. Neither he nor anyone else was nearly so vocal about a simultaneous and more concrete intimation of nuclear terror: the public announcement by the president of Iran, Mohammad Khatami, that his country planned to continue building a Russian-assisted nuclear power plant that might be a secret nuclear weapons operation. (That news was relegated to page five of *The New York Times*.)[26]

Uranium from Africa became the administration's favorite nuclear touchstone for the new year, a glittering and highly saleable accessory for the Iraq product. Rice thumped it in an Op-Ed article for the *Times* titled "Why We Know Iraq Is Lying," accusing Iraq of failing "to account for or explain" its "efforts to get uranium from abroad."[27] In his 2003 State of the Union address that same week, the president said, "The British government has learned that Saddam Hussein recently sought significant quantities of uranium from Africa. Our intelligence sources tell us that he has attempted to purchase high-strength aluminum tubes suitable for nuclear weapons production. Saddam Hussein has not credibly explained these activities. He clearly has much to hide."

The sales pitch reached its culmination on February 5, 2003, when Colin Powell, wielding props that included incriminating aerial photos of Iraq weapons sites and even a vial of "anthrax," made the American case to the United Nations and the entire world. It was almost self-consciously a television scene of high drama tantamount to Adlai Stevenson's appearance before the UN in October 1962, when he presented photographic proof of Soviet missiles in Cuba just after the Soviet representative denied their existence.

The Bush administration's sale was made. Just how successfully so could be seen by looking back to a CBS News/*New York Times* poll released two weeks after 9/11. Then only 6 percent of Americans thought bin Laden had collaborated with Saddam Hussein.[28] Now a CNN/*USA Today*/Gallup poll found that 66 percent thought Powell had made a "strong" case that Iraq had "ties" to Al Qaeda.[29] A CBS News survey showed that 53 percent believed Saddam had been "personally involved" in 9/11, and Knight Ridder found that half the country even believed that Iraqis were among the 9/11 hijackers.[30] It was all over except for the shouting, and there was not to be much shouting.

A month after Powell's show, on March 6, the president held his first prime-time press conference since a month after 9/11. It was certain to be his last before the war in Iraq. He had failed to persuade most of America's friends to come aboard. The economy was tanking. But the sleepwalking journalists at hand were so limply deferential to the president's boilerplate script—even Terry Moran, the ABC News White House correspondent, later said that his colleagues looked "like zombies"[31]—that the by-and-large ceremonial event played like black comedy. The scene almost uncannily resembled the satirical 1920s press conference in the year's Oscar champ, *Chicago*, in which Billy Flynn, a star defense attorney played by Richard Gere, browbeats a mob of reporters into believing that his client Roxie Hart (Renée Zellweger) did not murder her lover when in fact she did. "Now remember," Billy coaches Roxie, "we can only sell them one idea at a time." The idea: Roxie acted in self-defense. "We both reached for the gun," Roxie sings to the reporters, who obediently turn her lie into a rousing chorus, repeating it over and over in a production number that portrays them as marionettes, bowing and scraping to the tug of Billy's strings.

For history's sake, this spectacle might well be paired on the *Chicago* DVD with the actual Bush press conference. One reporter, April Ryan of American Urban Radio Networks, asked, "Mr. President, as the nation is at odds over war . . . how is your faith guiding you?"—a God-given cue for Bush to once more cloak his arrogance in the verbal vestments of humble religiosity. "My faith sustains me because I pray daily," came the president's reply. "I pray for peace, April, I pray for peace." Far be it from Ryan to ask a follow-up question about why virtually every religious denomination in the country, including Bush's own, opposed the war. She might as well have been Mary Sunshine, the sob sister reporter in *Chicago* who tosses Roxie an image-burnishing softball at her press conference by asking, "Do you have any advice for young girls seeking to avoid a life of jazz and drink?"

At Bush's sedated show there were no raised voices, not a single query about homeland security or bin Laden. As Billy Flynn says, one idea at a time is enough for the journalistic pack. In this case the idea was the administration's invasion of Iraq, which, like Roxie's killing of her lover, would be justified as an act of self-defense. And like its *Chicago* counterparts, the Washington press corps was more than willing to buy fictions if instructed to do so by the puppeteer. "Eight times [Bush] interchanged the war on Iraq with the attacks of September 11, 2001," wrote *The New York Observer,* "and eight times he was unchallenged."[32] The unproven but constantly reiterated White House claim of a Qaeda–Saddam Hussein connection had now become a settled fact, not to be questioned at a press conference any more than any *Chicago* reporter challenges the mythical pregnancy Billy Flynn flogs in his propaganda campaign to save Roxie Hart.

The movie's press conference ends with Billy Flynn's message spreading from the servile reporters' lips directly to the next morning's paper: "THEY BOTH REACHED FOR THE GUN" is the banner headline we see rolling off the press. At Bush's press conference, under the guise of "news," CNN flashed the White House's chosen messages in repetitive rotation on the bottom of the screen while the event was still going on–"People of good will are hoping for peace" and "'My job is to protect America.'" No less obliging were the puppets at CNN's rival, Fox News, whose Greta Van Susteren sharply observed, "What I liked tonight was that in prime time he said to the American people, my job is to protect the American people." (Van Susteren, a lawyer, had apparently forgotten that the presidential oath requires him to protect the Constitution.) Though Bush usually appeared on TV in front of White House backdrops stamped with the sound bite he wanted to sell, this time he didn't even have to bother. As he knew–and said, in his one moment of truth that night–the entire show was "scripted." It had been from the start.

THE NEXT DAY, March 7, the United States, Britain, Spain, and Bulgaria put forth a UN resolution–opposed by the major powers France, Germany, Russia, and China–to give Iraq a March 17 deadline to disarm completely or go to war. But that wasn't the only news that day. Hans Blix, the head of the UN weapons inspection team in Iraq, told the Security Council that Iraq's destruction of thirty-four Al-Samoud 2 missiles was a "substantial measure of disarmament," and that Iraq was now providing information on its biological and chemical weapons. He also said that a series of searches had found "no evidence" of the mobile biological production facilities in Iraq that had been so highly touted by Powell in his presentation to the UN. Blix asked for more time to finish his job, estimating that the remaining inspections "will not take years, nor weeks, but months." Mohamed ElBaradei, the director general of the IAEA and the chief nuclear arms inspector, also expressed some optimism about Iraqi disarmament, saying that "we have to date found no evidence or plausible indication of the revival of a nuclear weapons program in Iraq."

More intriguingly, ElBaradei announced that documents purportedly proving that Iraqi officials had sought uranium in Africa were "not authentic." The bogus letters between Iraqi agents and Niger officials were so crude that they didn't even have accurate names or titles for the correspondents. Equally inauthentic, ElBaradei said, was the persistent administration claim over the past six months that Iraq had tried to purchase aluminum tubes for use in centrifuges for enrichment of that nonexistent uranium. The IAEA investigators had found detailed records going back fourteen years, including invoices and blueprints, that showed that Iraq was trying to secure aluminum tubes for conventional rockets, not a nuclear program.

With America's March 17 deadline for war dominating the news, ElBaradei's pronouncements were widely ignored. The news of the forged uranium documents did not make any of the three network evening newscasts and did not appear in the following day's *New York Times*. (It would turn up a day later, in a four-hundred-word story on page A13.) But *The Washington Post* and the *Los Angeles Times* did give the forgeries front-page treatment, with the *L.A. Times* asking on March 8, "If U.S. intelligence is so good, why are United Nations experts still unable to confirm whether Saddam Hussein is actively concealing and producing illegal weapons?" That night a former diplomat who served in Iraq for the Bush I administration, Joseph Wilson, appeared as an analyst on CNN. "This particular case is outrageous," he said, adding that "it taints the whole rest of the case that the government is trying to build against Iraq." He called the U.S. government "simply stupid" because with "a couple of phone calls" it could have learned whether a deal between Iraq and Niger for uranium had taken place. "All this stuff is open," Wilson said. "It's a restricted market of buyers and sellers."

It took nearly a week, until March 14, and five subsequent press briefings before anyone in the White House press corps asked a single question about the forged documents on Niger uranium. That same day, Jay Rockefeller of West Virginia, the ranking Democrat on the Senate Intelligence Committee, asked the FBI to investigate the forgeries, writing to the agency's director, Robert Mueller, that "there is a possibility that the fabrication of these documents may be part of a larger deception campaign aimed at manipulating public opinion and foreign policy regarding Iraq." On March 16, Cheney was back on *Meet the Press,* painting a rosy scenario of the show to come in Iraq ("We will, in fact, be greeted as liberators") and disputing any contradictions of the administration casus belli for war. "I think Mr. ElBaradei frankly is wrong," Cheney said, accusing the IAEA of having "consistently underestimated or missed what it was Saddam Hussein was doing." As Hans Blix would later write in his book *Disarming Iraq,* Cheney's attacks on the IAEA, which were directly preceded by slightly less categorical criticisms by Powell and Rice, "were the first and only ones directed against the IAEA by a government regarding its inspections in Iraq."[33]

On the day after Cheney's blast at ElBaradei, March 17, a persistent Democratic critic in the House, Henry Waxman of California, sent a letter to Bush expressing doubts about the administration's characterization of Iraq's nuclear threat. On March 18, *The Washington Post* published an article by Walter Pincus and Dana Milbank headlined "Bush Clings to Dubious Allegations About Iraq." Among the dubious allegations was Cheney's claim, repeated yet again on the March 16 *Meet the Press,* that Iraq had "reconstituted nuclear weapons"– an assertion, the *Post* reporters pointed out, that Cheney himself contradicted moments later, saying it was "only a matter of time before [Saddam] acquires nuclear weapons." Whether Saddam had already reconstituted his bombs or was still trying to acquire them didn't much matter by this point. The vice president smothered such distinctions with a verbal blanket of doom, inviting Americans to imagine how much worse 9/11 would have been if Al Qaeda had "had a nuclear weapon and detonated it in the middle of one of our cities."

The *Post* article about the "dubious allegations" in the White House's case against Iraq ran on page A13. By then, the ides of March had come and gone, and Operation Iraqi Freedom was but one day away.

FIVE

"MISSION ACCOMPLISHED"

THE NIGHT the war began in prime time, there wasn't much to see. But there was already a TV drama: Peter Jennings was AWOL by network anchor standards, arriving at the studio a half hour later than his peers. As Baghdad presumably burned on CBS and NBC, *The Bachelor: Where Are They Now?* continued purring on ABC. It was a minor scandal. "The war has already claimed its first victim: ABC News," concluded the *Washington Post*'s TV columnist, Lisa de Moraes.[1]

But it was entirely possible that those Americans sticking with *The Bachelor* on ABC would be no less informed about the war than those watching the other networks. Television news was awash with exciting, if misleading, early reports of "a decapitation strike" in which cruise missiles and F-117 stealth fighters attacked a location where Saddam Hussein and his top brass had conveniently gathered for the Americans to take them all out at once on the very first night of the war. On CNN, where the title card read "Zero Hour for Iraq Arrives," the *New York Times* reporter Judith Miller said that thanks to "a slew of information from defectors" and other "intelligence sources"—the kind of information familiar from Colin Powell's "impressive speech to the United

Nations"—WMD sites would soon be overrun by American forces and disarmed. "One person in Washington told me that the list could total more than 1,400 of these sites," Miller said.

The official plan for the war's press coverage, at least as presented by the Defense Department, was to make this Gulf War more transparent to Americans than the one that had largely happened out of sight in 1991. Then, the Pentagon had imposed strict censorship, insisting on pool reporting that would preclude a role for renegade journalists doing enterprise reporting of their own; in place of vivid reports from the ground, the networks ran hours of press briefings laced with snazzy visuals that promoted the tactical and technological brilliance of the American effort and spewed inaccuracies that would not be corrected until well after Saddam had escaped the American noose. For the new war, the Pentagon had a different plan. More than five hundred journalists were "embedded" with American and British troops to offer grunt's-eye views of battle. The mastermind of the Pentagon media operation, the embed program included, was Torie Clarke, a PR star whose résumé included a stint at the National Cable Television Association, where she had accomplished the seeming mission impossible of ameliorating that industry's villainous image as a poster child for heinous customer service. Little in her Pentagon image portfolio would be left to chance: a production designer who had worked for Disney, MGM, *Good Morning America,* and the illusionist David Blaine was hired to give General Tommy Franks a confidence-inspiring $200,000 set for the briefings at Central Command headquarters in Qatar.[2]

The Pentagon's professed new openness notwithstanding, the administration's desire to control the press was more ferocious than ever. Just how much so was apparent a month before the war began, when Dan Rather, the CBS anchor, succeeded in getting an exclusive interview with Saddam Hussein, the first granted to an American journalist in a decade. The White House asked to give a rebuttal immediately after the interview aired, but when CBS said yes, as long as the rebuttal was by the president, vice president, or secretary of state, the administration balked. It wanted instead to field a PR man, either Ari Fleischer or Dan Bartlett. CBS said no, and the White House complained, much as it once had about networks broadcasting statements by Osama bin Laden. American television had no business trumpeting what Fleischer termed Saddam's "propaganda." Among the propaganda that roused the White House's ire, presumably, was the dictator's declarations about Iraq's lack of weapons of mass destruction. Asked by the CBS anchor if he was destroying the missiles prohibited by the UN, Saddam answered, "Which missiles? What do you mean? We have no missiles outside the specifications of the United Nations, and the inspection teams are here and they're looking. I believe the United States knows and the world knows that Iraq has none of what has been said at the higher political levels. So, the missiles . . . that are against the resolution of the United Nations, these do not exist. And they have been destroyed." Fleischer implied after the interview aired that it was almost unpatriotic to broadcast such obvious fictions. "If it's all lies," the White House press secretary said, "why put it on in the first place?"[3]

The show the White House *did* want the networks to put on was "Shock and Awe," the initial assault on Baghdad. On the war's first night, March 19, it became a ubiquitous title card on the cable-news networks—"shockinaw" to the news readers. (Later both Fox News and the perennially ratings-challenged MSNBC would brand their coverage with the official name of the military campaign, Operation Iraqi Freedom.) On-screen the pyrotechnics of Shock and Awe looked like a distant fireworks display, or perhaps the cool computer graphics of a *Matrix*-inspired video game, rather than the bombing of a large city. None of Baghdad's nearly six million people were visible.

The dazzlement of this picturesque bombardment immediately pumped up the limp American stock market ("I think the market's going to go up like a rocket!" Donald Trump promised on Fox News during the war's first weekend) and gave the country a presentiment of a quick and tidy war. Daytime coverage brought a similarly triumphal story line starring enthusiastic embeds in military khaki cruising across the desert like the youthful participants in a second-tier Olympic sport. "If you had hired actors, you could not have gotten better coverage," observed Kenneth Bacon, a former Pentagon spokesman.[4] But even before *Time* and *Newsweek* could hit the stands with their cover displays of Shock and Awe, the fireworks sputtered. Like the "lovely war" the British foresaw in the early going of World War I, the illusion of a painless engagement in Iraq was short-lived.

Suddenly there was a jump cut to new images, more up close and personal: an Aljazeera video of American troops who had been butchered or taken prisoner by Iraqi forces. When Donald Rumsfeld appeared on CBS's *Face the Na-*

tion on the war's first Sunday, the host, Bob Schieffer, showed part of that clip—at an inconvenient time, when the Pentagon was denying news reports that perhaps ten American soldiers had been captured or were missing. Such pictures were declared off-limits by the Pentagon henceforth; depicting POWs, it solemnly instructed, violated "the principles of the Geneva Conventions." But the discordant note of death couldn't be silenced. These images contained a novel element that the antiseptic, depopulated Baghdad pyrotechnics had not delivered: the human face of people visibly mauled by war. For the first time the viewers at home could smell blood, American blood, and while that was shocking, it was far from awesome.

It took only seventy-two hours for the upbeat, even giddy imagery of Americans spreading freedom like Johnny Appleseed to fade altogether. No longer were tanks speeding unimpeded across the desert and troops planting the flag in modest emulation of Iwo Jima. Injured marines could be seen being taken on stretchers from a battle near Nasiriya; a marine was seen ablaze as he ran out of a burning building in southern Iraq; firefights were captured on camera, whether in Aljazeera video replayed on CNN or in BBC reports watched directly via American satellite or cable.

The day before the war began, March 18, the president's mother had made a preemptive strike on ABC's *Good Morning America* to decry such coverage, telling Diane Sawyer that she for one would watch "none" of the war on TV. "Why should we hear about body bags and deaths and how many, what day it's gonna happen?" Barbara Bush asked rhetorically. "It's not relevant. So why should I waste my beautiful mind on something like that?" Now two top-tier anchors on the same network picked up the First Mother's thread, debating on camera about what should and should not be televised. When Charles Gibson, in New York, told Ted Koppel, embedded with the Third Infantry Division, that it would be "simply disrespectful" to show either the American or Iraqi dead, Koppel disagreed. Because the news media are "ginning up patriotic feelings" in covering a war, he said, "I feel that we do have an obligation to remind people in the most graphic way that war is a dreadful thing. . . . The fact of the matter is young Americans are dying. Young Iraqis are dying. And I think to turn our faces away from that is a mistake. . . . To sanitize it too much is a dreadful mistake."

But the sanitation had only just begun. "It's a news judgment where we would of course be mindful of the sensibilities of our viewers," a CNN spokeswoman said of the network's decision to minimize the savagery and blood of warfare.[5] All the American networks and much of print journalism made a similar decision about pictures (though not about the pictures that war correspondents could and did create with words). This choice was culturally counterintuitive. Only a few years earlier, movies such as *Saving Private Ryan* and *Black Hawk Down* had been widely applauded for the innovative realism of their battle scenes. Wouldn't it have made sense for media depictions of an actual war at least occasionally to adhere to the same standard? Apparently not. The prewar joke—that the war would be the ultimate reality show—came true. Its life-and-death perils were airbrushed whenever possible in the same soothing style as the artificial perils on *Survivor.*

Had such horrific images not been censored, it would have been tough, if not impossible, to sell commercials, which returned with accelerating frequency to 24/7 cable after the altruistic first few days of the war. (It was no coincidence that the BBC, which is commercial-free, refused to turn away when blood splashed on a cameraman's lens during an early firsthand report on a friendly fire incident that killed nineteen Kurds.)[6] Anthony Swofford, the former marine who wrote the bestselling *Jarhead* about his experience in the 1991 Gulf War, told *The Daily Show*'s Jon Stewart that he had shut off his TV entirely after three or four days of the new war and "stayed with the print." For all the TV images, he noted, "the actual experience of combat doesn't make it to the other side of the screen." Later, a research project conducted by Sean Aday of George Washington University's School of Media and Public Affairs would examine six hundred hours of television war coverage between March 20 and the fall of Baghdad, on April 9, and find that in 1,710 stories only 13.5 percent included any shots of dead or wounded civilians or soldiers, whether Iraqi or American. The coverage "did not differ discernibly" from that of the first Gulf War, the report concluded. "A war with hundreds of coalition and tens of thousands of Iraqi casualties" was transformed "into something closer to a defense contractor's training video: a lot of action, but no consequences, as if shells simply disappeared into the air and an invisible enemy magically ceased to exist."[7] A similar study by the Project for Excellence in Journalism at Columbia University found that "none of the embedded stories studied showed footage of people, either U.S. soldiers or Iraqis, being struck, injured or killed by weapons fired."[8]

For all the battalions of anchors and high-tech correspondents at work 24/7 on television, they seemed to be telling us less about what was going on than had the mere twenty-seven predigital newshounds who accompanied the American troops landing in Normandy on D-day. What most defined the war on cable TV was the networks' insistence on letting their own scorched-earth campaigns for brand supremacy run roughshod over the real action in Iraq. The conveying of actual news often seemed subsidiary to the networks' mission to out-flag-wave one another and to make their own personnel, rather than the war's antagonists, the leading players in the drama. The study at Columbia found that only in 20 percent of the reports by embedded television journalists did the journalists share the screen with anyone else. Soon even local New York weathermen were predicting rain in Kirkuk—every on-camera personality had to get into the act. TV viewers were on more intimate terms with Aaron Brown's and Shep Smith's perceptions of the war than with the collective thoughts of all those soon-to-be-liberated "Iraqi people" whom the anchors kept apotheosizing. Iraqis were the best seen-but-not-heard dress extras in this drama, alternately pictured as sobbing, snarling, waving, and cheering.

The connection, if any, between this war and the one on Al Qaeda was forgotten; news from Afghanistan, Israel, and the West Bank evaporated overnight. Even the villain at hand, Saddam Hussein, remained a vague figure from stock, since the specific history of his reign of terror got far less airtime than the tacky décor of his palaces. When Torie Clarke said in a Pentagon briefing that Saddam was responsible for "decades and decades and decades of torture and oppression the likes of which I think the world has not ever seen before," few journalists were going to gainsay the Pentagon mouthpiece by bringing up Hitler and Stalin. Few were going to question any official line. After just one week of war, Greg Mitchell of *Editor and Publisher* counted fifteen instances in which the American news media either got the story "wrong or misreported a sliver of fact into a major event."[9] Almost all the fictions erred on the side of a fast American victory. Among them were the first-night killing of Saddam and the "decapitation" of the Iraqi command; the surrender of an entire Iraqi division of eight thousand soldiers en masse; the capturing of a chemical plant that produced chemical weapons; the taking of Nasiriya and Basra; and Iraqi citizens greeting Americans as liberators. Anyone who wanted to learn what was really happening in Iraq had to turn to the more vivid accounts in the national American newspapers or foreign television or negotiate the bazaar of the Web.

American TV often marched in lockstep as much as Saddam's state-controlled TV had in Iraq. But eventually a war presented with minimal battle-field realism, canned jingoism, and scant debate was going to pall as television no less than it did as journalism, and sure enough ratings for coverage of Iraq started to fall fast. Only occasional signs of journalistic independence peeked through, though even the slightest of those breaks in form could spark heated political rows. After Donald Rumsfeld spoke in a post–Shock and Awe press conference of "the humanity" of American weaponry pinpointing noncivilian targets, ABC's Peter Jennings earned a spanking from the *New York Post* for re-marking on camera, "No offense to the secretary, but at this moment we sim-ply do not know whether that is the case." Such departures from patriotic political correctness, according to Rupert Murdoch's tabloid, amounted to "America-bashing, pessimism and anti-war agitation."[10] Jennings's real sin, how-ever, was to violate the unspoken rule that in the early stages of a war, journal-ists should junk the tools of skepticism and irony. But as Michael J. Arlen, then television critic for *The New Yorker,* wrote in the mid-1960s while observing cheerleading coverage of the first "living room war," Vietnam, "Trying to report a war without irony is a bit like trying to keep sex out of a discussion of the re-lations between men and women."

On Fox News, Murdoch's television outlet, there was no irony or ambigu-ity or anything other than all victory all the time. One anchor said that "objec-tively speaking" it is "hard to believe things could go much more successfully." Another announced "extraordinary news, the city of Basra under control!" just as Basra was teetering into guerrilla warfare. One of the many Bush appa-ratchiks among the network's commentators, Fred Barnes, called his competi-tors "weenies" for dwelling on casualties. So what if one Fox correspondent, Geraldo Rivera, was ordered out of Iraq after giving away American troop movements on camera? Fox saw itself as the patriotic standard-bearer. An idle news-briefing remark by General Richard B. Myers that "reporters just have to be fair and balanced, and that's all" was flogged by the network's anchors as an official endorsement of the network's "fair and balanced" advertising slogan.

Fox notwithstanding, some bad news had to seep out as the operation wore on. There was just too much of it. On the fourth day of the war, March 23, there was an ambush in Nasiriya, with reports of a dozen Americans killed or injured. The next day, Saddam resurfaced to give a twenty-five-minute televised speech taunting the United States and proving reports of his death greatly exaggerated. March 27 brought news of wounded Americans being flown (off-camera) to Landstuhl hospital in Germany and of Iraqi soldiers surprising Americans by fighting in civilian clothes. In rapid succession, American audiences learned of coalition troops mistakenly shooting a van full of Iraqi women and children, of ambushed Apache helicopters, of four American soldiers slaughtered in a suicide bombing at a checkpoint near Najaf. On March 30, Rumsfeld and Myers felt compelled to circulate on the network morning television shows to deny that troops were stretched thin or that planning had failed to account for tough resistance. On April 2, *The New York Times* ran the headline "Plans for Post-War Iraq Are Re-evaluated as Fast Military Exit Looks Less Likely."

Something had to break this spell of gloom, and in that day's headlines there was one bulletin of incredible feel-good news. Private First Class Jessica Dawn Lynch, a nineteen-year-old army supply clerk from Palestine, West Virginia, who had been missing in action in Iraq for nine days, had been found alive and rescued in the vicinity of Nasiriya.

This happy story had first broken on cable the night before, and as it happened, a video record later emerged of just how it had been disseminated. A feature documentary about Aljazeera, *Control Room*, that had its premiere at the Sundance Film Festival nine months later, included a sequence shot at the media center at Central Command headquarters in Doha, Qatar, where reporters were given the first, elaborately detailed briefing on the Lynch rescue. A veteran CNN correspondent, Tom Mintier, grumbled on camera about how this story had superseded the major news he and his colleagues had been waiting for that day: the fate of troops just entering Baghdad. "I was a bit upset that they spent so much time giving us all of the minute by minute, this happened, she said this, we said that," he told the documentary filmmakers, ". . . and on a day when you have forces going into Baghdad, it wasn't a part of the briefing. Seems like there is an effort to manage the news in an unmanageable situation. They tried it in the first gulf war, this time it was supposed to be different." The instant Lynch legend was moving too fast to be derailed, no matter what a reporter like Mintier might have to say about it. The military buttressed its account of Lynch's rescue by releasing a complementary video, shot and edited by its own movie crew: an action-packed montage of the guns-blazing Special Operations raid to rescue Lynch, bathed in the iridescent green glow of night-vision photography.

The breathless television accounts that resulted made much use of a picture of Lynch lying on a stretcher, conscious, with an American flag folded on her chest. The first *New York Times* story quoted an unnamed army official to the effect that Lynch "had been shot multiple times." A day later *The Washington Post* offered many more details in a front-page scoop headlined "She Was Fighting to the Death." Lynch was nothing less than a female Rambo who had tried to shoot her way out of an ambush. "She did not want to be taken alive," an unnamed U.S. official told the *Post* while testifying to Lynch's multiple gunshot and knife wounds.

Within days, someone who knew better, the commander of the Landstuhl hospital where Lynch had been evacuated for treatment, contradicted some of the *Post* story, saying that Lynch had not been shot or stabbed. Yet much of the press decided to use or embellish the *Post* account anyway, honoring the principle laid down in the classic John Ford Western *The Man Who Shot Liberty Valance:* "When the legend becomes fact, print the legend." Lynch was the cover of the April 14 *Newsweek,* which paid brief lip-service to the Landstuhl commander's statement that she had not been shot before immediately stating the reverse: "Surgeons discovered that she had been shot—and, according to a family spokesman in West Virginia, Dan Little, her wounds were 'consistent with low-velocity small arms.'" From there, the newsmagazine speculated about various dark scenarios for the "mystery" of "exactly how she was injured," suggesting that "she might have been shot after she'd been captured, rather than wounded in combat" and thus was possibly the victim of criminal mistreatment in the Iraqi hospital. "The possibility of mistreatment had been very much on the mind of President Bush," an unnamed "senior administration official" told *Newsweek*.

Almost all of this was false. On April 15, 2003, *The Washington Post* returned to the story, albeit on page A17. A doctor from the Iraqi hospital that treated Lynch called the rescue—the one so thrillingly packaged as a video by Centcom in Qatar—"a big show" and said that Lynch "was given special care, more than the Iraqi patients." After other news organizations—the *St. Louis Post-Dispatch*, the *Toronto Star*, and, in England, *The Guardian* (which called the Lynch story "one of the most stunning pieces of news management yet conceived")—further dismantled the *Post*'s original reporting, the paper published, in June, a front-page reinvestigation saying that Lynch had not killed any Iraqis and had not been shot or stabbed. The *Post* also questioned the whole point of the rescue Centcom had detailed so elaborately to reporters such as Tom Mintier the night of April 1: "The Special Operations unit's full-scale rescue of the private, while justified given the uncertainty confronting U.S. forces as they entered the compound, ultimately was proven unnecessary. Iraqi combatants had left the hospital almost a day earlier, leaving Lynch in the hands of doctors and nurses who said they were eager to turn her over to Americans." In all this, Jessica Lynch herself, unable to speak, was reduced to a mere pawn, an innocent bystander in the production of her own big-budget, action-packed biopic. When she emerged a year later, ABC's Diane Sawyer asked if it bothered her that she had been showcased by the military. "Yeah, it does," she answered. "It does that they used me as a way to symbolize all this stuff. I mean, yeah, it's wrong."

But such was the enforced jingoism in the early weeks of the Iraq War that journalists who questioned the official accounts were impugned rather than the Pentagon spinners who had created the fictions. Typical was the blogger Andrew Sullivan, who attacked a BBC reporter as a "far-lefty" and accused him of conducting a "smear" on Lynch after the BBC ran its own documentary debunking the original Lynch-as-Rambo Pentagon bill-of-goods. Meanwhile, the *Los Angeles Times* reported that Randy Kiehl of Comfort, Texas, the father of a soldier who went missing in the same ambush as Lynch, had to surf the Web to find Aljazeera images that might reveal the fate of his son, James.[11] The Pentagon media effort had left Lynch's fellow victim, whose death would later be reported, on the cutting-room floor.

As the air leaked out of the bloated saga of Jessica Lynch, a new feel-good image materialized to take its place: the toppling of a statue of Saddam Hussein in central Baghdad's Firdos Square, on the morning of April 9. On American television, it looked like—and was presented as—a spontaneous act of joy and defiance by liberated Iraqis. "Watching them," Rumsfeld said of the spectacle, "one cannot help but think of the fall of the Berlin Wall and the collapse of the Iron Curtain." Nearly everyone on camera followed his cue. "Not since the Berlin Wall have I seen anything quite like this," said Tim Russert on MSNBC. "You think about seminal moments in a nation's history . . . indelible moments like the fall of the Berlin Wall," Bill Hemmer said on CNN, "and that's what we're seeing right now." David Asman of Fox News said, "My goose bumps have never been higher than they are right now," only to be topped by his network's anchor, the normally reserved Brit Hume, who exclaimed, "This transcends anything I've ever seen."

It was left to television critics in the next day's newspapers, not television journalists on the air, to raise some skeptical questions about this glorious show. A brief discomforting moment when an American flag was thrown over the statue's face by a marine prompted Alessandra Stanley of *The New York Times* to observe that this was a "powerful reminder that unlike the Soviet empire, Iraq's regime did not implode from within" and that "in 1989, East Germans did not need American help to break down their wall." (An American tank had been required to finish off the toppling of the Saddam statue.) Tom Shales of *The Washington Post* noticed that "of all the statues of Saddam Hussein scattered throughout the city, the crowds had conveniently picked one located across from the hotel where most of the media were headquartered. This was either splendid luck or brilliant planning on the part of the military."

In late 2005, *The Journal of Broadcasting & Electronic Media* took a closer look. Its researchers found that "wide-angle shots show clearly that the Square was never close to being even a quarter full" and "never had more than a few hundred people in it (many of them reporters)." But the shots showing a fairly desolate scene started to disappear from American television coverage after the live broadcast of the real-time two-hour toppling of the statue; the networks generally kept instead to tight shots that conjured up a feverish popular uprising matching the administration's prewar promise that Americans would see liberated Iraqis celebrating in the streets. Some version of that festive statue-toppling was replayed every 4.4 minutes on average from 11:00 A.M. to 8:00 P.M. on Fox, and every seven and a half minutes on CNN.[12]

The wide-angle shots of the scene survive in *Control Room*. Samir Khader, a senior producer at Aljazeera who appears in the documentary, comments, "The Americans played the media element intelligently. . . . It was a show. It was a media show. After having bombed Aljazeera, and some part of Abu Dhabi television, they did this show, they brought with them some people—supposedly Iraqis cheering. These people were not Iraqis. I lived in Iraq, I was born there, I was raised there. I can recognize an Iraqi accent. . . . The show was meant for the international media—here we are in Baghdad. The war is finished." Deema Khatib, a young Aljazeera producer, adds, "I bet you they brought in these teenage guys who broke the statue, they brought them in with them because if you notice they are all sort of the same age, no women, and they all went in and it was the same people on the square. You couldn't see more people gathering from the houses around. No one came down to the street to see what was happening because people were scared. And these people who came in, how come one of them had the flag of Iraq before 1991 in his pocket? Has he been waiting there for ten years with the flag on that square? I don't think so. But this is not something the U.S. media will talk about."

That fighting continued elsewhere in Baghdad that same day was all but forgotten. While Martin Savidge, then of CNN, and Byron Pitts of CBS offered occasional oral reports of what CNN's morning anchor, Paula Zahn, mentioned in passing was "total anarchy" in the city, there were no pictures to back it up or to compete with the instant-replay iconography of the toppling statue. "Despite the fact that fighting continued literally blocks from Firdos Square," *The Journal of Broadcasting & Electronic Media* concluded, "apparently no camera crews were dispatched to capture those images. According to CNN and FNC [Fox News Channel], in other words, the war ended with the collapse of the statue of Saddam Hussein in Firdos Square." After that, "the battlefield itself disappeared," with all war coverage falling precipitously on every network, broadcast and cable alike. "Stories accompanied by visuals of fighting" were down 76 percent on Fox and 73 percent on CNN.

If fighting had disappeared from the American public's radar screen, another kind of chaos in Baghdad, albeit bloodless, had not vanished with the lightning American victory. The day after the Saddam statue fell, other, more rarefied artistic artifacts, from the National Museum in Baghdad, started tumbling into the hands of looters. There were many TV pictures of this hooliganism, and they didn't quite fit the euphoric story line of the morning after Saddam's fall. The American brass tried to make them do so, with well-chosen words. "What you are seeing is a reaction to oppression," said Ari Fleischer, arguing that looting, however deplorable, is a way station to "liberty and freedom." "Stuff happens," said Donald Rumsfeld, who likened the looting to the aftermath of soccer games and joked to the press that the scale of the crime was a trompe l'oeil effect foisted by a TV loop showing "over and over and over . . . the same picture of some person walking out of some building with a vase." It was just a minor incident in any event, an aberration, a trivial subplot to the grand drama of liberation. It would be "a stretch," Rumsfeld said in another of his briefing soliloquies, to view the rioting in any way as "a defect in the war plan." It would be "nonsense" for anyone to say to the Pentagon, "'Oh, my goodness, you didn't have a plan.'" The Americans who were now running Baghdad "know what they're doing. And they're doing a terrific job. And it's untidy. And freedom's untidy. And free people are free to make mistakes and commit crimes and do bad things. They're also free to live their lives and do wonderful things."

The administration's chosen story of an orderly post-liberation reconstruction of Iraq had been set forth by Rumsfeld and his deputy, Paul Wolfowitz, in congressional hearings some two weeks earlier. "Before we turn to the American taxpayer, we will turn first to the resources of the Iraqi government and the international community," the defense secretary had testified, saying that an "international donors' conference" would probably be convened to help foot the bill. Wolfowitz said that oil revenue would provide fifty to one hundred billion dollars over a two-to-three-year period: "We're dealing with a country that can really finance its own reconstruction and relatively soon." The looting was merely a blip, offering no larger insight into Iraq's state. "The one thing that is certain is Iraq is a wealthy nation," Ari Fleischer told the press.

When the outrage over the looting story refused to go away once the looting had subsided, the military came up with a new line to explain its lack of preparedness for the civil unrest. "I don't think that anyone anticipated that the riches of Iraq would be looted by the Iraqi people," said the Centcom PR man, Brigadier General Vincent Brooks. That was odd, since in the 1991 war, nine of Iraq's thirteen regional museums were looted, flooding the antiquities market with the booty for years.[13] Then *The Washington Times,* normally an administration ally, undid Brooks's spin by uncovering a Pentagon memo to the coalition command written less than three weeks before American troops entered Baghdad, listing sixteen sites that were crucial to protect in order of importance; number two on the list was the Baghdad museum.[14]

And so a new explanation was trotted out in early May 2003 to counter this discomforting story. Another American general, William Wallace, told reporters that nothing really terrible had happened anyway. "As few as 17 items" in the National Museum were unaccounted for, he said, so how big a deal could this rioting have been? He was backed up by the columnist Charles Krauthammer, a reliable unofficial spokesman for the administration's foreign adventures, who put the number of artifacts looted altogether at thirty-three. Anyone who said otherwise, he wrote, was an antiwar, Saddam-sympathizing leftist—the same kind of war critic who might accuse the U.S. government of "hyping" Iraq's weapons of mass destruction. Of course there were WMDs: "If Hussein had no chemical weapons, why did coalition forces find thousands of gas masks and atropine syringes in Iraqi army bunkers?" he wrote. Case closed.

It wasn't clear where Krauthammer's figure of thirty-three looted artifacts had come from—perhaps the same source who told General Wallace that only seventeen of those were unaccounted for. Already a UNESCO team of experts had estimated that at least two thousand to three thousand pieces were missing from the museum, and upward of one million volumes in the National Library and Archives, a site of unchecked arson, were now ash. The figure from the museum would turn out to be low; the real number was some fourteen thousand, according to Matthew Bogdanos, the Marine Reserve colonel who left his civilian life as an assistant district attorney in Manhattan after 9/11 and led the team searching for the missing treasures.[15] In 2005, Bogdanos received the National Humanities Medal in the Oval Office from President Bush, for his role in recovering some 5,500 of these treasures, but still lamented that few of the highest-quality objects had reappeared. That the looting of the museum might have been an early preview of the chaos yet to come in post-Saddam Iraq went unmentioned at Bogdanos's award ceremony, almost two and a half years after the Americans liberated Baghdad. Art stolen. Art found. Medal bestowed. Another case closed.

About the only discouraging words to be found in the American mass media about America's instant victory in Iraq was on a basic cable channel, Comedy Central, where a nightly news-parody show that had been around since 1996, and since 1999 with Jon Stewart as its host, was starting to gain some cultural traction. With Jay Leno wearing a flag pin, a growing, if still small, audience was identifying *The Daily Show* as one of the few reliable spots on the dial for finding something other than the government line. The Bush on *Saturday Night Live* was still a frat-boy cartoon, wishing that Shock and Awe had been named after *Tango & Cash,* but *The Daily Show* saw a more complex character. After the president told the Iraqis in a subtitled TV address that they were "a good and gifted people" who "deserve better than tyranny and corruption and torture chambers," Stewart cited this as proof that "condescension knows no borders." Often the show's writers found laughs by taking the facts of a news story more seriously than real TV journalists did. Right through the war, most TV reporters had mindlessly parroted the Pentagon speak of "coalition forces" without qualification, as if the dozens of allies in the White House's vaunted "Coalition of the Willing" were providing troops to the American war effort. On *The Daily Show,* by contrast, "Coalition of the Piddling" was from the start a continuing logo for reports on coalition partners such as Morocco, whose contribution to United States forces was two thousand monkeys, enlisted to set off land mines. (That was not satire; the story was reported by UPI.) Now, as the war started to disappear from real news, *The Daily Show* refused to take at face value the White House's professed devotion to postwar Iraq. "We won," said Stephen Colbert, one of the show's fictive Baghdad correspondents. "Rebuilding is for losers. Time to party! Then it's off to Syria for the next invasion."

In an interview, Stewart fended off the knee-jerk criticism of his show's supposed cynicism. "What's more cynical than forming an ideological news network like Fox and calling it 'fair and balanced'?" he asked. "What we do, I almost think, is adorable in its idealism. It's quaint." He was not wrong. During this war, the notion of exercising cant-free speech on an American TV network, even a basic-cable network, had proven to be idealistic, quaint, and usually restricted to Comedy Central at eleven o'clock.

NEXT TO *The Daily Show,* the White House's showmanship remained the epitome of slick. Just how much so became apparent soon enough. By the end of April 2003, the war was far from center stage. That spot had been usurped by a fertilizer salesman named Scott Peterson, from Modesto, California—in the heart of the Central Valley congressional district that Gary Condit had represented until being unseated in 2002. Peterson was arrested and charged with the murder of his pregnant wife, Laci, and the Laci mediathon was dominating the 24/7 news circus as Condit and Chandra Levy once had. But as always, the administration had a plan for retrieving the limelight at an opportune moment: the president would punctuate the end of Operation Iraqi Freedom by declaring victory in the most attention-grabbing way—in a speech given from the deck of a majestic aircraft carrier, the USS *Abraham Lincoln,* making him the first president ever to address the nation from a warship at sea.[16]

There were a few niggling details left unresolved, to be sure. In late April, the State Department had singled out Iran, not Iraq, for having the strongest ties to terrorism of any nation. The third member of the axis of evil, North Korea, was bragging that it had nuclear weapons and more were on the way. In Iraq, Saddam was still unaccounted for, though a White House "senior official" told *The New York Times* that "many members" of the Bush inner circle still believed he had been killed, if not on the war's opening night then later on, in the battle for Baghdad.

White House aides told reporters that Bush's speech would not be an official declaration that the war was over because, under the dictates of the Geneva Conventions, that would require the release of more than six thousand prisoners of war.[17] But such whispered asides notwithstanding, the glorious show they planned, a double feature for May Day, was designed to project a definitive message of closure to the nation and the world. First, Bush, dressed in a flight suit complete with parachute, would co-pilot a navy jet midafternoon on to the *Lincoln*'s deck. Then, after an intermission of some three hours, he would reemerge in a business suit and give his address, surrounded by uniformed troops. The speech was scheduled for prime time in the East, on the most watched night of television of the week, Thursday, home to the runaway hits *Survivor* and *Friends*–and in a heavily promoted Nielsen ratings "sweeps" month besides. A large and captive audience was guaranteed.

Though the Secret Service wouldn't let the president go through with his plan to fly "one of the sexier fighter jets," according to CBS News, his arrival in a four-seat S-3B Viking was more than sexy enough. He emerged from the cockpit draped in more combat gear than a Tom Cruise stunt double. On *Saturday Night Live*, Tina Fey subjected the photographic record of his getup to close scrutiny and wondered if Bush had stuffed "socks down the front of the jump suit."

Had he done so, it would have been consistent with a perfectly orchestrated production so painstakingly specific in its details that a White House media maven, Scott Sforza, had boarded the *Lincoln* days earlier to attend to them all. The plane the president flew, otherwise used for refueling, was renamed Navy One and was emblazoned with the legend GEORGE W. BUSH, COMMANDER IN CHIEF especially for the occasion. When Bush hopped out of the cockpit, he tucked his helmet under his arm while the *Lincoln*'s crew surrounded him–grateful subjects congratulating a conqueror on his triumph. "Yes, I flew it," the president told the press. "I miss flying, I can tell you that," he added, paying nostalgic tribute to his service in the Texas Air National Guard during the Vietnam War.[18]

On Fox News, Morton Kondracke, the pundit who helped out on the hagiographical Showtime movie *DC 9/11: Time of Crisis*, about Bush's derring-do, raved about the scene on the *Lincoln*: "This was fantastic theater." He likened it to the Hollywood blockbuster *Independence Day*, in which President Thomas J. Whitmore (Bill Pullman), a former fighter pilot, helps save the world from attacking aliens. Kondracke's admiration was ratified enthusiastically by the rest of the Beltway's amateur theater critics. David Broder of *The Washington Post* was agog over what he called the president's "physical posture," telling Tim Russert that "this president has learned how to move in a way that just conveys a great sense of authority and command." Inevitably, *Meet the Press* unspooled a classic Democratic rerun for contrast–Michael Dukakis's ill-fated 1988 photo op in a tank while running against the first George Bush. The columnist Robert Novak wondered aloud, "Could Joe Lieberman get into a jet pilot's jump suit and look credible?" and then answered his own question in the negative.

The president's speech came precisely at dusk in the West—Hollywood's so-called magic hour, much prized by cinematographers for the golden glow it bestows on any scene. Sforza, the master of the backdrop, had seen to it that a banner with the simple message MISSION ACCOMPLISHED was posted high up so that it appeared as a halo hovering over the president, much as the Statue of Liberty had appeared at Bush's 9/11 anniversary speech as the war's rollout began. The ranks of crew members who served as Bush's official audience and backdrop were in color-coordinated costumes as bright as the future.[19] "Officers and sailors of the USS *Abraham Lincoln,* my fellow Americans," the president declared, "major combat operations in Iraq have ended."

Bush went on to praise a military victory "carried out with a combination of precision and speed and boldness the enemy did not expect and the world had not seen before." He exulted in "the images of fallen statues" and "the images of celebrating Iraqis." He explained that "the battle of Iraq is one victory in a war on terror that began on September the eleventh, 2001, and still goes on" and that the battle had "removed an ally of Al Qaeda" and seen to it that "no terrorist network will gain weapons of mass destruction from the Iraqi regime, because the regime is no more." He invoked the carnage of the attacks that had so traumatized America twenty months earlier. "We have not forgotten the victims of September the eleventh, the last phone calls, the cold murder of children, the searches in the rubble," he said. "With those attacks, the terrorists and their supporters declared war on the United States, and war is what they got." That this war happened to be against a country that had had nothing to do with 9/11 was largely overlooked in the excitement of an American victory achieved in just over forty days with only 139 American casualties.

If there was a single aesthetic that dominated this rousing scene it was that of Jerry Bruckheimer, the hugely successful producer of *Armageddon, Black Hawk Down,* and *Top Gun,* the movie specifically reenacted by Bush in his flyboy landing on the *Lincoln.* Bruckheimer had enjoyed a happy partnership with the Rumsfeld Pentagon from the get-go. The gala premiere party for Bruckheimer's summer 2001 movie *Pearl Harbor,* which took place just four months before America's next real-life Pearl Harbor, had been held on the similarly impressive aircraft carrier USS *John C. Stennis.* The Bruckheimer–Defense Department collaboration had continued with the short-lived ABC prime-time entertainment series *Tales from the Front Lines,* which presented the

American mission in Afghanistan as an MTV-paced joy ride. As the *Stennis* had been generously dispatched from San Diego to Hawaii for the *Pearl Harbor* gala, so the return of the *Lincoln* and its eagerly homeward-bound troops to San Diego was stalled by a day to accommodate the pageantry of Bush's tailhook landing. One day, after all, was a relatively minor delay for troops whose deployment at sea had already been extended from six months to nearly ten, the longest by a carrier in thirty years, to help fill the maw of an understaffed war.[20]

Like *Pearl Harbor,* which turned its title attack and its aftermath into a pretty and blood-free victory jig, the new White House production sweetened reality. The *Abraham Lincoln* was not in the middle of the sea, as it appeared to the innocent television viewer, but only positioned to look that way: if the camera angle had been different, it would have revealed the San Diego skyline fewer than forty miles away.[21] The president's past as a pilot had been cleaned up in the editing room: no one mentioned that his attendance record had been spotty in the Texas Air National Guard, and his flying had been nowhere near a war. In this sense, the Bush celebratory May Day flight did the job as effectively as Ronald Reagan's 1984 D-day anniversary appearance in Normandy. Equipped with his own aircraft carrier backdrop, Reagan forever cemented the national fantasy that his own wartime service had been on the front rather than in the safe film-industry haven of Culver City, California.

But these were tiny details, intriguing only to nitpickers and dwarfed anyway by the big picture. Surely the cheering throng on the carrier and the jubilant banner above the president's head said it all. A nation that had traveled from the sleepy and self-satisfied 2001 summer of *Pearl Harbor* and Gary Condit to the complacent 2003 spring of "Mission Accomplished" and Scott Peterson had more or less arrived back where it first came in.

PART TWO

BUYER'S REMORSE

SIX

"WE FOUND THE WEAPONS OF MASS DESTRUCTION"

MAJOR COMBAT OPERATIONS in Iraq had ended, but there was still this discomforting hangover that wouldn't go away. Though no one was advertising the fact, anyone paying attention to the just-concluded American victory knew that none of Saddam Hussein's weapons of mass destruction had been found. Still, the country was confident they would be—two thirds of Americans said so to Fox News as Memorial Day approached. The administration had promised as much. "That is what this war was about," Ari Fleischer said midway through Operation Iraqi Freedom. Paul Wolfowitz, the deputy defense secretary, told the journalist Sam Tanenhaus of *Vanity Fair* that WMDs were "the one issue that everyone could agree upon" in the White House war counsels and "the core reason" for the war.[1]

Eventually, on May 29, a journalist got close enough to the president to raise the uncomfortable matter of the missing WMDs—a Polish reporter to whom Bush granted an audience on the eve of a thank-you visit to one of America's few European allies in the Iraq project. The interviewer prodded him: "But still, those countries that did not support the Iraqi freedom operation still use the same argument—weapons of mass destruction have not been

found." The president had an answer: "We found the weapons of mass destruction," he said, asserting that two mobile laboratories "to build biological
weapons" had been located. He promised "more" to come. "But for those who
say we haven't found the banned manufacturing devices or banned weapons,
they're wrong," he reiterated. "We found them."

Condoleezza Rice backed up Bush on CNBC, saying that "a mobile, biological weapons capability" was "already found"—evidence that "we are finding
these pieces that were described" by Colin Powell and others in advance of the
invasion. But Bush subtly revised his language on June 5 when visiting the
American base in Qatar—though perhaps only a careful listener would have noticed the difference, which was one of omission. "We recently found two mobile biological weapons facilities which were capable of producing biological
agents," he said, without reasserting his week-old claim to the Polish journalist
that "we found the weapons." As *Time* would report shortly afterward, the distinction between "facilities" and the actual weapons was suddenly very much
on Bush's mind. In the magazine's account of the president's meeting with his
Iraq commanders in Qatar, Bush "skipped quickly past the niceties" upon arrival to ask where the WMDs were. There was no answer. "Are you in charge of
finding WMD?" the president asked Paul Bremer, his newly installed head of
the provisional authority in Baghdad. When Bremer answered no, Bush repeated the question to General Tommy Franks and received the same response.
The exasperated president pressed on: so who is in charge of finding them?
When an aide coughed up the name Stephen Cambone, a Rumsfeld factotum
in Washington, Bush asked, "Who?"[2]

A leaked memo from the State Department's Bureau of Intelligence and
Research, surfacing in *The New York Times*, soon contradicted the entirety of the
president's CIA-sourced claim about "biological weapons facilities," saying
that the trailers found in Iraq did not amount to conclusive evidence of a Saddam biological weapons program.[3] Undaunted, administration officials continued to refer to "mobile biological laboratories" for the rest of the year. They
didn't have any other WMDs, theoretical or otherwise, to point to.

The failure to find biological or chemical weapons was not the administration's real political problem, however. It was nuclear weapons, that much-
brandished smoking gun that could come in the form of a mushroom cloud,
that had been the most prized and effective tool for selling the war. Now a few

questions, all of them off most Americans' radar screens, were being asked about the nuclear claims in particular. Not long after the invasion began, Seymour Hersh of *The New Yorker* had returned to the subject of the forged documents about supposed Iraqi transactions in Niger for weapons-grade uranium, also known as yellow cake. Given that "uranium from Africa" had been a major selling point in the case against Iraq in Bush's State of the Union speech, Hersh asked: "Was the Administration lying to itself? Or did it deliberately give Congress and the public what it knew to be bad information?"[4]

The issue was revisited after "Mission Accomplished" by Nicholas Kristof, a *New York Times* columnist, who broke the news that "more than a year ago" an unnamed "former U.S. ambassador to Africa" had been sent to Niger after "the vice president's office asked for an investigation of the uranium deal." The ambassador reported back to Washington his finding that speculation about such a deal was "unequivocally wrong." Patrick Lang, a former head of Middle Eastern affairs in the Defense Intelligence Agency, told Kristof that the office of the defense secretary had applied pressure on U.S. intelligence experts before the war, asking them "to think it over again" when they filed reports like that—reports skeptical about Iraq's WMDs. Lang added that any intelligence warning "that Iraqis would not necessarily line up to cheer U.S. troops and that the Shiite clergy could be a problem" was also unwelcome at Defense. Walter Pincus and Dana Priest of *The Washington Post* then filled in some specific details, reporting that Dick Cheney and his most senior aide, I. Lewis "Scooter" Libby, had frequently visited the CIA in the year before the invasion, pressuring intelligence analysts for assessments that backed up administration claims of Saddam WMDs and of an Iraq-Qaeda connection.

Over the next few weeks, chatter about the administration's prewar portrayal of Iraq's doomsday weapons kept simmering. On *Meet the Press,* Rice defended the State of the Union passage about African uranium by saying of the blatantly fake Iraq-Niger documents that "maybe someone knew down in the bowels of the agency, but no one in our circles knew that there were doubts and suspicions that this might be a forgery." The *Post's* Pincus then confirmed Kristof's account of a retired U.S. ambassador who had gone to Niger more than a year before the war began and learned firsthand that there had been no uranium transaction. Pincus added a new element: "senior administration officials" were now saying that the CIA had failed to pass on to the White House the results of the ambassador's investigation. The next day, June 13, Kristof further undermined the administration narrative: "My understanding is that while Director of Central Intelligence George Tenet may not have told Mr. Bush that the Niger documents were forged, lower CIA officials did tell both the vice president's office and National Security Council staff members." This was a flat contradiction of Rice's assertion that "no one in our circles" knew about the forged documents. Soon Pincus was back on page one of the *Post* with a new scoop, this time challenging the other key element in the administration's selling of the Iraq War, the Iraq-Qaeda link. According to Pincus, the prewar National Intelligence Estimate on Iraq, a classified consensus report from the U.S. intelligence community, had warned early on about the reliability of reports of Iraq-Qaeda connections. The notion that Iraq had "trained al Qaeda members in bomb-making and poisons and deadly gases," as Bush had claimed in his Cincinnati speech at the height of the Iraq rollout, was highly suspect. Though Democrats on the Senate Intelligence and Armed Services Panel had sought to see more of the ninety-odd-page NIE at that time, the CIA had given it only a twenty-eight-page "white paper" summary that had been scrubbed of many of the cavils and nuances in the full estimate seen by the White House.[5]

Finally, on the July Fourth weekend, just two months after "Mission Accomplished," the unnamed "retired U.S. ambassador" cited by both Kristof and Pincus stepped forward to identify himself: Joseph Wilson, the same man who had appeared on CNN before the war began in March saying that it was "simply stupid" for the U.S. government to have flogged claims about uranium that could have been disproved with "a couple of phone calls." Wilson had retired in 1998 after serving in both the first Bush and Clinton administrations; as a State Department chargé d'affaires in the Iraq embassy on the eve of the first Gulf War, he had risked his life to shelter eight hundred Americans from Saddam's threats. But he was not famous; few had noticed his CNN rant on the eve of the second war against Saddam. This was about to change. His coming out took the splashy form of an Op-Ed article for Sunday's *New York Times*, headlined "What I Didn't Find in Africa," and an appearance on *Meet the Press* that same day, July 6.

Later, on the same show, the columnist Robert Novak dismissed Wilson's significance. "Weapons of mass destruction or uranium from Niger," he said, "are little elitist issues that don't bother most of the people." Maybe he was right. The administration, though, seemed to be bothered quite a bit about these little elitist issues. In a press gaggle the next day, Ari Fleischer tried to deflect questions about the president's State of the Union uranium claims with "Who's on First?" doubletalk. "Well, there is zero, nada, nothing new here," he said. "Ambassador Wilson, other than the fact that now people know his name, has said all this before." Buck-passing and denials followed quickly throughout that week, as Bush, Powell, Rice, and Fleischer embarked on a five-country tour of Africa.

But the "nothing new" in Wilson's Op-Ed turned out to be something new after all. On July 8, 2003, an unnamed "senior administration official" sent a message through *The Washington Post:* "Knowing all that we know now, the reference to Iraq's attempt to acquire uranium from Africa should not have been included in the State of the Union speech." Wilson's charge had such force that the next day, July 9, only three days after Wilson's Op-Ed was published, Bush, when taking questions at a news conference in Pretoria with the South African president, Thabo Mbeki, referred to Saddam as having a weapons "program" rather than actual weapons. On July 10, when asked by Arkansas Democrat Mark Pryor at an Armed Services Committee hearing when he had learned that the reports of Iraq seeking uranium from Africa "were bogus," Donald Rumsfeld responded, "Oh, within recent days, since the information started becoming available." (ElBaradei's public branding of the Iraq-Niger documents as fakes had been more than four months earlier.) On July 11, Fleischer and Rice held a joint press conference at which Rice blamed the CIA for the State of the Union uranium language: "Knowing what we now know, that some of the Niger documents were apparently forged, we wouldn't have put this in the President's speech—but that's knowing what we know now." That was the cue for Bush to lower the boom on the intelligence agency as the sole scapegoat: "I gave a speech to the nation that was cleared by the intelligence services," he told reporters in Uganda. Within hours, in the media black hole of a Friday night, the CIA director, George Tenet, fell on the administration's sword, releasing a statement in Washington officially affirming that "these 16 words should never have been included in the text written for the President." The next day Bush reaffirmed his confidence in Tenet while in Nigeria. "The president has moved on," said Fleischer.

Yet even after the sixteen words about uranium from the State of the Union address were retracted by Tenet, the White House remained visibly preoccupied, if not obsessed, with Wilson, a figure still largely unknown beyond the Beltway. Rumsfeld and Rice fanned out to the Sunday shows to assert that, in the defense secretary's words, the State of the Union claim was "technically correct" because knowledge of Iraq's uranium search was attributed in the speech to "the British government," which still stood by its finding (without providing any corroborative evidence). In the press gaggle the day after Tenet's retraction, Fleischer tried to discredit the bottom-line conclusion of Wilson's report from Niger by saying (correctly) that it "never said anything about forged documents." Fleischer reiterated: "The President sees this as much ado, that it's beside the point of the central threat that Saddam Hussein presented. . . . Yes, the President has moved on. And I think, frankly, much of the country has moved on, as well." Two days later, on July 14, Fleischer, at least, did move on, leaving his job as press secretary. In a final briefing, he took one more stab at the subject: "I think this remains an issue about did Iraq seek uranium in Africa, an issue that very well may be true. We don't know if it's true, but nobody can say it is wrong." After a ritualistic thank-you to the press corps, he was presented with a farewell cake, prompting much laughter about whether it might be "yellow cake." "Well, if it is," Fleischer quipped, "I'm sure we'll find it."

No one at Fleischer's final briefing asked questions about a Novak column that had been published that morning, in which the columnist identified Wilson's wife, Valerie Plame, as a CIA "agency operative on weapons of mass destruction" and said that "two senior administration officials" had told him that sending Wilson on the Niger mission had been Plame's idea. No one noticed the Novak column at all until two days later, when David Corn, a columnist for *The Nation*, posed a question on his blog: "Did senior Bush officials blow the cover of a U.S. intelligence officer working covertly in a field of vital importance to national security—and break the law—in order to strike at a Bush administration critic and intimidate others?"

While Corn raised the issue of whether Bush officials had deliberately tried to strike at an administration critic, there was a faint hint of such an animus in another, minor dustup. Jeffrey Kofman, an ABC News correspondent embedded with the Third Infantry Division in Falluja, found himself the subject of gossip in Washington after he interviewed troops on the July 15 broadcast of

World News Tonight who complained angrily that their tour of duty had been extended yet again just a week after Rumsfeld had told them they were going home. One soldier told Kofman on camera that he'd like to ask the defense secretary "why we're still here, 'cause I don't, I don't have any clue as to why we're still in Iraq." ("I'd ask him for his resignation," said another.) As if on cue, an administration-friendly Web site, The Drudge Report, posted a story saying that Kofman was gay (and, worse, Canadian). Matt Drudge attributed the information to "someone from the White House communications shop."[6] As it happened, Kofman was openly gay (and even openly Canadian), but the gossip had a circumstantial Karl Rove touch to it. A whispering campaign questioning Ann Richards's sexual orientation had been a feature of the successful Bush-Rove campaign to unseat her as Texas governor. The simultaneous hits on Kofman, Wilson, and Wilson's wife prompted a few questions to the new press secretary, Scott McClellan, but they soon faded away.

Questions about the WMDs did not. In tandem with Bush's downgrading of Iraq's weapons to weapons "facilities," some of the most prominent prewar proponents of Saddam's doomsday stash started adjusting their own language. Two weeks after Wilson's Op-Ed, a new report by Judith Miller in the *Times* attributed much of the empty-handed search of "578 'suspect sites' in Iraq" (down from the figure of 1,400 she had used on CNN the first night of the war) to inept execution by the Pentagon—"chaos, disorganization, interagency feuds, disputes within and among various military units, and shortages of everything from gasoline to soap." Four paragraphs into the story, which ran on page A12, Miller wrote: "To this day, whether Saddam Hussein possessed such weapons when the war began remains unknown."[7] The deputy defense secretary Paul Wolfowitz, then making a visit to postwar Iraq, was no longer calling WMDs a "core reason" for the war. "I'm not concerned about weapons of mass destruction," he told reporters on July 21. "I'm concerned about getting Iraq on its feet."[8]

Maybe Saddam's WMDs were nowhere to be found, but conventional weapons were killing Americans in Iraq at an alarming rate. Only two months after major combat operations had "ended," 25 soldiers had been killed in action and 177 wounded.[9] Pressed for a reaction, the president told reporters, "There are some who feel that the conditions are such that they can attack us there." Then he thrust his hand forward in defiance. "My answer is: Bring 'em on. We've got the force necessary to deal with the security situation." Bring 'em on they did. When the subject of WMDs returned with a vengeance in the fall, it was in syncopation with the constant drip of bloodshed.

David Kay, the head of the American team searching for weapons in Iraq, would release an interim report in early October finding "an intent" on the part of Iraqi's leaders "to continue production at some future point in time," but no "actual weapons." (No American weapons inspectors, including Kay's successor, Charles Duelfer, would ever find any actual weapons.) But while Bush had tried to drop the subject, the issue wouldn't stay dropped. As it became more and more likely that Saddam's WMD cupboard had been bare before Operation Iraqi Freedom, there was an opening for Joseph Wilson to flog his I-told-you-so-about-uranium story, which had been half forgotten after the initial flurry created by his Op-Ed and Novak's outing of his wife in July. A natural grandstander exulting in his newfound celebrity (both Wilsons would later pose for a glamorous photo for *Vanity Fair*), he poured oil on the dying embers of his fifteen minutes of fame after Labor Day by saying that it was Karl Rove who had revealed his wife's identity to Novak, potentially a felony. "At the end of the day," the retired diplomat announced in a public forum, "it's of keen interest to me to see whether or not we can get Karl Rove frog-marched out of the White House in handcuffs."

"That's just totally ridiculous," said Scott McClellan in response to Wilson's accusation against Rove. When Rove himself was ambushed by an ABC News producer in front of his house, and asked "Did you have any knowledge or did you leak the name of the CIA agent to the press?" Rove answered more categorically: "No."[10] The story might have ended there. But apparently unbeknownst to Rove, there was a new development on the way, just twelve hours after his flat denial of guilt. On the night of September 29, 2003, the Justice Department, acting on a request from George Tenet, notified Alberto Gonzales, the White House counsel, that it had officially opened an investigation into whether the leak of Valerie Plame Wilson's name was illegal.[11] For reasons that were never explained, Gonzales sat on this news overnight before notifying the White House staff and asking them to preserve all documents relevant to Justice's investigation.[12]

Now forced to address the Wilson issue for the first time, Bush said, "If there is a leak out of my administration, I want to know who it is," he said. "If the person has violated the law, the person will be taken care of." But this new attention to the Wilson case would last only a few days; it couldn't begin to compete with the exciting political story on the other coast, the recall of the California governor, Gray Davis, and the emergent political career of the movie star Arnold Schwarzenegger. A week after his stern initial remarks about leakers, the president suggested that the whole affair was probably going to disappear into official Washington's vast dead-letter office anyway. "This is a town full of people who like to leak information," he said, "and I don't know if we're going to find out the senior administration official." McClellan told the press corps that he had spoken with three senior administration officials whose names had entered the gossip pool and had been personally assured that they had neither leaked nor authorized the leak of Valerie Plame Wilson's identity: Rove; the vice presidential aide Scooter Libby; and Elliott Abrams, who had pleaded guilty to two offenses in the Reagan administration Iran-Contra scandal and now served on Bush's National Security Council. McClellan added that "the President made it very clear that we should cooperate fully with the Department of Justice." What he did not make explicit was that the investigation would be supervised by John Ashcroft, not just a White House loyalist but a former Rove client during his political career.

WITH THE LEAK CASE safely cordoned off out of sight in a closed-door investigation, the White House had to deal with the ongoing story that could not be so easily locked away in a back room: growing chaos in Iraq. On the first anniversary of that crucial interlude in September 2002, when the top administration brass had rolled out its new war with aluminum tubes and mushroom clouds, crowned by Bush's exquisitely staged Ellis Island address, a major presidential speech about the war was once again televised in prime time, this time from the Cabinet Room. Bush asked for Congress to appropriate sixty-six billion dollars for Iraq and Afghanistan operations, but reassured the country that no new troops would be needed; his commanders had advised him that "the current number of American troops" (nearly 130,000) was enough to handle the mission. Besides, there were "now some 60,000 Iraqi citizens under arms, defending the security of their own country"—with "accelerating" training soon to add more. He implied that Iraq's own new Governing Council ("25 leaders representing Iraq's diverse people") was on its way to running the whole show.

But despite three invocations of 9/11, this presidential rerun was a flop, and it wasn't clear that it would have played better even had the Statue of Liberty once more been enlisted as a backdrop. The president's viewership was way down—to half of what it had been for the State of the Union address in January—and repeated polls chronicled the same downbeat fallout: instead of making Americans feel better about their victory in Iraq, Bush had called attention to the setbacks and the price tag. Typical was a *Washington Post*/ABC News poll finding that 55 percent of the country thought the administration had not had a clear plan for Iraq and 85 percent were concerned the United States might get bogged down there in a long and costly mission.[13]

The White House concluded that this poor response was the press's fault. "The best way to get the news is from objective sources," Bush told a sympathetic interviewer, Brit Hume of Fox News, "and the most objective sources I have are people on my staff who tell me what's happening in the world." The news sources that the rest of America had to rely on, by contrast, were suspect. "There's a sense that people in America aren't getting the truth," the president said as the White House launched a new PR campaign. "I'm mindful of the filter through which some news travels. And sometimes, you just have to go over the heads of the filter and speak directly to the people." The mainstream news media just couldn't be trusted to get anything right, not even the point of the MISSION ACCOMPLISHED banner crowing Bush's victory speech in May. To correct the record on that score, Rice went on *Meet the Press* in late September and explained that the banner signified only that "the mission of those forces that he went to greet had been accomplished."

To do an end run around "the filter" and speak directly to "the people," Bush gave a round-robin of interviews in mid-October exclusively to the anchors of regional TV companies such as Tribune Broadcasting, Belo, and Hearst-Argyle. He hammered in how much "good progress" America was making in the war. A government-run "good news" operation was started in Iraq concurrently with the president's PR offensive at home. To help kick it off, the secretary of commerce, Don Evans, made a brief trip to the front to point to the "thousands" of new businesses that had started since Iraq's liberation, citing as one example two boys he'd seen with a roadside soft-drink stand.[14]

But it wasn't so easy to choke off the bad news at its source. While Bush was using regional anchors to tell the people that congressional delegations were returning from Iraq with happy progress reports, Fox News and *Newsweek* were reporting that these delegations were spending their nights in the safety of Kuwait, not Iraq. *Stars and Stripes,* the Pentagon-financed armed forces newspaper, reported that half the troops it had polled had low morale. "Some troops even go so far as to say they've been ordered not to talk to V.I.P.'s because leaders are afraid of what they might say," the paper's Jon Anderson told the commander, Lieutenant General Ricardo Sanchez, in a confrontational interview.[15] *The Washington Post*'s Dana Milbank reported that dead troops were being kept as tightly under wraps as live ones: the Bush administration had quietly started banning all news coverage of flag-draped coffins returning to military installations such as Dover Air Force Base, in Delaware, with the ban extending to interim stops such as the Ramstein Air Base, in Germany. A Pentagon spokeswoman said that the policy dated from November 2000, the end of the Clinton administration. But it had not been put into practice by the Bush White House until the eve of the Iraq invasion. Before then, the last enforced ban had been in 1991, when the first President Bush halted coverage of coffins returning to Dover from the Persian Gulf War after a network used a split screen to juxtapose his appearance at a news briefing with the procession of the dead. For the current Bush, though, the ban on coffin photos was not enough. He went a step further to ward off vivid news coverage of casualties: breaking with the practice of every president since Carter, he did not attend any memorials or funerals for troops killed at war.[16]

In sync with the White House habit of keeping top policy makers, like dead soldiers, out of reach of "the filter" whenever possible, Rice, Powell, Rumsfeld, and Cheney all declined to be interviewed by PBS for a *Frontline* documentary about prewar intelligence that was broadcast in the midst of the president's regional-anchor PR tour. But Greg Thielmann, who a month earlier had left his high-level post in the State Department's Bureau of Intelligence and Research, did talk, telling *Frontline* that the administration practiced "faith-based intelligence" by "cherry-picking" his department's intelligence to suit its case for war.[17]

That wasn't the only cherry-picking that had gone on. The documentary added details about a small Pentagon intelligence office set up to counter the intelligence coming from the CIA and other agencies in the run-up to the war in Iraq. This special unit, which had been reported on as early as October 2002 by *The New York Times*[18] and the Knight Ridder Washington bureau,[19] produced alternative assessments of Iraq intelligence for administration hawks to use in arguing the case for an invasion. A major source for this alternative intelligence was Ahmad Chalabi, who had provided information on what he said was Iraq's active WMD operations and its supposed connections to Al Qaeda.

When a *Frontline* producer, Martin Smith, pressed Chalabi on camera to produce "documentary evidence of any kind" of a Saddam-Qaeda link, it was in vain. Chalabi, who had now been appointed by the Americans to the new Iraqi Governing Council celebrated by Bush in his prime-time speech, promised to produce a document showing "money changing hands between Saddam Hussein's government and Al Qaeda." But he never did. Equally damning was the *Frontline* account of the administration's decision to ignore the State Department's prescient "Future of Iraq" project. Some fifteen working groups, drawn from several hundred Iraqi exiles, had anticipated the likely difficulties in postwar Iraq, from maintaining law and order to providing utilities—the very issues that the Americans were proving ill-prepared to deal with as stuff happened in the aftermath of "Mission Accomplished."

In the face of all this unwanted news, Dan Bartlett, the White House PR guru, went on the October 15 *Nightline* to carry the president's complaint about the mainstream media to Ted Koppel, a network anchor who was rarely, if ever, given access to Bush, Cheney, Rumsfeld, or Rice. Knocking the national broadcasts and newspapers that didn't give "the full picture" of the "incredible amount of progress being made in Iraq," Bartlett said there "should be a debate about the content as well as the judgment of what makes news." Yes, violence is news, he conceded, but it was old news: "Violence has been with Iraq for more than thirty years." The new news in Iraq is "freedom." Koppel countered by reminding Bartlett that the content of the administration's own news was sometimes suspect: "For example, the director of USAID was on this broadcast [and] told me that he anticipated that the total cost of the U.S. contribution to the rebuilding of Iraq was going to be $1.7 billion. Clearly, totally off the mark. Paul Wolfowitz made it quite clear that he thought oil production in Iraq was going to be able to pay for the reconstruction of that country. Clearly isn't going to happen." Bartlett waved away this line of questioning. "I strongly disagree with the premise," he told Koppel. "I disagree with the fact that the administration was telling the American people or the Congress or the media one thing, while we completely knew something different." Wolfowitz, Bartlett continued, "did not put a time frame" on Iraq's ability to pay for its own reconstruction "but what he did say is that Iraq's own oil resources will go a long way to help rebuild the country." In fact Wolfowitz had testified before Congress just six months earlier that "we're dealing with a country that can really finance its own reconstruction, and relatively soon."

Hardly had the "good-news" offensive begun than the Gannett News Service discovered that scripted good news had somehow been planted in the American press. At least eleven newspapers around the country had run identical letters from different soldiers "describing their successes rebuilding Iraq," at the precise moment when public opinion on the mission was going south. (A *USA Today* poll on September 23 showed that the percentage of Americans who believed that "the situation in Iraq was worth going to war over" had dropped from 73 in April to 50 in September, as those suspect letters to the editor were published.) In the letters, the soldiers wrote that "the quality of life and security for the citizens has been largely restored" and described grateful Iraqis greeting them as liberators, much as Cheney had promised before the war. When the various signatories were contacted, some of them didn't know anything about the letters. Others said they had been asked to sign a form letter. The father of Private First Class Nick Deaconson, who had been hospitalized with shrapnel in both legs after a grenade explosion, recounted a phone conversation he had with his son: "When I told him he wrote such a good letter, he said: 'What letter?' This is just not his [writing] style." A spokesman for the army brigade where the letters originated said that a public-affairs unit had not been involved, but he offered little other explanation for the letters' organized dissemination throughout the United States, saying that he had been told a soldier wrote the letter "but he didn't know who."[20]

The administration's posture toward news about the Americans actually under fire in Iraq was evident. The troops were allowed to appear in "the filter" if they were alive and on script, but were discouraged from mouthing off to correspondents like ABC's Kofman, and hidden away entirely if they had the ill grace to be killed or injured. After spending the day visiting the military wounded at Walter Reed Army Medical Center, Cher, of all people, crystallized the game plan. She called into C-SPAN to tell of her experience talking with "a boy about nineteen or twenty who had lost both his arms" and then asked: "Why are none of Cheney, Wolfowitz, Bremer, the president—why aren't they taking pictures with all these guys? Because I don't understand why these guys are so hidden and why there aren't pictures of them."

If the White House was particularly desperate, the troops could be invoked in absentia to be blamed for the administration's own PR mishaps. When reporters revisited Bush's May victory jig, the president told them that "the 'Mission Accomplished' sign, of course, was put up by the members of the U.S.S. *Abraham Lincoln,* saying that their mission was accomplished," adding, "I know it was attributed somehow to some ingenious advance man from my staff. They weren't that ingenious, by the way." But in fact the sign had been produced by Scott Sforza, the former ABC producer on the White House PR team who'd been bivouacked on the ship. Later, Scott McClellan would revise the president's words, saying that the banner "was suggested by those on the ship" before being produced by Sforza. (The "those" who suggested it never came forward to take credit.) Wesley Clark, the general soon to run for president in the Democratic primaries, was offended by the president's effort to shift responsibility for his own overreach to enlisted men who couldn't speak for themselves. "I guess the next thing we're going to hear is that the sailors told him to wear the flight suit and prance around on the aircraft carrier," Clark said.[21]

The administration's now-you-see-them, now-you-don't presentation of the troops was put to a severe test on November 2, when a Chinook helicopter was shot down near Falluja, leading to the death of sixteen soldiers and the wounding of at least twenty, the single deadliest attack since Operation Iraqi Freedom began. Only the day before, the U.S. commander in Iraq, Lieutenant General Ricardo Sanchez, had tried to relieve anxiety on the home front by dismissing what seemed to be a growing insurgency as "strategically and operationally insignificant." Now Americans were watching the most literal replay imaginable of the most catastrophic war image of recent years, the downing of a helicopter that led to eighteen American casualties in Mogadishu in 1993—a memory that had been refreshed by the Jerry Bruckheimer Hollywood retelling, *Black Hawk Down.* That movie was said to be a favorite of Saddam's, and not without reason. American officials believed it had been distributed by the Iraqi command to its officers before the war as an instructional video guide to American defeat.

In broadcasting early bulletins of "Chinook Down" on a Sunday morning, the normally unflappable Bob Schieffer of CBS News raised his voice as he said, "If this is winning, you have to ask the question: How much of this winning can we stand?" Later that day, on ABC, the correspondent John Berman captured a *M*A*S*H* moment when a military medic attending the American wounded looked directly at the camera and said, "'All major combat operations have ceased' "–after which he winked and, with a roll of his eyes, added a sarcastic "Right!" The president pointedly stayed off-camera on his ranch after the Chinook disaster, idling before a new round of campaign fund-raisers, and sent out only a written statement of grief. In Iraq, the military kept the press away from the scene of the crash, reducing pictures of the incident to long-shot miniatures. Reporters seeking access to Ramstein Air Base were told that the Defense Department would not lift its policy prohibiting photographs of flag-draped coffins for the Chinook casualties.

The following Sunday, November 9, as it happened, NBC broadcast *Saving Jessica Lynch*, its unofficial dramatization of the nineteen-year-old private whose ambush and rescue had been fictionalized as *Rambo* redux by the military and a credulous press back in April. Lynch had passed through her recovery and was about to publish her memoir of her experiences. Few of this war's images had had such longevity or proven more pliable than that of the smiling face of Pfc. Lynch. In the seven months of virtual silence since her rescue from a Nasiriya hospital, she had become the Mona Lisa of Operation Iraqi Freedom. Americans had been able to read into her pleasant but unrevealing snapshot whatever story they chose, and those stories, usually imposed on her by others, had become a Rorschach test for home-front mood swings. When American forces were bogged down in the war's early days, Lynch was the happy harbinger of an imminent military turnaround: a superheroine who had tried to blast her way out of the enemy's clutches, taking out any man who got in her path. When those accounts turned out to be largely fiction, she became a symbol of Bush administration propaganda and the press's credulity in buying it. Then came her months of muffled recuperation: a metaphor for the low-grade fever of inertia and unease that set in at home in the months after the

Saddam statue fell. The NBC movie, trying to stick to the actual facts of Lynch's story rather than the *Rambo* remake, inevitably sacrificed drama for the sake of integrity. If anything, it was more candid than much of the reportage on Iraq, including that at MSNBC, NBC's sibling network, where correspondents had enthused about Bush's *Top Gun* antics as "the president's excellent adventure." In its revisionist way, *Saving Jessica Lynch* brought forth yet another Lynch, appropriate to the current moment in the war: a lowly pawn of larger, mysterious forces operating in the shadows, whether in Baghdad or Washington.

As was the case when the fictional Lynch tale had first been told, things once again did not seem to be going well in Iraq, and as the holiday season arrived, the White House could not let the Chinook tragedy remain in the public mind as a defining index of the war's progress. The PR antidote was a two-and-a-half-hour surprise Thanksgiving trip to Baghdad for the president and his national security adviser, who traveled with a small pool of reporters sworn to secrecy. Much was made of the intrigue that surrounded this festive trip once it was publicized. Bush gleefully described the scene of driving from his Crawford ranch to a Waco airstrip with a small Secret Service contingent: "They pulled up in a plain-looking vehicle with tinted windows. I slipped on a baseball cap, pulled 'er down—as did Condi. We looked like a normal couple."[22] The prize picture of the trip put Bush back in uniform surrounded by welcoming troops, much like the *Top Gun* reenactment on the USS *Lincoln,* but this time he was in an army jacket and presenting a huge platter of turkey that looked as if it had been styled for a food magazine. In fact, it was: the perfect bird was a decoration, not one of the turkeys actually being served from a steam table buffet.[23] The whole production was orchestrated by the pet Pentagon contractor, the Halliburton subsidiary KBR.[24]

This image in turn was superseded two weeks later by an even stronger one: the video of the captured Saddam Hussein, found in a rathole and looking like the rat he was. Yet not even the nailing of Saddam was quieting the questions about why the United States had invaded Iraq in the first place. Making a rare appearance on "the filter," the president sat down for a prime-time interview with Diane Sawyer of ABC just after the Saddam capture. She pressed him as no journalist yet had, repeatedly asking him about the nonexistent weapons of mass destruction, the Kay report, the sixteen retracted words about "yellow cake in Niger." Bush was as testy as he had been a few weeks earlier about the provenance of the MISSION ACCOMPLISHED banner: "Well, you can keep asking the question," the president said, "and my answer's gonna be the same. Saddam was a danger. And the world is better off because we got rid of him." When Sawyer tried to draw a line between Saddam actually having "weapons of mass destruction as opposed to the possibility that he could move to acquire those weapons," Bush snapped back, "So what's the difference? . . . If he were to acquire weapons, he would be the danger. That's, that's what I'm trying to explain to you. A gathering threat, after 9/11, is a threat that needed to be dealt with. And it was done after twelve long years of the world saying the man's a danger. And so, we got rid of him. . . . Diane, you can keep asking the question. I'm telling you, I made the right decision for America."

Christmas was at hand, but there was still no peace. Americans found more reassurance, however subliminal, in the season's runaway movie blockbuster, *The Return of the King*, the final installment of the Hollywood adaptation of J.R.R. Tolkien's *Lord of the Rings* trilogy. The film portrayed a clear-cut war between good and evil in which the bad guys were very visible, unlike the unseen, supposedly insignificant enemy in Iraq.

Almost lost in the thick of a holiday season was a story that appeared on the front page of many newspapers on the very last day of 2003. With scant explanation, John Ashcroft, who had been criticized for three months by Democrats for refusing to recuse himself from the investigation of the leaked identity of Valerie Plame Wilson, suddenly decided to do exactly that. He turned the case over to James Comey, Jr., a former Manhattan prosecutor who had become deputy attorney general just three weeks earlier, and Comey in turn assigned the case to a special counsel whom he appointed on the spot, a U.S. attorney in Chicago named Patrick Fitzgerald. Ashcroft was nowhere to be found and offered no public explanation for his turnabout. Fitzgerald also avoided the press, instead having his Chicago office issue a four-sentence press release. "Consistent with the usual practice concerning investigations, Mr. Fitzgerald does not intend to comment any further," it said.[25]

But George Santangelo, a defense attorney who had done battle with Fitzgerald in a case involving the Gambino mob family, had a comment of his own about the new special counsel, which served as the "quotation of the day" in the New Year's Eve edition of *The New York Times*. "If John Ashcroft wanted any favors on this one," Santangelo said, "he went to the wrong guy."

SEVEN

"SLAM DUNK"

JUST WHEN IT SEEMED that all analogies between Iraq and Vietnam, real and bogus, had exhausted themselves, the crypt of America's darkest foreign adventure opened and out stepped . . . Robert McNamara. The old defense secretary from the Camelot era, now pushing ninety and as spectral as any ghost of Christmases past, had given hours of interviews to the filmmaker Errol Morris for a documentary titled *The Fog of War: Eleven Lessons from the Life of Robert S. McNamara.* Whatever McNamara's motives—a hard-to-gauge admixture of guilt and egomania—he talked nonstop to the press to promote the film. When prodded, he coyly walked up to comparisons between the two wars of choice, only to hastily retreat, saying he didn't think it was proper for a former Cabinet officer to criticize a sitting president. It was a most eccentric final bow, more comic than tragic. A brilliant man who knew that Vietnam was lost by the time he left the Johnson administration, he never spoke up about the debacle during the seven costly years of war that followed his exit. Given a second chance all these years later, McNamara still lacked the courage to speak out. He proved once again that, for him at least, discretion was hardly the better part of valor.

At least one Bush Cabinet member, the first treasury secretary, Paul O'Neill, did not share McNamara's inhibitions. Like McNamara, the onetime wunderkind of Ford, O'Neill was a highly prized former CEO (of Alcoa) whose venture into public service ended with a Texas wartime president firing him. But O'Neill wasn't going to wait decades before revisiting his tenure in the executive branch and criticizing a war he found half-cocked. Just thirteen months after his departure, it was payback time. O'Neill reclaimed the spotlight to publicize a score-settling book, *The Price of Loyalty,* written with his co-operation (and his trove of nineteen thousand White House documents) by the former *Wall Street Journal* reporter Ron Suskind. The timing was exquisite: the kickoff for the publication was an interview on *60 Minutes* on January 11, a week and a half before the president's 2004 State of the Union address.

O'Neill described an administration that was fixated on Iraq from its very first National Security Council meeting—ten days after the inauguration, more than eight months before 9/11. He quoted Donald Rumsfeld as saying at the second NSC meeting that removing Saddam Hussein would "demonstrate what U.S. policy is all about." O'Neill added: "From the start, we were building the case against Hussein and looking at how we could take him out and change Iraq into a new country. And, if we did that, it would solve everything. It was all about finding *a way to do it.* That was the tone of it. The President saying, 'Fine. Go find me a way to do this.'"[1] O'Neill didn't buy the way they finally found. "In the 23 months I was there, I never saw anything that I would characterize as evidence of weapons of mass destruction," he told *Time,* suggesting that the administration, rather than gather "real evidence," had shaped its intelligence conclusions to suit its own preconceptions.[2] O'Neill's accusation implicitly floated one obvious Vietnam parallel that McNamara couldn't bring himself to say aloud: the Bush administration's selling of the imminent threat of Saddam's WMDs recalled the Johnson administration's manipulation of the Gulf of Tonkin incident in its own zeal to rush to war.

The Bush White House didn't just deny O'Neill's version of events; it struck back. The Treasury Department asked its inspector general to investigate the brandishing of a "secret" government document on O'Neill's *60 Minutes* segment. Though nothing came of this threat, it alone seemed to prompt the former secretary to soften his original line. But the book hit the bestseller lists nonetheless, just as word started to spread that David Kay, the U.S. weapons inspector in Iraq, was resigning without finding any WMDs. Facing the flak from both O'Neill and Kay, the president was prompted to change his tune, too. In his State of the Union address, Bush resorted to tortured language that moved him even further away from his claims before and after the Iraq invasion. He now referred to "dozens of weapons of mass destruction–related program activities," whatever they were. Just a year earlier, some two months before Shock and Awe, his State of the Union address had meticulously specified the weapons he knew to be in Saddam's possession.

In the new speech, given on January 20, Bush emphasized the liberation of Iraq over the smoking gun Saddam had once pointed at America. For illustration, a smiling Ahmad Chalabi, one of the new democratic Iraqi leaders, was seated behind Laura Bush as TV window dressing. But however salutary the liberation of Iraq, the president did not want Americans to lose their taste for war, which had done so much to burnish his reputation as a leader since 9/11 and would be central to his reelection campaign. "I know that some people question if America is really in a war at all," Bush said, then added a stern admonition: "After the chaos and carnage of September the 11th, it is not enough to serve our enemies with legal papers." This was a swipe at the supposedly soft-on-terrorism pronouncements of John Kerry, who had just vanquished Howard Dean in the Iowa caucuses to become the Democratic front runner. It was the opening salvo in what would become a Republican motif of characterizing political opponents as less manly than the *Top Gun* president.

Though Bush sounded as if he might be backing away from his prewar assertions about Iraq, his vice president kept the old message percolating. At least three times in the weeks bracketing the State of the Union, Cheney reiterated his claims of "overwhelming evidence" (as he put it on NPR) for a pre-9/11 Iraq-Qaeda connection or spoke of "a couple of semi-trailers" found in Iraq that were proof of a program for "mobile biological weapons labs." But following close behind Paul O'Neill on both *60 Minutes* and the bestseller lists was another eyewitness to inner doings in the Bush White House who challenged administration credibility. In a new book titled *Against All Enemies,* Richard Clarke, a pugnacious veteran Beltway in-fighter who had served in every administration since Reagan's and was the antiterrorism czar under Bush in 2001, corroborated O'Neill's and others' accounts of an administration obsessed with Iraq over all else. Clarke also portrayed the White House as being clueless about terrorism for too long, a case he drove home with a Tom Clancy–style dramatization of events in the Situation Room and other corridors of power before, during, and after 9/11.

The timing of Clarke's book was even more devastating than that of O'Neill's. The 9/11 Commission had finally begun its hearings; Clarke's publisher moved up the book's publication by a week so that it would be on sale just in time for his televised testimony before the commission.[3] CBS energetically promoted the Clarke *60 Minutes* segment in advance, running a teaser for five nights during the NCAA men's basketball tournament: "Who says the president dropped the ball on terrorism to go to war in Iraq? One of his own former White House advisers." The interview itself, conducted by Lesley Stahl, was incendiary. Speaking of White House meetings after the 9/11 attacks, Clarke said that Osama bin Laden and Al Qaeda were all but lost in the shuffle: "Rumsfeld was saying that we needed to bomb Iraq, and we all said, but no, no. Al Qaeda is in Afghanistan. We need to bomb Afghanistan. And Rumsfeld said there aren't any good targets in Afghanistan, and there are lots of good targets in Iraq. And I said, well, there are lots of good targets in lots of places, but Iraq had nothing to do with it. . . . Invading Iraq or bombing Iraq after we're attacked by somebody else, you know, it's akin to what if Franklin Roosevelt after Pearl Harbor, instead of going to war with Japan, said, let's invade Mexico." Clarke also belittled the administration's thesis of a link between Iraq and Al Qaeda: "I think they wanted to believe that there was a connection, but the CIA was sitting there, the FBI was sitting there, I was sitting there saying, 'We've looked at this issue for years. For years we've looked for a connection, and there's just no connection.'" And then he went straight for the jugular, asserting that George Tenet had repeatedly warned the president in daily intelligence briefings throughout June, July, and August of 2001 that "a major Al Qaeda attack is going to happen against the United States somewhere in the world in the weeks and months ahead."

The next morning, on March 22, *The New York Times* ran on page A18 an article by Judith Miller recounting Clarke's accusations. The story gave the response of the White House flack, Dan Bartlett—who "dismissed Clarke's charges as 'politically motivated,' 'reckless' and 'baseless'"—before getting to the charges themselves.[4] But by wielding the weapon of television, Clarke had created an unquenchable firestorm just after the White House had staged a production to mark the Iraq War's first anniversary (a Bush address to representatives of eighty-three nations, most of which did not support the war). What's more, Clarke had no intention of retreating from the fray under pressure, as O'Neill had. He appeared on all three network morning shows the day after *60 Minutes,* prompting the White House to send Rice to the same programs to try to refute him. Far from neutralizing her antagonist, however, Rice's interviews forced another round of questioning about why the White House would not permit her to appear under oath at the 9/11 Commission hearings.

That morning Clarke's own revelations were compounded by *The Wall Street Journal,* which reported that the 9/11 Commission was unearthing discrepancies in the White House's account of its own actions on that day. The chief of staff, Andrew Card, had previously said that Bush left the Florida classroom within seconds after Card whispered in his ear about the second plane crashing into the World Trade Center. Not so: "[U]ncut videotape of the classroom visit obtained from the local cable-TV station director who shot it, and interviews with the teacher and principal, show that Mr. Bush remained in the classroom not for mere seconds, but for at least seven additional minutes" during which he "followed along for five minutes as children read aloud a story about a pet goat" and then "stayed for at least another two minutes, asking the children questions."[5]

As the morning after *60 Minutes* turned into afternoon, other members of the administration started manning the barricades. Appearing on Rush Limbaugh's radio talk show, Dick Cheney said Clarke "wasn't in the loop, frankly, on a lot of this stuff." There was an obvious inconsistency to this line of attack that others immediately leapt on. "You can't have it both ways," said Wesley Clark on CNN, noting that Clarke "either was the counterterrorism czar and was responsible and knew what was going on or the administration gave him a title and didn't put any emphasis on terrorism and that's why he wasn't in the loop." Some White House surrogates, noting Clarke's long friendship with Rand Beers, a foreign-policy adviser to John Kerry, tried to paint him as a Kerry campaign operative. But Clarke had nothing to do with the Kerry campaign and said he would not accept a job, if offered one, in a Kerry administration. For his part, Kerry was on vacation skiing in Idaho, where he said he would wait for his staff to FedEx "several chapters" before he responded to Clarke's book.[6] (Presumably fax machines hadn't yet made it to Sun Valley.) Other leading Democrats, including the senators Joe Lieberman and Joe Biden, refused to endorse Clarke's charges, giving the benefit of the doubt to the president.

By the time Clarke's appearance before the 9/11 Commission arrived, three days after his *60 Minutes* interview, he had booted Hillary Clinton and *The South Beach Diet* from the top of Amazon.com's bestseller list. His television performance in the Senate hearing room began on another note of high drama—a gratuitous but arresting apology to the families of the 9/11 victims, some of whom were front and center in his audience (while others, he pointedly noted, were "watching on television"). "Your government failed you," Clarke told them. "Those entrusted with protecting you failed you. And I failed you. We tried hard, but that doesn't matter because we failed. And for that failure, I would ask, once all the facts are out, for your understanding and for your forgiveness." It was the 9/11 families' incessant campaign for an inquiry that had forced the Bush administration to end its resistance to the establishment of the commission in the first place. Their applause when a sharp Clarke riposte one-upped a Republican interrogator, the supercilious former Illinois governor James Thompson, played mightily on-screen, as did their tearful embraces of Clarke after his testimony. For a man who had spent his entire career in the shadowy bowels of the Washington bureaucracy, Clarke proved to be a natural before the camera. With his sonorous voice, secret-agent aura, and vaguely intimidating body language, he was as commanding in his weird way as Orson Welles in full noir. His menacing stare in response to another antagonistic interrogator on the commission, John Lehman, seemed to brush back Lehman much as Clarke's verbal darts eventually drove Thompson from the hearing room altogether.[7]

Bizarrely, the president chose the same night as Clarke's testimony at the 9/11 hearings to press ahead with a comedy routine about his administration's failure to find weapons of mass destruction in Iraq. The stage was the dais at an annual black-tie dinner for broadcast journalists in Washington, televised by C-SPAN. The bit was a jocular slide show in which a mugging Bush was seen searching for Saddam's arsenal here, there, and everywhere in the Oval Office. The video was quickly picked up by the networks. Viewers who had watched Clarke mourn the unnecessary loss of American life on 9/11 now saw the president make light of the rationale that had necessitated the sacrifice of an additional five hundred plus Americans (so far) in the war fought in 9/11's name.

Rice continued to dog Clarke on the air, and that same evening, Tom Brokaw, generally the least contentious (and most watched) of the three network anchors, took the startling step of giving her the first hard slap of her heretofore charmed life in the public eye: "Dr. Rice, with all due respect, I think a lot of people are watching this tonight, saying, 'Well, she can appear on television, write commentary, but she won't appear before the commission under oath. It just doesn't seem to make sense.'"

The White House, so often masterly in its TV management, particularly when it came to guarding its 9/11 franchise in an election year, was wildly off its game. Among other strategic mistakes, Scott McClellan at first said that Bush was too busy to watch the commission hearings—making the president sound as if he were dismissive of the 9/11 families and of those viewers throughout the country glued to their sets. The repeated attempt to chastise Clarke for promoting a self-serving book during an election year also backfired. Bush's once and future communications czar, Karen Hughes, was just days from starting a nonstop TV tour to hype her own self-serving book about her White House tenure, 9/11 included. Bill Frist, the Senate majority leader, raised the level of invective even higher and less productively, attacking Clarke's book as an attempt to profiteer on his inside access and on "highly classified information." Not for the first or last time did Frist, a fount of self-righteous arrogance even by Senate standards, prove to have an incomplete command of the facts and a propensity for shooting himself in the foot. Presumably temporary amnesia had made him forget—as others would immediately remind him—that he had capitalized on his own insider status to publish a post-9/11 book, the particularly cheesy *When Every Moment Counts: What You Need to Know About Bioterrorism from the Senate's Only Doctor.* As for Clarke's release of "highly classified information," the White House itself had vetted Clarke's book for possible security transgressions and had approved it.

Of all the White House efforts to take down Clarke, perhaps the most revealing surfaced only briefly: CNN's Wolf Blitzer, attributing the information to "administration officials," spoke on air of some unspecified "weird aspects" in Clarke's life without specifying who those "officials" or what those "aspects" were. Coincidentally or not, the anchor indulged in this innuendo just as a few right-wing bloggers started speculating on-line about Clarke's sexual orientation. A week later, under fire in a *Times* column by Paul Krugman, Blitzer offered a convoluted explanation of what he had meant, now saying that he was referring to only a single administration official and that the only weird aspect in Clarke's life was his alleged tendency to indulge in *X-Files* scenarios about terrorists.

By then, the White House had little choice but to move on. On *Meet the Press* following his 9/11 testimony, Clarke checkmated any further character assassination from the Bush legions by showing on camera a handwritten adulatory note from Bush himself. Two days after that, in an abrupt reversal, the White House folded on its last resistance to the 9/11 Commission. It agreed to let Rice testify in public and under oath and dropped the restrictive terms it had sought on private interviews for Bush and Cheney.

The dirty little secret about the uproar over Clarke's revelations was that many of them had been previously revealed by others, well before he published his book. But as the Bush administration knew better than anyone, perception was all, and perception began with images on television. Clarke had given the charges a human face.

There were many more whipsaw battles on TV yet to come as two presidential campaigns began to heat up in earnest and continued to vie over 9/11. The Bush-Cheney reelection campaign had scheduled the Republican National Convention in the unfriendly confines of New York City at an unusually late date for no other apparent purpose than to ensure that Bush's renomination would be as close geographically and chronologically as feasible to Ground Zero on the attacks' third anniversary. Already the Bush-Cheney campaign had run TV ads that made pictorial use of the ruins and the flag-draped corpses of the World Trade Center. The White House's prohibition on photos of flag-draped coffins from Iraq, it seemed, did not extend to the politically useful pictures of casualties from 9/11.

Images from Iraq nonetheless remained the skeletons that kept rattling no matter how hard the administration tried to lock them away. The week following Clarke's book blitz brought pictures so graphic in their violence that the news media debated whether to show them. Four Americans working for Blackwater Security Consulting of Moyock, North Carolina, one of the many private contractors augmenting American troops in Iraq under murky, mercenary-like arrangements, were ambushed, murdered, and dragged through the streets of Falluja, the Sunni-dominated city west of Baghdad. Two of the mutilated corpses were strung up on a bridge over the Euphrates River as mobs chanted "Falluja is the graveyard of Americans!" In sharp contrast to the news media's behavior after the similarly violent downing of a Black Hawk helicopter in Somalia eleven years earlier, CNN, Fox News, and NBC all decided to skip the most graphic images. However unintentionally, that decision lent support to the White House's ever-greater determination to downplay the bloodshed. To further keep this horrific story on the down low, Scott McClellan delivered a minimalist message of sorrow and outrage over the killings. The president made no mention of the incident at all in his one semipublic appearance afterward, at a two-thousand-dollar-a-seat fund-raiser, his last for the campaign year.[8] CBS and ABC did use some of the Falluja images, blurring the bodies of the dead and prompting the executive producer of the *CBS Evening News,* Jim Murphy, to take the rare step of criticizing a competitor. "CNN showed so much restraint it wasn't really covering the story," he said.[9]

With or without the pictures, the incident didn't fit the White House's own story line, which had the Americans turning over sovereignty to a liberated, mostly pacified Iraq on June 30, just three months hence. Rumsfeld told reporters that any remaining violence was due to "thugs," "gangs," and "terrorists," scattered dead-enders from Saddam's regime, not to a growing insurgency. The administration also claimed that Iraq had two hundred thousand troops of its own ready to step up in a variety of policing capacities as the Americans got out of the way.[10]

In the first ten days of April 2004, this narrative imploded. There was now an all-out battle in Falluja. At least a dozen marines were killed in fighting in Ramadi. Militia loyal to the anti-American Shiite cleric Moktada al-Sadr mounted an assault on Najaf. At least six cities were torn by war. There now seemed to be two separate but equally lethal and large insurgencies spreading at once—one by the Sunnis, though not exclusively Sunnis once loyal to Saddam, and another by Shiites, though not exclusively those loyal to Sadr. What any of these combatants had to do with bin Laden or Al Qaeda was unclear. Nor was it easy to find those Iraqis who were said to be greeting the Americans as liberators. The homegrown Iraqi troops recruited to help the Americans in battle were either deserting their posts or refusing to fight as the violence escalated.

With the 9/11 hearings and the uptick in conflict in Iraq playing out simultaneously, television was overrun by another potent image: grieving families. Whatever the Iraq War's synergies with Vietnam, the ubiquity of families on TV was beginning to recall the media dynamics of the most dramatic previous American confrontation with Islamic radicals: the 1979 hostage crisis that helped speed the demise of the Carter presidency. Back then, the attenuated siege in Iran had prompted the inventive ABC News impresario Roone Arledge to create a nightly late-night news show, *America Held Hostage* (later to be made permanent as *Nightline*). What made this unprecedented series a hit was not so much its insights into the Ayatollah Khomeini or the largely out-of-view hostages themselves but its sometimes soap-operatic fixation on the hostage families back home. The families collectively proved "a new kind of figure in American public life," wrote Melani McAlister, the author of a subsequent study.[11] By giving interviews, staging their own press conferences, and attending commemorative events in their own communities, the families gained "a powerful status as moral agents in the realm of politics," McAlister found. Precisely because they were allied with emotions and domesticity "rather than diplomacy, officialdom or politics," a powerful narrative, often quite political, could spring up around them.

Such was the phenomenon now repeating itself. If Vietnam was the living-room war, Iraq extended the media battlefield to actual living rooms where, in a 24/7 news world unimaginable in 1979, families of any and every American tragedy, whether those of war, natural disaster, or crime, sat for interviews whenever the networks came calling, not just during the *Nightline* time slot. Such families, with their tales of dead or absent fathers and children, were not-to-be-underestimated guerrillas in the battle for public opinion, and the administration, gradually realizing what it was up against, knew the former had to be pacified along with the insurgents in Falluja.

The Bush White House's first step to counter the 9/11 families was to sic its media allies on the so-called Jersey Girls, the four telegenic suburban widows of 9/11 who had forced the administration to reverse its stonewalling of the 9/11 Commission. Limbaugh labeled the most outspoken of the four, Kristen Breitweiser, a Democratic operative (though, in fact, she had been a Republican who voted for Bush in 2000) and said the widows were not "grieving family members" but were "obsessed with rage and hatred."[12] Bill O'Reilly on Fox sounded the alarm that "some 9/11 families have aligned themselves with the far left." But this stab at damage control went nowhere. Knocking widowed "Jersey girls" was as un-American as badmouthing Bruce Springsteen. Rice's long-delayed testimony before the 9/11 Commission, arriving just as the insurgency roared in Iraq, only enhanced the families' outrage and authority. Rice acknowledged on camera that the special intelligence briefing presented to the president in Crawford at his request on August 6, 2001, was titled "Bin Laden Determined to Attack Inside the United States."

On April 12, 2004—two weeks into the eruption that had begun in Falluja—all three morning network news shows, the programs that reach a vast audience of American women of voting age, aired reports on aggrieved families or interviews with them or their immediate neighbors: either the families of 9/11 victims, the families of American troops in Iraq (whether those killed there or those forced to extend their stay), or the families of Americans taken hostage in Iraq. CBS's *Early Show* ingeniously managed to cook up a smorgasbord of all three. Perhaps the most wrenching of those stories involved a Wisconsin family, the Witmers, that had lost one of three sisters who were serving in the National Guard in Iraq, prompting a television debate about whether the other two sisters should return to the war. (They eventually decided not to.)

The White House, which had been so determined to keep the president away from mourning families in public, was suddenly desperate to get with the program. It sent Bush out for a press conference the next day so that he could hit scripted talking points about the families a half-dozen times. "I feel incredibly grieved when I meet with family members," he said at one point, adding, "and I do quite frequently." (Message: I care—more than my father ever seemed to.) "I've met with a lot of family members," he reiterated, "and I do the best I do to console them about the loss of their loved one." (Message: I care as much as Bill Clinton did after Oklahoma City.) Bush's motivation was naked. "Nobody likes to see dead people on their television screens," he said.

Still, the bad news, like the families, kept arriving on those television screens—both from Iraq and from *60 Minutes*. Just four weeks after Richard Clarke's appearance on the CBS newsmagazine, Bob Woodward was on hand to promote his new book about the Bush administration, *Plan of Attack*, which was enthusiastically greeted by many who had criticized the previous *Bush at War* for its hagiography. Another instant bestseller, the book confirmed and expanded upon the revelations of previous administration insiders, revealing that Bush had asked Rumsfeld to start a war plan for Iraq in secret on November 21, 2001, and that Tenet had told the president that intelligence about Iraq WMDs was "a slam dunk" even though the National Intelligence Estimate and other reports had left reason for doubt. Woodward also confirmed Clarke's assertion that before 9/11, the administration had "largely ignored the terrorism problem."

As the questions raised by Woodward's account rattled through the mediasphere, the first photos of coffins bearing the Iraq War dead surfaced in defiance of the Pentagon ban on them. The photos, published in *The Seattle Times* on April 18, were taken by a contract worker (who was soon fired) and showed flag-draped caskets being loaded onto a transport plane in Kuwait. Days later, a Web site, the Memory Hole, posted more than three hundred images from the Dover Air Force Base—the fruits of a successful Freedom of Information Act request. It was just the grim reminder of the war's toll that the administration had feared, coming in a month that would yield 135 American casualties—far more than any other month since the invasion began and only a few casualties short of the total number of American dead during the six weeks of "major combat operations" a year earlier.

The time could not have been riper for an inspiring story that might elevate the nation's mood, if not change the subject—one that could remind Americans of the committed, brave troops sacrificing on behalf of freedom. Lo and behold, on the same day that a White House spokesman criticized the publication of coffin photos as a violation of the privacy and sensitivities "of the families of the fallen," such a story just happened to materialize. It was the news on April 23 of yet another American war casualty—and a more uplifting story than the cold-blooded murder of anonymous hired guns in Falluja. This time the victim was the most famous military recruit of the entire war. His heroism under fire had unfolded not in the war in Iraq, but in the original, half-forgotten war prompted by 9/11 to liberate Afghanistan from the grip of the Taliban.

The casualty was Pat Tillman, twenty-seven, who had been a starting safety for the Arizona Cardinals football team and had walked away from a $3.6 million NFL contract to enlist and fight terrorism in the aftermath of Al Qaeda's attacks on America. While Tillman was the best-known American soldier, he had never sought publicity for his service. When he and his brother, Kevin, a former minor-league baseball player, enlisted together, they drove from Phoenix to Denver to do so, hoping to avoid any celebrity treatment that might set them apart from their fellow troops. They never gave interviews and were so eager to avoid any special attention that they had declined to appear in person to receive the Arthur Ashe Courage Award at the ESPY Awards sponsored by ESPN.

There would be plenty of publicity for Pat Tillman now. A military spokesman, Lieutenant Colonel Matthew Beevers, gave a vivid description of the circumstances surrounding the young soldier's death on April 22, 2004. Tillman had been part of an elite Army Ranger unit in the rugged mountains on the Afghanistan-Pakistan border, the area believed to be the hideout for bin Laden and his deputy, Ayman al-Zawahiri. Beevers wouldn't say precisely what role Tillman's unit might have been playing in the continuing search for the Qaeda leaders—that would have compromised security, of course—but he added some details about the hero's demise. After Tillman's patrol came under fire, he and his fellow troops left their vehicles to pursue their attackers. Tillman was killed by enemy fire during the ensuing sustained firefight of some fifteen to twenty minutes.

A week later, on April 30, 2004, an official army press release awarded a Silver Star to Tillman and filled in still more details of his last battle. The release said that he had been storming a hill to rescue ambushed soldiers pinned down by enemy fire—"Through the firing, Tillman's voice was heard issuing commands to take the fight to the enemy forces emplaced on the dominating high ground"—even as he "personally provided suppressive fire with an M-249 Squad Automatic Weapon machine gun."[13] On May 3, thousands turned out for a nationally televised memorial in Tillman's hometown of San Jose, California, at which the First Lady of California, Maria Shriver, and a war hero from Tillman's football home of Arizona, John McCain, both spoke.

But national attention for that ceremony was limited. Tillman's heroic death was being overrun by a dizzying succession of new images from Iraq. After three weeks of a siege following the murder of the four American contract workers, the marines had retreated from Falluja. The military spokesman, Brigadier General Mark Kimmitt, explained that "this is not a withdrawal, it's not a retreat," but his words couldn't eradicate news video of an American tank literally going into reverse while pulling out.

The retreat took place on the eve of the first anniversary of the president's May 1, 2003, celebration of the end of "major combat operations." This time it was Falluja's citizens who were celebrating, dancing in the streets to gloat about their victory over the American liberators whom, it was once thought, they would be welcoming with flowers. The coup de grâce was an image that negated the war's one unambiguous accomplishment, the toppling of Saddam. In the wake of the departed marines, a man in the olive-green uniform and beret of Saddam's Republican Guard took command in Falluja, looking for all the world like one of those Saddam doubles Americans had been warned about before the war. But instead of toppling this Saddam stand-in, the Americans were resurrecting him and returning him to power as part of a new Iraqi-American "military partnership" promising "peace and stability." The U.S. military spokesman professed ignorance of the commander's background, but the press had no trouble discovering that he was a ranking officer in one of the special Republican Guard units that had been closest to Saddam. The war had now reached a point where the old Marx Brothers gag was coming into play: "Who are you going to believe—me or your own eyes?" Americans were beginning to believe their own eyes.

Through the cruel accident of timing, such troubling images from Iraq were in turn cross-cut on television with a retread of a Bush standing under the MISSION ACCOMPLISHED banner of a year earlier. "I wish the banner was not up there," Karl Rove told a newspaper editorial board in the swing state of Ohio. Not "I wish that we had planned for the dangers of post-Saddam Iraq before recklessly throwing underprepared and underprotected Americans into harm's way." No, Rove had his eye on the big picture: better political image management through better set design. In prewar America, presidential backdrops reading STRENGTHENING MEDICARE and STRENGTHENING OUR ECONOMY had worked just fine. If only that one on the USS *Lincoln* had said STRENGTHENING IRAQ, everything would be hunky-dory now.

The defeat in Falluja, however, was only one element in a perfect storm of unwanted Iraq images that filled the weekend on the first anniversary of "Mission Accomplished." The nation's news media, after forty-eight hours of stunned semi-silence and excessive caution, were belatedly picking up on a shocking story broken by CBS News on its Wednesday night newsmagazine *60 Minutes II* about the abuse of detainees by American guards at Abu Ghraib, a notorious prison outside Baghdad that had previously been used by Saddam to torture his own captives. CBS had obtained photos taken by the American guards showing the fruits of their cruelty: the detainees were forced to simulate sexual acts, to form a naked human pyramid, and to cower from dogs snarling at close range. In one photo broadcast by the network, a prisoner, his head hooded, was perched on a box with wires attached to his body; he had been threatened with electrocution if he lost his balance and fell. Other snapshots revealed the American guards in exuberant poses, giving thumbs-ups and enthusiastically pointing at the victims of their sadistic sexual games. These intimations of rape, with Americans cast as the rapists and Iraqis as the victims, needed no commentary to be understood in any culture.

Almost simultaneously, ABC unveiled another set of pictures from the war—less grotesque but still highly upsetting. To mark the first anniversary of the end of "major combat operations," Ted Koppel decided to read aloud the names of the American fallen in Iraq and show their portraits on *Nightline*. It was an unbearably poignant roll call. One young soldier could be seen cradling his infant child; others were still wearing the cap and gown of high school and college graduations. The acknowledged prototype for Koppel's memorial was a famous *Life* magazine cover story "The Faces of the American Dead in Vietnam: One Week's Toll," from 1969. It was also in 1969 that a little-known reporter, Seymour Hersh, broke the story of the 1968 massacre at My Lai, the horrific scoop that now found its match thirty-five years later in Hersh's *New Yorker* follow-up to CBS's Abu Ghraib scoop. Hersh had obtained a fifty-three-page army report detailing "numerous instances of 'sadistic, blatant and wanton criminal abuses'" at the prison. His story was illustrated by another set of appalling pictures of the abuses.

The profusion of bad news prompted a Vietnam-like uproar. At first the administration, quite successful so far in enforcing its story no matter what, underestimated the Abu Ghraib pictures' impact. In hasty congressional testimony, Rumsfeld seemed less focused on the apparent crimes than on the challenge of containing them in an "Information Age" when lowly enlisted men were "running around with digital cameras" e-mailing ugly images all over the world. Even after making that discovery, neither he nor General Richard Myers, chairman of the Joint Chiefs, had bothered to get ahead of the story—or familiarize himself with its particulars—when CBS gave them a full two weeks of heads-ups before broadcasting the *60 Minutes II* segment.[14] In its wake, Myers went on three Sunday morning talk shows to say that only "a handful" of Americans had engaged in such heinous activities—though that low estimate was contradicted by the two-month-old internal army report uncovered by Hersh. After such official diffidence failed to quiet the rancor, the auxiliary force of right-wing bloviators stepped in. Limbaugh was especially creative. The Abu Ghraib abuses "look like standard good old American pornography," he said. The guards were just "having a good time" and their actions looked "just like anything you'd see Madonna or Britney Spears do onstage. . . . I mean, this is something that you can see onstage at Lincoln Center from an NEA grant, maybe on *Sex and the City*."[15]

Other cheerleaders for the war attacked *Nightline*. William Kristol told *The New York Times* that the program's tribute to the fallen was a "stupid statement." The Sinclair Broadcast Group, a large nationwide station owner whose top executives were Bush donors, ordered its eight ABC affiliates, in cities as large as St. Louis and Columbus, not to air that *Nightline* at all. A spokesman, Mark Hyman, explained: "Someone who died thirteen months ago—why is that news?"[16] Such protests raised a question: If the country was as firmly in support of this war as Bush loyalists claimed, by what logic would photographs of its selfless soldiers, either of their faces or of their flag-draped coffins, undermine public opinion?

Only the day before the Koppel show aired, Paul Wolfowitz revealed the ardor with which the administration, subconsciously or not, wanted to downplay casualties by testifying before Congress that those casualties numbered only five hundred, when the actual count had passed seven hundred. A few weeks later, as the casualty count continued to bulge, Wolfowitz attacked the press, which he saw as suppressing all the good news coming out of Iraq: "Frankly, part of our problem is a lot of the press are afraid to travel very much, so they sit in Baghdad and they publish rumors." (After fierce criticism, he apologized; already thirty-four of those theoretically frightened journalists had died in Iraq, including such high-profile reporters as NBC's David Bloom and *The Atlantic Monthly*'s Michael Kelly.)[17] In a less incendiary fashion, General Myers also saw the press as being at the root of the problem. As he noted in a briefing, he found inaccurate reporting nearly everywhere, from CNN to the morning papers.

As an alternative to such shoddy journalism, Dick Cheney gave a public testimonial for Fox News, because in his experience that network was "more accurate" in reporting "those events that I'm personally involved in than many of the other outlets."[18] (The Web site thesmokinggun.com would discover two years later that the vice president's demands for a "downtime suite" when on the road required that every television "be preset to the Fox News Channel.")[19] Fox illustrated what Cheney meant on the disastrous May Day weekend by disparaging the images ubiquitous elsewhere. Fox's O'Reilly worried that *Nightline* might undermine morale if it tried to "exploit casualties in a time of war"— only days after he had used his own program to exploit the death of Pat Tillman for flag-waving purposes.

But still more images kept coming: notably, the video of the beheading of Nick Berg, an idealistic twenty-six-year-old from suburban Philadelphia who had gone to Iraq to do good in the Iraq reconstruction effort and ended up being captured by Islamic terrorists. Even the one safe area in Iraq under American command, the heavily fortified Baghdad Green Zone that served as coalition headquarters, was penetrated by a suicide bomber, who killed the president of the Iraqi Governing Council, among others, at the entrance checkpoint.

As the nation moved toward the election-year summer pastime of political conventions, it was hard to see how the news could be worse for the White House. The 9/11 Commission concluded that the vice president's favorite evidence of an Iraq-Qaeda collaboration, a Mohamed Atta meeting in Prague with a Saddam intelligence officer months before the attacks, had never taken place. A Senate Intelligence Committee report on prewar intelligence found much of it unfounded and could not confirm the administration claims about Niger and uranium. The president, with a private lawyer present, sat, off-camera, for an hour-plus interview with Patrick Fitzgerald, the special counsel in the Valerie Plame Wilson leak case. And though the United States beat by two days its June 30 deadline for turning over sovereignty in Iraq to the new prime minister, Ayad Allawi, it did so in a modest meeting in Allawi's Green Zone office with only a few dozen witnesses. This much-awaited ceremonial milestone looked forlorn on video. After it was over, the American majordomo of the occupation, L. Paul Bremer III, posed for photographers in the doorway of his getaway plane. But the plane was a decoy to thwart a possible insurgent attack. The photo op done with, Bremer deplaned to hitch a ride with a helicopter, which took him to another part of the airport, where his plane to Jordan awaited. "What started with neoconservative fantasies of cheering Iraqis greeting American liberators with flowers and sweets ended with a secret ceremony and a decoy plane," observed the diplomat Peter W. Galbraith.[20] The image of Bremer fleeing Iraq furtively by helicopter stuck. It did not leave an impression of stability—or of so much as minimal security.

Even the Pat Tillman story turned out to be spin. Less than a month after the army had released a stirring description of the circumstances of Tillman's death charging up a hill in Afghanistan, Central Command issued a perfunctory new release saying that Tillman had died instead "as a probable result of friendly fire while his unit was engaged in combat with enemy forces." As with the good-news form letters from the front, the authorship of the fictional press release about Tillman's firefight remained a mystery.

It would be many months before the real story would begin to emerge, and then only because of the relentless pressure put on the Pentagon by Tillman's parents, who shared their quest to uncover the truth about their son's death with reporters. The *San Francisco Chronicle* eventually found that General John Abizaid, the top American officer in Iraq, and others in his command had learned by April 29, 2004, that friendly fire had killed their star recruit. That was the day before the army released its fictitious press release of Tillman's hillside firefight and four days before a nationally televised memorial service back home enshrined the fake account of his death. Yet Tillman's parents, his widow, and his brother (who served in the same platoon), as well as politicians such as John McCain, who spoke at the memorial, were kept in the dark for another month. "The administration clearly was using this case for its own political reasons," said Patrick Tillman, Pat Tillman's father, who learned that crucial evidence in the case, including his son's uniform and gear, had been destroyed almost immediately. "This cover-up started within minutes of Pat's death, and it started at high levels."[21]

The political motives for this scheme were obvious enough. Tillman's death followed the worst month of bad news for the country and, more pertinently, for the Bush-Cheney reelection campaign, since the start of the Iraq War. Against this backdrop, it would not do to have it known that the most famous volunteer of the war might have been a victim of gross negligence or homicide. It wouldn't do to have reporters asking too many questions; they might discover, as they eventually did, that Tillman, who had enlisted after 9/11 out of a patriotic urge to fight Al Qaeda, was adamantly against the Iraq War. "They could have told us upfront that they were suspicious that it was a fratricide but they didn't," his mother, Mary Tillman, told *The Arizona Republic.* "They wanted to use him for their purposes. It was good for the administration. It was before the elections. It was during the prison scandal. They needed something that looked good, and it was appalling that they would use him like that." Tillman's father was convinced that "all the people in positions of authority went out of their way to script" the fictional narrative of his son's death because "they blew up their poster boy."[22]

The press release containing the month-old revelation that Tillman had died "probably" because of friendly fire was deliberately withheld by the army until Memorial Day weekend—where it would be a tiny, little-noticed footnote next to the major story of the dedication of the new World War II memorial before a crowd of two hundred thousand in Washington. The sheer extent of the cover-up would not begin to become known until newspaper accounts started appearing in 2005. Not until 2006, after relentless hounding by Tillman's parents and politicians supportive of their cause, did the Pentagon's inspector general demand a review of three previous, incomplete investigations into Tillman's death.[23]

If the successful Tillman cover-up was a time bomb with a very slow fuse, accounts of two other famous American soldiers in Iraq were inescapable. Perhaps no images better captured the change in the war's fortunes over its first year than those of the pair of young working-class women from opposite ends of West Virginia who had gone off to fight. One was blond and had aspirations to be a schoolteacher. The other was dark, a smoker, divorced, and carrying an out-of-wedlock baby. The first, Jessica Lynch, became the heroic poster child for Operation Iraqi Freedom, the subject of a laudatory book and TV movie; the second, Private Lynndie England, the most exuberant of the guards in the Abu Ghraib photos, became the hideous, leering face of American wartime criminality, Exhibit A in the indictment of America's descent into the gulag. England, said *Time,* was "a Jessica Lynch gone wrong." But America's thirteen-month journey from Lynch's profile in courage to England's profile in sadism was less a tale of two women at the bottom of the chain of command than a gauge of the hubris with which those at the top were losing the war in both the international and American courts of public opinion. As the thrilling Pentagon-made movie that was Saving Private Jessica symbolized how effectively the military and administration controlled the news during Operation Iraqi Freedom, so the photos of England and her cohorts symbolized the government's utter loss of that control now.

Given the speed with which the White House was losing the war of images from Iraq by the summer of 2004, it was hard to imagine how it could fail to lose a presidential election at home that fall. All the opposition needed to do was tell a credible alternative story of its own.

EIGHT

"REPORTING FOR DUTY"

IT WAS IN MARCH 2004, a year after the war began, that the gap between the White House's narrative and the reality on the ground in Iraq was first captured in a gruesome dramatic split screen on TV: as Dick Cheney delivered a speech at the Ronald Reagan Presidential Library, bashing his and the president's presumptive opponent, John Kerry, and boasting of the administration's progress in the war, his sour certitude was paired on cable with an especially lethal car bombing in central Baghdad.[1]

But all was not lost for the vice president: Kerry was already proving a genius at self-destruction, handing the White House loaded weapons with which to mow him down. Just the day before Cheney's speech, the Massachusetts senator had given what would prove an indelible response when asked to reconcile his vote to authorize the use of force in Iraq with his later vote against the eighty-seven-billion-dollar appropriation to pay for the war and Iraqi reconstruction. "I actually did vote for the $87 billion before I voted against it," Kerry said. Cheney, though not exactly a natural comedian, brought down the house at the Reagan library simply by repeating Kerry's words and underlining them with a deadpan punch line, "It's a true fact."

A Republican campaign theme was born. Later, at Madison Square Garden, the party's conventioneers waved rubber flip-flops to mock Kerry, and Kerry did his best to help the metaphor along throughout the year with a string of self-contradictory pronouncements and photo-op malapropisms. (He had a particular penchant for striking zigzag poses on camera while pursuing the upper-crust pastimes of skiing and windsurfing.) But until Election Day—indeed right up through Election Day, when misleading early exit polls at first confirmed the Republicans' worst fears of defeat—the Bush-Cheney campaign had good reason to worry about its opponent, and did.

The Republicans had been hoping for an adversary who, unlike the stolid Kerry, could be effortlessly caricatured as a flake or unreconstructed 1960s radical. And the Democrats had at first given them some reason to believe their dream would come true, thanks both to the former governor Howard Dean, a smart but strident dark-horse presidential candidate from the Ben & Jerry's principality of Vermont, and to Michael Moore, the in-your-face documentary filmmaker whose movie eviscerating Bush, *Fahrenheit 9/11*, was an instant media sensation.

Unburdened by a Senate vote authorizing the war in Iraq, Dean was the toughest Bush critic and had brilliantly exploited the Internet to rally supporters and raise cash. But in retail politics, he was trounced by Kerry and John Edwards in the Iowa caucuses, and he compounded the loss with a hoarse-voiced concession stem-winder that made him look like a madman once replayed incessantly on 24/7 cable, late-night talk shows, and the Web. Dean had been shouting to be heard over a cheering crowd of supporters, but the microphone captured solely his voice, not the roar of the crowd in the background, isolating his vein-throbbing yelping and making him sound more ludicrous than he actually did.[2] That a technical miscalculation, more than an issue of substance, sped his demise mattered no more in the era of The Image than whether there had been actual tears or melted snowflakes on Ed Muskie's cheeks at the New Hampshire press conference that ended his presidential candidacy in 1972. The image of a raving maniac stuck, and that was the end of the story for Dean's presidential bid.

Moore emerged as a force as the summer began, when *Fahrenheit 9/11* had its premiere at the Cannes Film Festival. The movie was in part a tendentious, over-the-top replay of a Bush-hater's greatest hits: Katherine Harris, the Supreme Court, Harken Energy, the lazy Crawford vacation of August 2001, the Patriot Act. But the movie filled in some missing pieces of the first-term Bush narrative with devastating new video; Moore secured the amateur recording of Bush continuing to read "The Pet Goat" in the Florida schoolroom for minutes after Andrew Card notified him that a second plane had crashed into the World Trade Center. He also showed the actual dying of American troops and Iraqi civilians, with all the ripped flesh and spilled guts that American television avoided. Not least, *Fahrenheit 9/11* for the first time raised the curtain on horrific American injuries, with vignettes of troops in clinics at Walter Reed and at Blanchfield Army Community Hospital in Fort Campbell, Kentucky, where multiple severed limbs and grave brain injuries were daily fare.

The movie is powerful when it focuses on the war in Iraq. By the standards of documentaries, it did business like no other in the history of American film. But that's a low bar; *Fahrenheit 9/11* was only the seventeenth-highest-grossing movie of 2004 and had an audience only a third the size (if that) of the year's top Hollywood box-office hits. None of this deterred any grandstanding from Moore, whose ego and sense of entitlement could match any in show business. He took to making hyperbolic pronouncements about his movie's appeal to red-state audiences and turned himself into a ubiquitous sound-bite Vesuvius, venting loudly in the overbearing style made famous by his rant about Bush during his 2003 Oscar acceptance speech for *Bowling for Columbine*. The Republicans couldn't have found a better choice to cast as Out of the Mainstream Democratic Lefty, and Moore was only too glad to act the part to, and often past, the hilt.

But he wasn't the Democrats' candidate, and the man who was, Kerry, not only kept his distance from Moore but also posed a considerable challenge to Bush's wartime bona fides. When the White House media trust had the president dress up as the circa 1986 Tom Cruise of *Top Gun* to dance a victory jig, it didn't reckon that he might later face an opponent who could be typecast more persuasively in his own, weightier, Tom Cruise role. Kerry was in real life a comrade of Ron Kovic, whom Cruise played in the 1989 film *Born on the Fourth of July*. Both Kerry and Kovic were decorated Vietnam soldiers who, upon coming home, became star activists for Vietnam Veterans Against the War.

In a pivotal scene in *Born on the Fourth of July*, delegates at the 1972 Republican National Convention in Miami Beach eject Kovic and his fellow protesting vets from the hall, call him a traitor, and spit on him. It's powerful stuff, reflecting the passions of the film's director, Oliver Stone, who had been at Yale with Bush and Kerry and, like Kerry, had gone on to combat in Vietnam, won a Bronze Star, and then turned against the war. It was no secret that that same summer of '72 presented a political problem for Bush all these decades later. It fell into the missing months in the president's résumé—a time when, in the undocumented White House account, the young Bush was completing his National Guard service while campaigning for a senatorial hopeful in Alabama. There was no record of him as being on duty in Alabama, but he had attended the Republican convention with his father. There he may well have watched from afar as Kovic and his fellow veterans were dispersed in a paroxysm of tear gas and rage.

Somehow Bush was always on the sidelines during the Vietnam War, neither demonstrably pro nor con—a peculiar anomaly for a draft-age man of his generation and background. As president, he tried to avoid the subject as much as possible; to mention it was implicitly to raise questions about his own service then and about the growing Vietnam-like credibility gap afflicting his administration's explanations of the Iraq War's rationale and progress now. In an interview with Tim Russert, Bush volunteered that what troubled him about Vietnam was that it "was a political war—we had politicians making military decisions." Given that his own secretary of defense, Rumsfeld, made military decisions about Iraq much as Robert McNamara did in the Kennedy and Johnson administrations, even that single lesson didn't seem to have taken hold.

By 2004, most Americans could probably no longer identify Nguyen Van Thieu or the Tet Offensive. Communism and the domino theory had been relegated to history's junk heap. And yet even as the actual war had faded in memory, Vietnam still loomed as a festering culture war, a permanent fixture of the national collective unconscious, always on tap for fresh hostilities. The wounds of Vietnam could not be healed by the fashionable early-twenty-first-century American panacea of closure.

With Kerry, the right saw an opportunity to rip open those wounds and peg the candidate as the dangerous radical it wanted Bush to run against. Angry Internet vigilantes took on Kerry for his antiwar activism, attacking him and his fellow antiwar vets from Vietnam Veterans Against the War as vociferously in 2004 as their ideological forebears had assaulted Kovic's band of brothers at the 1972 Republican Convention. One group calling itself Vietnam Veterans Against John Kerry circulated a photo of an antiwar demonstration that placed Kerry (barely) in proximity to Jane Fonda, the Michael Moore of her day. The likely Democratic standard-bearer was branded a radical, a traitor, and, worst of all, "hippie-like." *The Weekly Standard* struck a similar theme, pointedly characterizing the antiwar Vietnam veterans who camped out in protest at the National Mall as "hairy men, many with *Easy Rider* mustaches."

There was a method to this archaic culture-war madness. It was meant to contrast an ostensibly wild-and-wooly Kerry with the widely seen Vietnam-era photo of a decidedly clean-shaven, un-hippie-like Bush at the moment he joined the Texas Air National Guard. The photo showed Bush's beaming father, then a congressman, as he prepared to pin second lieutenant's bars to his son's uniform. But the senior Bush's appearance in the picture was not an unalloyed blessing for the White House. His presence raised the unanswered question of just how the future president got into the Guard, in those days a safe haven from combat duty, ahead of one hundred thousand others then on the national waiting list. At the time, 250 Americans a week were dying in Vietnam.

When badgered about the president's military service, the White House had a stock answer: "The issue is settled." The issue might have remained settled had Bush not set the stage for Iraq-Vietnam parallels by donning the fly-boy uniform of his own disputed guard duty while prematurely declaring victory in Iraq the previous spring. But the issue was in play now, and an Achilles heel for Bush. Whatever the names anyone called Kerry, he had actually served in Vietnam and was hard to tar as "hippie-like"—he was just too dull and patrician, even in his protest days. His potential as a political threat to the president was real. Unlike Bush, Gore, or McCain, Kerry was the first candidate in either party to have been both a leader in combat in Vietnam *and* a leader in the antiwar movement; he represented the establishment that fueled the misadventure in Southeast Asia and was also an antiestablishment (albeit non-hippie) representative of the movement that challenged the powers that be when the war turned sour. To his critics he might have been hypocritical, but to many others he was prototypical. It took years of body bags and falsely optimistic White House predictions for an American majority to turn against the Vietnam War. Once the country did change its mind, however, it stayed changed. To argue in 2004 that antiwar protesters were traitors, especially those who took bullets for their country in the Mekong Delta and saved their buddies' lives, could be a tough sell.

There had to be a clever way for Bush's operatives to demolish the first half of Kerry's Vietnam biography, his war heroism, and leave his antiwar second act intact—and, as it turned out, there was. The Rove minions, so brilliant at creating fictional stories for their own man, would simply create a fictional biography for Kerry and impose it on him, no matter what Kerry himself might have to say about it. In this revised biography, the war hero would have to be stripped of his battle heroics—indeed literally stripped of his medals—so that he would be on the same footing as a president whose Vietnam service consisted of sporadic participation in the Texas "champagne unit" stateside.

The makeshift organization that assumed the task of giving Kerry an involuntary image makeover named itself Swift Boat Veterans for Truth; its prime mover was John O'Neill, now a Houston lawyer, who had not become a Swift Boat commander until at least two months after Kerry had concluded his tour of duty in 1969 and who had first battled with Kerry when he was recruited by Richard Nixon's henchman Charles Colson for a debate about the war on *The Dick Cavett Show* in 1971. The Swift Boat Veterans' opening gambit in 2004 was to hold a press conference in May questioning Kerry's heroic war record. Almost no one noticed, and the group did not surface again until August.

Before it did reappear, Kerry placed most, if not all, of his chips on presenting himself as a military hero at the July Democratic Convention in Boston. The point was to show that Democrats could be trusted to be strong in defending the country at a time of terrorism—and to minimize the antiwar chapter of Kerry's story that followed his navy service. Much like Bush—with whom he had in common a New England blue-blood genealogy, a Yale degree, and a life of fabulous wealth—Kerry also wanted to repackage himself as a macho Joe Six-Pack of sorts. It seemed a preposterous ambition, but if George Walker Bush could get away with it, why not John Forbes Kerry? As Bush playacted at ranching in Crawford, so Kerry rode a Harley-Davidson onto Jay Leno's set. Both men hewed to the same Hollywood dictum: If you can fake authenticity, you've got it made.

But for all the chumminess between the Democrats and the movie industry—Meryl Streep, Whoopi Goldberg, Chevy Chase, and Paul Newman

had headlined an early Kerry-Edwards fund-raiser at Radio City Music Hall–
Kerry's image-making stagecraft was amateur compared with that of the Bush
showmen. In a lame attempt to stage his own version of "Mission Accomplished" five months after the prototype, he had traveled to the unlikely setting
of Mount Pleasant, South Carolina, in September 2003 to formally announce
his presidential campaign against the flag-and-veterans-bestrewn backdrop of
the aircraft carrier *Yorktown.* (The *Yorktown,* unlike Bush's aircraft carrier, was
docked.) Even hokier was the soundtrack: a recording of a military band playing "Anchors Aweigh."[3]

Kerry's theatrics did not improve as the primary campaign wore on. The
Massachusetts senator all but asked Republicans to ridicule him, with ad-libs
such as "Who among us does not love NASCAR?" In an interview in the men's
magazine *GQ*, he joined the reporter for a beer (alcoholic–no teetotaler he!)
while confessing to a modicum of lust for Charlize Theron and Catherine
Zeta-Jones. One day during the campaign he invited reporters to follow him
around on a "day off," when his errands included buying a jockstrap.[4]

The night of Kerry's acceptance speech at the Democratic Convention, in
Boston, July 29, such posturing was supersized. The nominee made a grand entrance from the rear of the FleetCenter, then mounted the stage to greet, one
by one, his old navy crewmates, who had been arrayed in a formation worthy
of "March of the Tin Soldiers." At last came the nominee's opening line, so
highly prized by his handlers that it had been withheld from the advance text.
"I'm John Kerry, and I'm reporting for duty," he said, while raising his hand in
a snappy salute. Though Steven Spielberg had had a hand in the Kerry documentary that preceded his entrance, the candidate's own climactic scene was
more suitable for a high school assembly than prime time.

In the speech that followed there was more than a little rhetorical bait
and switch. Twice Kerry invoked both "band of brothers" and "greatest
generation"–a patent effort to inoculate service in a controversial war with
phrases that, courtesy of HBO and Tom Brokaw, had become the culture's indelible brand for World War II's unambiguous heroism. The hope was that
Vietnam might blur with the earlier war, or at least that no one would think
about what happened after the Vietnam band of brothers came home and split
apart, at which point Kerry's antiwar role pushed him into closer political proximity to memories of My Lai than Iwo Jima.

That hope was dashed soon enough. In August, the Swift Boat vets started placing television commercials challenging Kerry's heroics in Vietnam and showcasing the antiwar activities he engaged in upon his return. An accompanying book, *Unfit for Command: Swift Boat Veterans Speak Out Against John Kerry*, co-written by John O'Neill and marketed by the right-wing Regnery Publishing, quickly rose up the bestseller list, with a boost from talk radio and the Murdoch media, led by Fox News.

As the press would report, many of the Swift Boat vets' charges were easily debunked. One act of heroism that the group was particularly eager to tear down involved Kerry's Bronze Star. He had received it for turning around his Swift Boat and facing enemy fire rather than leave behind a soldier who had fallen overboard. The soldier he rescued, Jim Rassmann, had sought out Kerry for the first time since the war during the Iowa caucuses. Identifying himself as a Republican, he told his story publicly, helping to reignite the then-stalled Kerry campaign. But the Swift Boat vets now said there was no enemy fire and that Kerry's rescue effort was routine; one member of the group, Jack Chenoweth, accused Rassmann of lying. Actually, it was the Swift Boat vets who were lying. *The Washington Post* retrieved Kerry's Bronze Star citation, which confirmed Rassmann's account, referring to "automatic weapons fire" and "enemy bullets flying" as Kerry carried out his rescue.[5]

Blatant fictionalizing was typical of the Swift Boat assault. In one television commercial, a doctor named Louis Letson testified, "I know John Kerry is lying about his first Purple Heart because I treated him for that injury." Letson claimed that Kerry's wound was merely a self-inflicted scratch. But Letson's name did not appear on any of Kerry's medical records, where another, now-deceased doctor was listed as the "person administering treatment." Some of the other Kerry attackers were, if possible, even more shameless in their dishonesty. Veterans who had in the past publicly saluted Kerry as "among the finest of those Swift Boat drivers" or an exemplar of courage now turned up on camera in Swift Boat ads attacking his leadership and integrity.[6]

Many of the vets in this group had at most a tangential connection to Kerry anyway; only one of them had served in the same boat he had. But those funding, leading, and advising the group's campaign of character assassination had far-from-merely-tangential connections to the Bush political circle. A communications consultant for the Swift Boat veterans, Merrie Spaeth (who may have learned something about myth-making during her brief career as a teenage Hollywood actress in the 1960s[7]), had previously been the spokesperson for Republicans for Clean Air, a fly-by-night front for a two-million-dollar barrage of ads paid for by the longtime Bush supporter Sam Wyly to attack John McCain as an environmental menace during crucial 2000 Republican primaries. Spaeth's late husband, Tex Lezar, had run for Texas lieutenant governor on the Bush ticket in 1994. The Swift Boat ads were produced by the same team that had done the spots for Bush's father in 1988 mocking Michael Dukakis's efforts to shore up his military cred by driving a tank. The largest contributor to the Swift Boat vets campaign, Bob J. Perry, had been an associate of Karl Rove's since the 1980s.[8] A legal adviser to the group was Benjamin Ginsberg, the national counsel for Bush-Cheney 2004, who resigned from the reelection campaign after his role with the Swift Boat smear effort was exposed.[9]

Eventually the *Los Angeles Times* discovered that the Sinclair Broadcast Group, the same nationwide station owner that had refused to air Ted Koppel's *Nightline* roll call of the Iraq War's American dead on its ABC affiliates, had ordered all sixty-two of its stations, reaching 24 percent of the country's television viewers, to broadcast a "news" special featuring a film, *Stolen Honor: Wounds That Never Heal,* that trashed Kerry along the same lines of the Swift Boat ads. Sinclair's top executives, all maxed-out Bush-Cheney contributors, scheduled the show for just before the election.[10] Only after advertising cancellations, threatened lawsuits, and a drop in the Sinclair stock price made their overt support of the Swift Boat vets fiscally untenable did they blink and substitute a more neutral election special.[11]

Through all this ruckus, the White House purported to have no involvement with the Swift Boat vets or their charges. "We have not and we will not question Senator Kerry's service in Vietnam" was the standard line. As in every Rove character assassination of a Bush political opponent, there was just enough distance between those doing the dirty work and Rove himself to assert there was no direct link. Kerry, who initially found the Swift Boat assault too absurd to merit a serious response, did not get around to fighting back in earnest until late August, after weeks of suffering the slings and arrows. By then damage had been done, and the Republican Convention was setting up shop in New York.

Like the Democratic Convention, the Republican pageant built its infotainment on militarism and masculinity. As Kerry tried to change the subject
from Vietnam to World War II, so Bush did the same—though in his case from
Iraq to World War II. Laura Bush, Tommy Franks, the apostate Democratic
senator Zell Miller, and Dick Cheney all made allusions to Franklin D. Roosevelt in their convention speeches, with the vice president going so far as to
note that he and Roosevelt shared the same birthday. Rudy Giuliani one-
upped them all by equating Bush with Churchill. Of course these World War II
flashbacks had to come to a screeching halt before identifying the present Hitler,
Osama bin Laden. To take the analogy that far would have been to remind
the audience that the administration had diverted troops and money from the
essential war against Al Qaeda and Islamic fanaticism to open an optional second front against Iraq's secular despot.

In thematic keeping with Bush's careening down a runway in a *Top Gun*
flight suit, a special Madison Square Garden runway was built for Bush's acceptance speech, a giant phallus thrusting him into the nation's lap. ("To me that
says strength" was how his media adviser, Mark McKinnon, previewed the set's
intent to *The New York Times*.) The White House had already publicized the
president's proud possession of Saddam Hussein's captured pistol, which, in
another not-so-subtle piece of phallic stagecraft, was said to be kept in the same
study where the previous incumbent squandered his own weapon of masculinity on Monica Lewinsky.[12] Instead of the minstrel antics of the 2000 convention, which were designed to fictionalize the party as a utopia of racial diversity,
the 2004 model laid on the testosterone. The prime speakers were the former
New York mayor who had not dallied to read a children's story on 9/11, a senator who had served in the Hanoi Hilton rather than the Texas Air National
Guard, and a newly elected governor from California who could play the role
of a warrior on-screen more convincingly than a former cheerleader.

But no sooner did the Republicans leave New York than word spread that
CBS News was poking anew into the president's National Guard stint, a Pan-
dora's box of unanswered questions. Bush's slender official account of his military service as put forth in *A Charge to Keep*, his 1999 campaign biography
crafted by Karen Hughes, was vague and suspect; it suggested that Bush just
happened to slide on his own into one of the "several openings" for pilots in
the Texas Guard in 1968 and that he continued to fly with his unit for "several

years." In 2000, *The Boston Globe* reviewed 160 pages of documents and learned that Bush did not perform drills or fly while working on a senatorial campaign in Alabama in 1972—raising the issue of whether he had been absent without leave for months. It was also apparent that Bush had not fulfilled the six-year commitment he made to the Guard at the time of his enlistment.[13]

Shortly after Labor Day the anchor Dan Rather and the producer Mary Mapes—the same team that had broken the Abu Ghraib story months earlier—broadcast a dramatic investigative report on the Wednesday edition of *60 Minutes* about Bush's service during Vietnam. Newly found documents from the files of his Texas squadron commander, now dead twenty years, indicated that the future president failed to meet performance standards in the Guard and that there had been pressure to sugarcoat his record because of his father's political clout.

The piece had barely aired when conservative bloggers started to question the documents, whose fonts looked anachronistic and whose provenance was ambiguous. After two weeks of standing firmly behind the story as more and more doubts were raised, CBS folded, saying that it could not authenticate the four documents it had used to make its charges. The network's source, a former guardsman, had by then confessed to lying about how he had first obtained the papers. Though an inquiry at CBS followed, leading to Rather's premature retirement as the evening news anchor and the firing of Mapes and others who had worked on the story, no one ever did find out where the documents came from—or who forged them, if that was the case. Nor has anyone ever found out for certain where Bush disappeared for months at a time when in the Guard or why he didn't report for required physicals. (Bush antagonists had their theories, most of which had to do with drugs.)

The fallout of the *60 Minutes* fiasco on the campaign was immediate: the lingering questions about Bush's Guard history were immediately off the table. Bush's suspect past during Vietnam became a nonissue while Kerry's honorable past remained a subject of debate. Only in an election year ruled by fiction could a rich kid who used his father's connections to escape Vietnam turn an actual war hero into a girlie-man. Even a ten-thousand-dollar reward offered by the cartoonist Garry Trudeau couldn't smoke out a credible eyewitness to support Bush's contention that he showed up for duty in Alabama in 1972.[14] Yet Kerry, who without doubt shed his own blood and others' in the vicinity of the Mekong, not the Mississippi, had been transformed into a deserter and wimp by outright lies.

There was another, little-noticed side effect of the CBS News flap as well. Intimidated by its critics, who accused it of making its reportorial mistakes because of an anti-Bush agenda, *60 Minutes Wednesday* scrapped a planned report—an investigative piece that had been held a week to make way for the National Guard story—about another set of false papers: the forged documents that the administration had leaned on to make the case that Saddam had tried to secure uranium from Niger for nuclear weapons. *Newsweek* learned that CBS had obtained the first on-camera interview with the Italian journalist who had received the fake documents and sent them to the United States embassy.[15] The network announced that it would postpone the report until after the election. The interview didn't surface on *60 Minutes* until April 2006.

A MONTH BEFORE the election, the country's mood was captured with startling acuity in a newly published Philip Roth novel, *The Plot Against America*. The book's resonance with ongoing events may have been part of the reason why it became Roth's biggest seller in years, joining a bestseller shelf crowded with books about George W. Bush.

The Plot Against America offers an alternate history of the World War II era. Its what-if scenario has the isolationist and anti-Semitic aviation hero Charles Lindbergh running for president as a Republican in 1940, defeating FDR, and signing nonaggression pacts with Germany and Japan to keep America out of the war abroad. But the threat of war hovers over Roth's characters nonetheless. The very first sentence of the book sets its tone: "Fear presides over these memories, a perpetual fear."

In Roth's story, that fear is ultimately borne out by scattered pogroms in early 1940s America. But "perpetual fear" also defined early-twenty-first-century America—and the ruthless election-year politics of autumn 2004—as succinctly as what Roth tagged "the ecstasy of sanctimony" defined the Monica summer of 1998, the setting of his novel *The Human Stain*. And though Roth denied that his plainspoken Lindbergh was meant to evoke the current American president, the resemblance between the real and fictional Republican presidents is striking. Roth describes his protagonist as "normalcy raised to heroic proportions, a decent man with an honest face and an undistinguished voice who had resoundingly demonstrated to the entire planet the courage to take charge and the fortitude to shape history." He is for "entrepreneurial individualism" and against governmental tyranny. He opposes bigotry. He reassures Americans that every decision he makes in the White House, including his willingness to blow off former allies opposed to his go-it-alone foreign policy, is "designed solely to increase their security and guarantee their well-being." He flies around the country in his own plane to advertise his military readiness. In domestic policy, his signature invention is named Just Folks—"a volunteer work program introducing city youth to the traditional ways of heartland life," administered by an Office of American Absorption "to raze those barriers of ignorance that continue to separate Christian from Jew and Jew from Christian." The only problem with this benign-sounding faith-based initiative is that any non-Christian who abstains from the "voluntary" indoctrination into the "traditional ways of heartland life" is instantly branded as less than Just Folks, or, in other words, as something less than American.

In unintentional symmetry with the Lindbergh presidency imagined by Roth, faith and fear were always foremost in Bush's reelection campaign. The invocation of faith—or more specifically, Christianity—had always been a prime Bush selling point. He had cited Christ as his favorite "political philosopher" during the Republican primary process in 1999; his fateful fortieth-birthday hangover in Colorado Springs was marketed like a station of the cross in his campaign biography. After 9/11, his view of faith as a Manichaean scheme of black and white to be acted out in a perpetual war between good and evil was synergistic with the violent poetics of popular culture favored by his religious-right political base—the Armageddon-embracing, bestselling *Left Behind* novels by Tim LaHaye and Jerry Jenkins and Mel Gibson's gory cinematic blockbuster *The Passion of the Christ.* While Bush quickly retreated from his early reference to the war on terror as a "crusade," that pious note was sometimes sounded by his subordinates. The general in charge of tracking down Osama bin Laden, William G. Boykin, earned cheers (and no official rebuke) for giving speeches at churches proclaiming that Bush was "in the White House because God put him there" to lead the "army of God" against "a guy named Satan."[16] At the Republican Convention in New York, a Family, Faith and Freedom rally for the religious right distributed a DVD, *George W. Bush: Faith in the White House,* laced with clerical (mainly evangelical) endorsements for the president and presenting him as a prodigal son with the "moral clarity of an old-fashioned biblical prophet."[17]

The Bush-Cheney flogging of fear for political advantage had come into its own after 9/11. But in election years, they really pulled out the stops. For the midterm of 2002, that meant hyping Saddam's potential for unleashing a "mushroom cloud." For 2004, it was time for the terrorists who attacked America on 9/11 to make a comeback. The manipulation of the voters' fears was designed to be both perpetual and highly theatrical. Back in March, *Time* had reported that the Department of Homeland Security, however overtaxed it might be by its appointed tasks, had been tapped to round up one terrorism-fighting photo op a month for the president.[18]

As always, the principal player in the scare tactics was John Ashcroft, a born camera hog. Though the attorney general's on-screen persona needed work—he tried to come off like Robert Stack in *The Untouchables* but more often impersonated the hapless W. C. Fields in *The Bank Dick*—his resources as a showman were considerable. He had a bigger budget than most filmmakers and could command far more free TV time for promoting his wares. His press conferences, whether to showcase his latest, implicitly single-handed victory in the war on terrorism or to predict the apocalypse he wanted to make certain he wouldn't be blamed for, became as ubiquitous as spin-offs of *CSI* and *Law & Order*. While FDR once told Americans that they had nothing to fear but fear itself, Ashcroft was delighted to play the part of Fear Itself, an assignment in which he let his imagination run riot.

He started the election-season terror alerts rolling just before Memorial Day weekend, when he declared that terrorists would "hit the United States hard" either on the Fourth of July or during the political conventions or on Election Day. Flanked by the FBI director and photos of seven wanted terrorists, he enlisted Americans as junior G-men—"be aware of your surroundings, remain vigilant"—while sowing the seeds of hopelessness that would keep the pot of fear at a full boil. "Unfortunately, we currently do not know what form the threat may take," he said. "And that is why it is so important that we locate the seven individuals."

His show looked plausible enough when it led the evening newscasts. Only on further examination did it prove to be mostly bluster. The seven individuals he had asked the audience to help track down were not believed to be in the United States, other officials soon told *The New York Times*. Six of the seven culprits, in fact, were recycled from previous warnings, one of them dating back to a similar Ashcroft press conference twenty-eight months earlier.[19] Another fictional flourish was Ashcroft's claim that a Qaeda "spokesman" had "announced" in March that preparations for the imminent attack were 90 percent complete. The announcement was not from Al Qaeda at all, Lisa Myers of NBC News reported two days later, but from a Web site run by a group that "has no known operational capability and may be no more than one man with a fax machine." (The same group had also taken credit for a 2003 Northeast power blackout that had no terrorist involvement.)

For the Democratic Convention, fear impresarios in the administration revised a trick they had used to deflect attention from the FBI whistleblower Coleen Rowley in 2002. Then Ashcroft had held a press conference from Moscow to announce disrupting "an unfolding terrorist plot" involving a "dirty bomb" even though the suspect, José Padilla, had actually been arrested a month earlier in Chicago.[20] This time, when Kerry unveiled John Edwards as his running mate, it was the cue for Tom Ridge to grab away the media spotlight by predicting that Al Qaeda was poised to "disrupt our democratic process." It was in truth the Bush-Cheney campaign that was disrupting the democratic process, by manipulating terror alerts to upstage its opponents. Ridge conceded that he had no "precise knowledge" of the attack he was warning about and no plans to raise his color-coded threat level. But his real mission, to wield fear as a weapon of mass distraction, had been accomplished. (The alerts would magically disappear after the election.) Democrats couldn't be blamed for wondering if Ashcroft or Ridge would time the next doomsday press conference to coincide with Kerry's acceptance speech.

That did not happen. But in the fear game, the Democrats were the visiting team, always playing at a serious disadvantage. Out of power, they couldn't suit up officials at will to go on camera to scare the country to death. Kerry was reduced instead to incessantly repeating the word "strength" and promising to put "a national coordinator for nuclear terrorism" in the Cabinet. That was not enough to cut it against his cunning opponents. Every time a Bush administration official announced that the apocalypse was on its way, the president bragged that he had made America safer. The message was in the bad news–good news contradiction: the less safe Americans felt, the more likely they would play it safe on Election Day by sticking with the protector they knew rather than take a chance on the devil they didn't.

Two weeks before the election, Dick Cheney played the fear card one last time. Touring Ohio, the vice president belittled Kerry as a weak foe against terrorism and ramped up his Armageddon rhetoric as he had during the run-up to the war in Iraq during the election season of two years earlier. "The biggest threat we face now as a nation," he said, "is the possibility of terrorists ending up in the middle of one of our cities with deadlier weapons than have ever before been used against us–biological agents or a nuclear weapon or a chemical weapon of some kind–able to threaten the lives of hundreds of thousands of Americans." As he summoned this deadly specter, John Ashcroft harmonized in Washington, where he implied that God had spared America from an attack since 9/11 because President Bush's team was assisting "the hand of Providence."[21]

When Osama bin Laden surfaced in a new videotape the weekend before Election Day, looking healthy and raising the anxiety level even higher, he was widely thought to have played into the Bush-Cheney campaign's hands and ensured Kerry's defeat. Americans wouldn't want to switch horses in mid–terror alert, period. But the story of the election of 2004 was not that simple.

Washington wisdom had it that Kerry had sabotaged his own campaign by bringing up Vietnam–both because it roused the Swift Boat veterans and because Vietnam was ancient history, an irrelevant distraction from the issues of the current war. But both Kerry's Vietnam service and Vietnam itself were entirely relevant to a campaign unfolding during an unpopular, ineptly executed, and attenuated war in Iraq that was spawned by the executive branch in similarly cloudy circumstances. And the Vietnam-like news from Iraq, from Falluja to Abu Ghraib, only got worse throughout the campaign year.

"What you're seeing on your TV screens," the president had said when minimizing the Iraq insurgency in May, was "desperation by a hateful few." It was a hard case to maintain as the election season progressed. A late-June *USA Today*/CNN poll showed that 55 percent of Americans felt less safe because of the war in Iraq–a figure that had spiked twenty-two points in merely six months.[22] Insurgent attacks had gone from a daily average of six in May 2003, the announced end of major combat operations, to as high as eighty-seven in

August 2004.[23] The American casualty rate kept rising after the turnover of sovereignty to the provisional Iraqi government in June. When the White House invited its handpicked Iraqi prime minister, Ayad Allawi, to Washington for a series of photo ops in September 2004, the stunt was far from the reassuring dog and pony show of Iraqi self-sufficiency that had been intended. Allawi delivered so many sound bites that were identical to his host's that he came across as even more of a puppet than Ahmad Chalabi had in his State of the Union cameo sitting behind Laura Bush; the whole charade played out like a lost reel of *Duck Soup*. A few days later, in the hours before the first Bush-Kerry debate, television was flooded with graphic reports from Baghdad of car bombs that had killed some thirty-five Iraqi children.

Having brought up Vietnam against the backdrop of this incipient quagmire, Kerry then choked. It turned out he had almost nothing to say about the subject except that his military service proved that he was manlier than Bush. Yet nearly anyone could look manlier than a president who didn't even have the guts to visit with the 9/11 Commission without his vice president as a chaperone. Kerry was a man's man not just because he had volunteered to fight in the war and Bush had avoided it. Kerry had also been brave when he came home from Vietnam and forthrightly fought against the war, on grounds that history upheld. But he hadn't been man enough to stand up for that part of his past during the campaign, and because he hadn't been, he was now doomed to keep competing with Bush to see who could best play an action figure on TV. In that race, it's not necessarily the man with the best military record but the best actor who wins. And Bush was easily the more practiced actor, with the more accomplished studio behind him besides. Kerry never understood that it takes a certain kind of talent to play dress-up and deliver lines like "Bring 'em on" with a straight face.

If there was a day when Kerry lost the election it may have come in August, when he took reporters' questions while posing against the macho landscape of the Grand Canyon. Asked if he still would have voted to authorize the use of force against Saddam Hussein if he had known then that there were no weapons of mass destruction, Kerry answered yes. Would Kerry also have answered that a senator should have voted to authorize the Vietnam War even if he knew that the Johnson administration had hyped North Vietnamese attacks on American ships in the Gulf of Tonkin? Hardly. His answer about Iraq was a moment of supreme intellectual dishonesty that sullied his own Vietnam past as surely as the sleazy Swift Boat character assassins had.

As a practical political matter, the answer left Kerry in essence endorsing the White House's message: that the road from 9/11 had led inevitably to Operation Iraqi Freedom. Throughout the campaign, the only definable alternatives he offered to the president's stay-the-course prescription for the war were vague and toothless half measures—the enlistment of international cooperation (without clarifying how), the deployment of forty thousand more troops (without explaining from where). He barely even mentioned the Abu Ghraib scandal. Yet it was a measure of how badly the war was going that a candidate as slandered and ineffectual as Kerry lost by only some three million popular votes in November, holding a president who had been king of the world after 9/11 to a bare 51 percent majority.

WHEN THE DUST settled from the wartime presidential election of 2004, the press and political establishment promptly declared that the election hadn't been about Iraq or war after all, no matter what the two campaigns might have had to say about it. The inspiration for this revisionist history was an exit poll conducted by the Associated Press and the television networks—the same poll that had lulled trigger-happy news-organization gossips (and the bloggers who love them) into believing that Kerry was pulling ahead on the afternoon of Election Day. No matter; the morning after, one sloppily worded question from the poll was suddenly elevated to the punditocracy's holy grail. Asked to pick which of seven issues had most influenced their presidential vote, 22 percent of those questioned selected "moral values"—a higher percentage than any other, including Iraq and the economy.

Although this meant that nearly four fifths of those polled did *not* choose "moral values," the 22 percent morphed into a landslide overnight. "It really is Michael Moore versus Mel Gibson" was Newt Gingrich's summary of the election. The Super Bowl halftime show fracas of the preceding February—the brief exposure of the singer Janet Jackson's right breast on network television—was belatedly crowned by William Safire on *Meet the Press* as "the social-political event of the past year." Karl Rove also subscribed to this interpretation: "I think it's people who are concerned about the coarseness of our culture, about what they see on the television sets, what they see in the movies." Robert Novak put an even finer point on it in a column: the "moral values" number was proof that "the anti-abortion, anti–gay marriage, socially conservative agenda is ascendant." Jon Stewart summed up the new consensus with a joke: the election was the red states' revenge on *Will & Grace.*

In this reading, the rising mayhem in Iraq, the revelations of Abu Ghraib, and the escalating terror alerts (real or contrived) had been irrelevant to Bush's victory. The 2004 election was retrofitted to a revised list of red-letter events led by Jackson's "wardrobe malfunction" in her MTV-produced duet with Justin Timberlake; the Kerry-Edwards Radio City benefit in which Whoopi Goldberg notoriously made a raunchy joke about George Bush's surname; the anti–gay marriage constitutional amendment that was endorsed by the president; the similar (and successful) initiatives on the ballot in eleven states (including the crucial swing state of Ohio); and John Kerry's reference to Mary Cheney, the vice president's openly gay daughter, as a lesbian in a presidential debate. (Republicans howled, insisting that the love that dare not speak its name could not be spoken of by name by anyone except Mary Cheney's father, who had previously mentioned her orientation in public.)

The press, which knows a sexy angle when it sees one, especially if the angle has something to do with sex (in this case a presumed national abhorrence of it), ran with the "moral values" story line. Yet it was patently, even farcically, false. If you added up the AP poll respondents who picked terrorism (19 percent) and Iraq (15 percent) as their top issues, it was clear that national security was of greater concern to more Americans than "moral values." Nor was there a definition by the pollsters of what "moral values" meant—the term could refer to anything from abortion to aiding the poor to being nice to your mother. A Pew Research Center analysis discovered that the format of the exit poll was also deficient: "moral values" was an appealing way for a voter to answer "none of the above" because it was less specific than the other issues offered. When voters were asked which issue influenced them most but were given *no* menu of suggestions to choose from, Iraq, the economy, and terrorism led by far, and issues that might be labeled as "values" polled in the low single digits. The popular verdict on those values was not overwhelmingly conservative anyway, according to Pew. Sixty percent of those polled supported either same-sex marriage (25 percent) or civil unions (35 percent), and 55 percent were in favor of abortion being legal in all or most instances.[24] Gary Langer, director of polling for ABC News, observed that the "moral values" bandwagon in the press "created a deep distortion—one that threatens to misinform the political discourse for years to come."[25]

He was right. After the election, Democrats took to flagellating themselves with a vehemence worthy of *The Passion of the Christ*. They spoke incessantly of their need to find religion and connect with "values voters." They sought out liberal evangelical leaders such as Jim Wallis to tutor them en masse in ostentatious piety. The Republican right, for its part, saw an opening to use the "values" mandate as a means to shove its own values down people's throats.

In the new and skewed post–exit poll profile of the electorate, the fact that *both* parties' candidates opposed same-sex marriage was forgotten. (With typical maladroitness, Kerry had defended his stand by defining marriage as "an institution between men and women for the purpose of having children and procreating," a standard not met by his own post-procreation second marriage.) Also forgotten in the rush to recast American political fault lines according to "moral values" was the fact that the three top-billed speakers at the Republican Convention—Schwarzenegger, McCain, and Giuliani—were all pro–gay rights opponents of the same-sex marriage amendment. (Two of the three—McCain being the exception—were also pro-choice.) The biggest values scandals leading into the election—Schwarzenegger's fondling escapades, William Bennett's gambling obsession, Bill O'Reilly's settlement of a vivid sexual harassment lawsuit detailed at thesmokinggun.com—had all starred Republicans. A former TV critic and an enterprising blogger, Jeff Jarvis, discovered that even the indecency uproars set off by the Janet Jackson brouhaha were built on numbers as misleading as the "moral values" percentage in the exit poll. With a Freedom of Information Act request, he obtained the actual viewer complaints that had driven the Federal Communications Commission to threaten the Fox network and its affiliates with the largest indecency fine to date—$1.2 million for the sins of a reality "matchmaking" program called *Married by America*. Though the FCC had cited 159 public complaints in its legal case against Fox, the documents showed that there were actually only 90 complaints, written by 23 individuals. Of those 23, all but two were identical repetitions of a form letter posted by the Parents Television Council, the right-wing e-mail-and-fax mill at the center of many of these media culture wars. Bottom line: the total of actual, discrete complaints about *Married by America* was three.[26]

Kerry's defeat notwithstanding, it was blue America, not red, that was inexorably winning the culture war, and by a landslide. Yes, according to a *Newsweek* poll, there was a Christian-right Republican base that subscribed to the *Left Behind* belief that Armageddon was imminent, but it totaled just 17 percent of the country. Everyone else was watching ABC's salacious new hit *Desperate Housewives,* which, according to the Nielsen ratings, was a bigger hit in Oklahoma City than in Los Angeles, bigger in Kansas City than in New York. Lycos, the Internet search engine, reported that the number of searches for the Janet Jackson "wardrobe malfunction" tied the record set by 9/11-related searches on and just after 9/11.

"That a single breast received as much attention as the first attack on United States soil in 60 years is beyond belief," wrote Aaron Schatz, the columnist on the Lycos top-50 site. It said perhaps more than anyone wanted to know about American "moral values" that a waning pop star's breast now loomed as large in the culture as the day that was supposed to have "changed everything." But three years later, the day that was supposed to have "changed everything" wasn't what it used to be. A cataclysmic event had been downsized in the nation's memory and robbed of its urgent original meaning by the new narrative of Iraq. The battleground for the initial American response to the first attack on U.S. soil in sixty years—Afghanistan, now starting its tumble back into chaos and Taliban control—was a distant memory. When, midway through the election year, a twenty-ton granite cornerstone was laid at the World Trade Center to mark the start of construction of a new Freedom Tower, few outside New York knew or cared. Ground Zero had become figuratively—and, given the absence of any construction on the site, literally—a void.

NINE

"WHEN WE ACT, WE CREATE OUR OWN REALITY"

S O STRONG WAS the perceived "moral values" juggernaut in the immediate aftermath of the 2004 election that within days it claimed an unexpected cultural casualty. A Veterans Day broadcast of Steven Spielberg's 1998
World War II movie *Saving Private Ryan,* a sacred text of the pre-9/11 greatest
generation/*Band of Brothers* craze, was scrapped by sixty-six ABC stations, even
though it had been nationally broadcast by ABC on Veterans Day in both
2001 and 2002 without incident.[1] Media owners who once might have disre-
garded complaints by the Parents Television Council or the American Family
Association were now fearful that the Bush administration's FCC would reward the Republican base and impose sanctions if actors playing American soldiers said curse words while dying on-screen. In McCarthyism, "moral values"
style, merely the fear of reprisals was enough to push television stations or a
network onto the slippery slope of self-censorship before anyone in Washington even bothered to act.

What made the *Private Ryan* case alarming was that it was not about sex but
about the presentation of war at a time when the country was fighting one.
Some of the companies whose stations refused to broadcast the movie also

owned major American newspapers in cities as various as Providence and Atlanta. If these media outlets were afraid to show a graphic Hollywood treatment of a sixty-year-old war starring the beloved Tom Hanks because the feds
might fine them, toy with their licenses, or deny them regulatory permission to
expand their empires, might they curry favor with Washington by softening
their news divisions' efforts to present the ugly facts of an ongoing war? The
pressure groups that were incensed by both *Saving Private Ryan* and risqué
programming were often the same ones who campaigned against any news
organization that was not toeing the administration political line in lockstep
with Fox.

The same week that the ABC stations censored the Spielberg movie, the
right extended its muscle into the news arena by targeting Kevin Sites, a freelance TV cameraman in the employ of NBC News, who caught on video a
marine shooting an apparently unarmed wounded insurgent prisoner in a
mosque during the new effort by American troops to retake Falluja. To NBC's
credit, it ran Sites's report on its evening newscast. Sites avoided giving any
snap judgment, pending the marines' own investigation of the shooting, cau-
tioning that a war zone is "rife with uncertainty and confusion." But loud
voices in red America wanted him silenced anyway. On right-wing sites such
as freerepublic.com the cameraman was branded an "anti-war activist" (which
he was not), a traitor, and an "enemy combatant." Sites's own blog, touted by
the anchor Brian Williams on the air, was full of messages from the relatives of
marines profusely thanking the cameraman for bringing them news of their
sons in Iraq. But that communal message board soon had to be shut down because of death threats against Sites. The attempt to demonize and censor him
simply for doing his job was no anomaly. Earlier in the year the *New York Post*
smeared Associated Press television cameramen as having "a mutually benefi-
cial relationship with the insurgents in Falluja" simply because their cameras
had captured the horrific images of the four American contract workers slaughtered there.

In this climate, it was no surprise that the torture story had all but vanished
from television since the initial photographs surfaced from Abu Ghraib. There
had been continued revelations in major newspapers and magazines such as
The New Yorker, The New York Review of Books, and *Vanity Fair,* but if a story isn't
on TV in America, it's MIA in the culture. The first full-scale court-martial

to be generated by the prison abuse scandal—of Charles Graner, the Army Reserve specialist who was the father of Lynndie England's child—unfolded at Fort Hood, Texas, during the pre-inaugural week in January. It was broadcast on the evening news almost exclusively in brief, mechanical summary, when it was broadcast at all. It surely didn't lack for drama; the Graner trial was *Judgment at Nuremberg* turned upside down. The defendant's lawyer, Guy Womack, explained in his closing courtroom statement: "In Nuremberg, it was the generals being prosecuted. We were going after the order-givers. Here the government is going after the order-takers."[2] The trial's judge, Colonel James L. Pohl of the army, would not permit witnesses to say which officers knew of the abuses or what orders the officers had given. While Graner was the ringleader of the horrors seen in the Abu Ghraib snapshots, the entire chain of command above him, including the officers in his immediate proximity at the prison, was spared prosecution.

The public was spared any further discomforting details of these war crimes, much as it had been many explicit details of the war itself. If Americans had to be protected from Spielberg's reenactment of World War II and the closed coffins of Iraq casualties, then certainly they could not be exposed to real-life stories involving forced group masturbation, electric shock, rape committed with a phosphorescent stick, the burning of cigarettes in prisoners' ears, involuntary enemas, and beatings that ended in death. When one detainee witness at the Graner trial testified in a taped deposition that he had been forced to eat out of a toilet, his story was routinely cited in newspaper accounts but left unmentioned on network TV newscasts. The evening news was fixated instead on the "clown prince" of England, Harry, who had dressed up in Nazi regalia for a costume party given on the theme "native and colonial."

As the Graner trial was getting under way, *The Washington Post* reported that a secret August 2002 Justice Department memo, prepared in consultation with then–White House counsel Alberto Gonzales, authorized the CIA to use interrogation practices that included "waterboarding,"[3] a form of simulated drowning that had been the torture device of choice for military regimes in Argentina and Uruguay in the 1970s. This revelation also failed to make the cut on network news; actual criminal behavior under the category "native and colonial" wasn't as sexy as a dim-witted prince wearing a swastika armband while partying at a British country house. Nor was much television attention paid to revelations that the prisoner abuse was widespread and systemic, stretching from Afghanistan to Guantánamo Bay to unknown locales where "ghost detainees" were being held.

Thanks to the spotty vigilance of the press and the Democrats' new obsession with values, which they searched for as fruitlessly as David Kay had for Saddam's WMDs, the White House tried to keep unpleasant Iraq news on the q.t. A typical day of unreality in the nominal war capital of Washington was December 5, when the annual Kennedy Center Honors were bestowed upon celebrities at the center's opera house, in a bipartisan gala taped for holiday broadcast on CBS. That day, the morning newspapers told of more deadly strikes by suicide bombers in Mosul and Baghdad, leaving at least twenty-six Iraqi security officers dead, including eight in a police station near the capital's protected Green Zone. There were also reports of at least four American casualties in firefights. But the war went unacknowledged among the Washington revelers preening for a network audience.

Less than seventy-two hours after appearing adjacent to the same-sex marriage proponent Elton John in his box at the Kennedy Center event, the president donned a snappy muted-green "commander in chief" jacket—a "Casual Friday" version of the full *Top Gun* costume he had worn on the USS *Lincoln*—to address marines at Camp Pendleton, in California. Back at the time of "Mission Accomplished," the Pentagon had estimated that the American occupation would end in December 2004. But on this December day in 2004, Pearl Harbor Day, the troops in the president's audience were going to war, not coming home; Camp Pendleton's population had contributed almost one fifth of the year's U.S. combat fatalities so far.[4] Now the base was providing another handsome made-for-TV tableau for the commander-in-chief.

But that feel-good message was contradicted the next day, December 8, halfway across the world, in Kuwait. There an American soldier asked an unexpected question during the secretary of defense's own photo-op town hall meeting in an aircraft hangar. Specialist Thomas Wilson, a scout with a Tennessee Army National Guard unit about to head into Iraq, spoke of troops having to search through landfills for so-called "hillbilly armor" to protect their trucks. "Why don't we have those resources readily available to us?" he asked as his fellow troops cheered and clapped. Rumsfeld promised more armor soon, but asked the assembled to make do in the meantime. "You go to war with the Army you have, not the Army you might want or wish to have at a later time," he said.

For some Americans, this intimation of an inadequately supplied army was jaw-dropping news, as was Rumsfeld's what-me-worry response. For others, the soldier's question was tantamount to sedition, especially once it became known that he had batted around its phrasing with an embedded newspaper reporter before asking it. Specialist Wilson, Rush Limbaugh said, was guilty of "near insubordination" for asking about armor; the poor defenseless defense secretary "was set up," whined the *New York Post*. The blame-the-press line was happily embraced by Rumsfeld, who continued on to Iraq for a PR tour in which he used more compliant troops as photo-op accessories and fielded a softball question about negative war coverage, a question he applauded as "not planted by the media." Surely the defense secretary was entitled to the same deference that the president and Condoleezza Rice had received a year earlier, on their excellent Thanksgiving adventure in Iraq.

In truth, Specialist Wilson's question should not have been news at all. It was no secret, and especially not to Rumsfeld, that American troops had been undersupplied and often poorly supported in Iraq. The *Los Angeles Times* was chronicling the complaints of National Guard soldiers about being shipped to war from Fort Bliss, California, with "broken guns and trucks with blown transmissions."[5] Dana Priest of *The Washington Post* told MSNBC's Chris Matthews of hearing soldiers ask the defense secretary similar questions about their body armor when she traveled with him a year earlier. Just before the election, twenty-three members of an Army Reserve unit disobeyed a direct order to deliver fuel, partly because they had decided that the vulnerability of their trucks would make the journey tantamount to a suicide mission.[6] Months earlier, the service newspaper *Stars and Stripes* reported that desperate troops were using sandbags as makeshift vehicle armor.[7]

When Rumsfeld responded to his questioner in Kuwait that the only reason the troops still lacked armor was "a matter of production and capability," it was exposed instantly as a lie. The manufacturers that supplied the armor told the press that they had been telling the Pentagon for months that they could increase production, in the case of one company, ArmorWorks, in Arizona, by as much as 100 percent.[8] Yet even seven months after the Wilson-Rumsfeld exchange—in June 2005—Michael Moss of *The New York Times* found that the Pentagon was still failing to secure safer trucks for the troops. While Rumsfeld and other dignitaries visiting Iraq, including congressmen, were loaned safe steel vehicles from the private contractor Halliburton, fighting men and women had to make do with vulnerable Humvees.[9] In January 2006, almost three years after the war began, Moss would discover a similar uncorrected shortfall in body armor: a secret Pentagon study revealed "that as many as 80 percent of the marines who have been killed in Iraq from wounds to the upper body could have survived if they had had extra body armor" and that while such armor had been available since 2003, "until recently the Pentagon has largely declined to supply it to troops despite calls from the field for additional protection."[10]

But in December 2004, the issue of insufficient armor was quickly drowned out by the cable and talk-radio arguments over whether Specialist Wilson should or should not have consulted with an embedded reporter about the wording of his question to Rumsfeld. By the time the president appeared in the East Room of the White House a week later to award the highest civilian honor, the Presidential Medal of Freedom, to the war's prime movers, the inadequate armor had been forgotten. The three medals were given to the men who had lost Osama bin Laden (General Tommy Franks), botched the Iraq occupation (Paul Bremer), and called prewar intelligence on Saddam's WMDs a "slam dunk" (George Tenet). That the bestowing of an exalted reward for high achievement on such incompetents incited little laughter was a measure of how much the administration, buoyed by reelection, still maintained control of its embattled but not yet dismantled triumphalist wartime narrative.

The next set piece in this narrative was the inauguration. While FDR decreed that the usual gaiety be set aside at his wartime inaugural in January 1945, there was no such restraint in the $40 million, four-day extravaganza planned this time, with its top ticket package priced at $250,000. Television had to be served in a way that would enhance the White House's portrayal of the war in Iraq. The official theme of the show was "Celebrating Freedom, Honoring Service." The trick for its producers was to market the military effort while keeping all of its costs off-screen so that no unpleasantness or difficult questions like Specialist Wilson's might spoil the party or Bush's message of victory around the corner.

On inauguration morning, Dick Cheney told the radio host Don Imus that "we can bring our boys home" and that "our mission is complete" once the Iraqis "can defend themselves." The time line for this was more than a little vague. Bush and the new Iraqi prime minister, Allawi, announced in September that there were "nearly 100,000 fully trained and equipped" Iraqi security forces ready to carry out that self-defense. Rice told the Senate Foreign Relations Committee that there were 120,000. *Time* reported that the actual figure of fully trained ground soldiers was 14,000. The administration made no effort to sort out these contradictions for the public. There was no percentage in talking about specifics in Iraq.

Indeed Bush did not mention the word *Iraq* in his inaugural address. The patriots at the lavish bash thrown at Washington's Ritz-Carlton for the grandees of the Christian right by the Reverend Lou Sheldon of the Traditional Values Coalition barely mentioned the war either; they kept Iraq out of sight in their ballroom much as they had kept *Saving Private Ryan* off ABC affiliates two months earlier. Television's ceremonial coverage of the inauguration, much of which resembled the martial pageantry broadcast by state-owned networks in banana republics, dutifully parroted the White House message that the four-day bacchanal was a salute to the troops. The only commentator to rudely call attention to the disconnect between that fictional pretense and reality was Judy Bachrach, a writer for *Vanity Fair,* who dared say on Fox News that the inaugural's military ball and prayer service would not keep troops "safe and warm" in their "flimsy" Humvees in Iraq. She was promptly given the hook.

There were no television cameras to capture what might have been the week's most surreal "salute" to the troops, the "Heroes Red, White and Blue Inaugural Ball" attended by Rumsfeld and Paul Wolfowitz. The event's celebrity headliners included the Fox correspondent Geraldo Rivera, who had been booted from Iraq at the start of the war for compromising "operational security" by telling his viewers the position of American troops. He joked to the crowd at the gala that his deployment as an "overpaid" reporter was tantamount to that of an "underpaid hero" in battle. The attendees from Walter Reed Army Medical Center and Bethesda Naval Hospital, some of whose long-term care had to be picked up by private foundations because of government stinginess, responded with "deafening silence," reported Roxanne Roberts of

The Washington Post. The party's big act was still to come: Nile Rodgers and Chic sang the lyrics "Clap your hands, hoo!" and "Dance to the beat" to soldiers who had lost hands and legs.[11]

The inaugural festivities led seamlessly to the Iraqi election—another much-publicized light at the end of the Iraq tunnel signifying that American troops were almost, just-about-to-be on their way home. It was the fifth V-I day so far, following the liberation of Baghdad (April 9, 2003), Bush's declaration that "major combat operations in Iraq have ended" (May 1, 2003), the arrest of Saddam Hussein (December 14, 2003), and the handover of sovereignty to the new provisional Iraqi government (June 28, 2004). Iraq was starting to seem like Vietnam on speed—the false endings of that tragic decade reenacted and compressed in jump cuts, a quagmire retooled for the MTV attention span. At the State of the Union address, always a prized opportunity for the administration to broadcast its latest propaganda, Republicans celebrated the latest milestone by holding up index fingers dipped in purple ink, emulating the images of Iraqi voters that had flooded television three days earlier. Now, surely, a peaceful transition to democracy was at hand.

Two weeks before the 2004 election, *The New York Times Magazine* had published its widely discussed article in which a senior presidential adviser told the journalist Ron Suskind that there was no longer any need for the "reality-based community" epitomized by journalists and vowed that the administration would create its "own reality." The conversation between the adviser and Suskind dated back to the summer of 2002—just before the White House started to roll out its new product of an Iraq war. The adviser's words explained much of what happened thereafter, from the hyping of Saddam's nuclear weapons and Qaeda connections to the Operation Iraqi Freedom double bill of "Shock and Awe" and "Saving Private Lynch" to the president's premature announcement of the end of major combat operations. A week after that May 2003 victory, which was surely the grandest of the administration's alternative realities, a reporter had queried Rumsfeld in a Pentagon press briefing about journalistic reports "that a sense of public order is still lacking" in Iraq. The secretary of defense, echoing the adviser Suskind talked to, responded dismissively to the news of a growing insurgency, ridiculing reporters for showing only "slices of truth." He had the full truth, of course: according to the administration's own reality, the reconstruction effort was right on track.

Given all the setbacks that followed, it was no small feat that the White House's fictional apparatus in Iraq was still going full blast a year and a half later. It reached a new high in artifice in the second battle for Falluja, just after Bush's reelection. In another case of Vietnam déjà vu, a city of 250,000 had essentially been destroyed to "save" it from the enemy. The information the administration put out about this quixotic victory was brazenly at odds with the known facts. "There are over 3,000 Iraqi soldiers who are leading the activity," said the deputy secretary of state, Richard Armitage, as the operation began and those crack Iraqi troops were paraded before the television cameras. But a "reality-based" reporter, Edward Wong of *The New York Times*, found that the Iraqis had actually turned up in battle only after the hard work had been done, their uniforms "spotless from not having done a lick of fighting."[12] When other "reality-based" news spread that many of the insurgents had melted away before the coalition forces engaged them, an oft-repeated Pentagon policy of not providing enemy body counts was sacrificed to the cause of manufacturing some good news to drive out the bad. Suddenly there was a government body count of 1,200 to 1,600 insurgents in Falluja, even though reporters on the scene found, as the *Times* reported, "little evidence of dead insurgents in the streets and warrens where some of the most intense combat took place."[13] By inflating both body counts and the fighting prowess of the local army against guerrillas, the Bush administration had constructed a "Mission Accomplished II"–soon to be followed by a happy Iraqi election for dessert.

The White House's ability to create its own reality worked in tandem with its facility for vilifying and shutting out those reality-based pests of the press who kept trying to poke holes in its story line. By the start of 2004, the president had held only eleven solo news conferences, compared with his father's count of seventy-one by the same point in his presidency and even with the criminally secretive Nixon's twenty-three. Bush's count was the lowest in history. His administration's critique of journalists echoed that of the Nixon vice president Spiro Agnew, who, as scripted by the speechwriter Pat Buchanan, tried to discredit the press as an elite–"a tiny, enclosed fraternity of privileged men." Some of the actions by the Bush White House–or its Rovian surrogates– to punish these elitists were also distinctly redolent of the Watergate era.

Back then, Nixon's special counsel, Charles W. Colson, pursued a ruthless program of intimidation that included threatening antitrust action against the networks if they didn't run pro-Nixon stories. When Colson boasted in Watergate tapes and memos of "destroying the old establishment," he sounded very much like the founding father of the new century's blogging lynch mobs. He exulted in bullying CBS to cut back its Watergate reports before the '72 election. He enlisted NBC in pro-administration propaganda by browbeating it to repackage ten-day-old coverage of Tricia Nixon's wedding as a prime-time special. It was the Colson office as well that compiled a White House enemies list that included journalists who had had the audacity to question administration policies.

So little of this history was remembered that when Bob Woodward and Carl Bernstein's Watergate source Deep Throat was finally revealed in the spring of 2005 as the FBI official W. Mark Felt, Colson was repeatedly trotted out on television, without irony, to pass moral judgment on Felt for dishonoring "the confidence of the president of the United States" (as he put it on NBC's *Today* show). It didn't matter that Colson had dishonored the law, proposed bombing the Brookings Institution, and gone to prison for his role in the break-in to steal the psychiatric records of *The New York Times*'s Deep Throat on Vietnam, Daniel Ellsberg. None of Colson's TV interviewers ever specified his criminal actions in the Nixon years. Some shows identified him on-screen only as a "former White House counsel."

Had anyone been so rude (or professional) as to recount Colson's sordid past, the genealogical line between his Watergate-era machinations and those of his present-day successors would have been all too painfully visible. The Bush administration, like Nixon's, was obsessed with news management and secrecy from the day it arrived in the White House. If Nixon had instituted "an unprecedented, government-wide effort to control, restrict and conceal information," as a contemporaneous special National Press Club study had concluded, Bush went further, hoping to ensure that any papers he wanted to hide would be off-limits to future historians, not just present-day journalists. By executive order he quietly gutted the Presidential Records Act of 1978, the very reform enacted by Congress as a post-Watergate antidote to pathological Nixonian secrecy. Even reporters circulating at Bush inaugural balls were assigned minders, to send the signal to the revelers that Big Brother was watching should they be tempted to say anything remotely off-message.[14]

But Bush had two powerful weapons to use against the press that his paranoid predecessor did not. The first was the horror of 9/11, which the White House and its surrogates still invoked to besmirch the patriotism of any journalist who reported the war unblinkingly, as Kevin Sites most recently had discovered. The second weapon, handed to Bush by the press itself, was journalism's own screwups. In May of 2003, *The New York Times,* in a seven-thousand-word exposé, had revealed what it called "a low point in the 152-year history of the newspaper," the fabrications and plagiarism of a twenty-seven-year-old reporter named Jayson Blair. Though Blair's bogus stories were not nearly as important in content as the credulous WMD accounts that would later embarrass the paper, they were a blow to the credibility of an institution known for its rigorous standards. The CBS "memogate" scandal in reporting on Bush's National Guard record did similar damage to an establishment news organization that was known for the legacy of Edward R. Murrow, Walter Cronkite, and *60 Minutes.*

These scandals played perfectly into the administration's insidious efforts to blur the boundary between its reality and actual reality. The White House could exploit them as part of its plan to demolish the very idea that there could possibly be an objective and accurate free press. The same conservatives who once deplored postmodernism and moral relativism were now eagerly promoting a brave new world in which it was a given that there could be no empirical reality in news, only the reality you wanted to hear (or that they wanted you to hear). Every time "the filter" reported news unflattering to the administration, the White House and its amen chorus used the news media's self-inflicted injuries to undermine the unwanted story at hand.

A classic example occurred a week before 2004's Election Day, when the *Times* reported that nearly 380 tons of powerful conventional explosives had been looted at a huge facility called Al Qaqaa that was supposed to be under American control. CBS's *60 Minutes* had also been pursuing the story.[15] The Bush administration and its Fox-blogosphere media cohort pounced immediately on the news, repeatedly denouncing it as a case of liberal bias or out-and-out hogwash. The story was later corroborated not only by United States Army reservists and national guardsmen who spoke to the *Los Angeles Times*[16] but also by Iraq's deputy minister of industry, who told *The New York Times* that Al Qaqaa was only one of many such weapon caches hijacked on America's undermanned post-invasion watch. Not that anyone knew or much cared whether the story was true or whether some of these munitions might now be used by insurgents to kill American troops.[17] The White House and its auxiliaries saw to it that the *Times* and CBS became the subject of the media firestorm instead.

A similar stunt was pulled on *Newsweek* in May 2005, after the magazine ran a ten-sentence item in its Periscope section including the accusation that American interrogators at Guantánamo Bay had flushed a copy of the Koran down a toilet to inflame the Muslim inmates. The item went unnoticed for days, until anti-American riots broke out in Pakistan and Afghanistan and some of the ringleaders cited the *Newsweek* story to further inflame the rioters' rage. This sudden scrutiny forced the magazine to recheck the item. It discovered that its single, anonymous source for the Koran anecdote was wrong, and the magazine retracted the story.

The White House promptly pinned the deaths of some seventeen people in the riots on *Newsweek*, a preposterous exaggeration of the magazine's role. Both Richard Myers, the chairman of the Joint Chiefs of Staff, and Hamid Karzai, Afghanistan's president, said that neither the riots nor the deaths had had anything to do with *Newsweek*.[18] But the administration had two larger aims in mind. First, it saw a new opportunity to knock "the filter" as ideologically biased, untrustworthy, and unpatriotic—a hard case to make in this particular instance, given that the reporter who had erred on the story, Michael Isikoff, was a hero of the right for his dogged investigative pursuit of the Lewinsky story during the Clinton years. Second, the White House saw a chance to pinpoint a single paragraph in a single magazine as the fount of all anti-American rage in the Muslim world and cover up its own considerable missteps in that regard.

"Our United States military personnel go out of their way to make sure that the Holy Koran is treated with care," said the White House press secretary, Scott McClellan, as he eagerly and sanctimoniously made the magazine the scapegoat for the riots. McClellan was so fixated on his bosses' desire to destroy *Newsweek*—and on mouthing his own phony PC pieties about the Koran—that by omission he whitewashed the rioters themselves, Islamic extremists who routinely misused their holy book as a pretext for murder, including the mass murder of 9/11. In what could be taken as a Freudian slip, Richard Boucher, a State Department spokesman, chastised *Newsweek* for using "facts that have not been substantiated"—strange words coming from the man whose boss, Colin Powell, had delivered the unsubstantiated and, as it turned out, fictional recitation of Saddam Hussein's weapon capabilities before the United Nations Security Council on the eve of the war. Rumsfeld chimed in, too, channeling Ari Fleischer's admonition to Bill Maher after 9/11 by warning that "people need to be careful what they say . . . just as people need to be careful what they do."

Again, the sins of the press were used to draw attention from the administration's mismanagement of the war. And few areas had been more mismanaged than America's image in the Muslim world. As the Abu Ghraib photos showed, there was substantial evidence that American interrogators had abused Muslim detainees with methods specifically chosen to hit the prisoners' religious hot buttons, Korans flushed down toilets or not. A cable signed by Lieutenant General Ricardo S. Sanchez in September 2003 called for interrogators to "exploit Arab fear of dogs."[19] (Muslims view them as unclean.) A Defense Department memo of October 2002 authorized such Muslim-baiting practices as depriving prisoners of "published religious items or materials" and forcing the removal of beards and clothing.[20] Only the day before *Newsweek*'s story was published, *The New York Times* reported that a former American interrogator at Guantánamo corroborated a detainee's account of guards tossing Korans into a pile and stepping on them, prompting a hunger strike among the detainees.[21]

The administration put such a low priority on winning hearts and minds in the Muslim world that Karen Hughes, the third appointee since 9/11 in the revolving-door job of undersecretary of state for public diplomacy, was permitted to set up a shop with no Muslims at the top—and then to go AWOL. The administration saw so little urgency in her assignment that after nominating her for the job in March 2005, it allowed her to take six months off to attend to family matters before beginning her confirmation process in the fall.[22] The *Newsweek* controversy was just one of many flare-ups that occurred unattended during her hiatus.

For all this, the White House asked the world to believe that anti-American animus among Muslims throughout the Middle East was all a newsmagazine's fault. The punch line to this dark joke occurred two weeks after the *Newsweek* imbroglio, when a Pentagon report certifying desecrations of the Koran by American guards was released at 7:15 P.M. on a Friday,[23] to ensure that it would miss the evening newscasts and be buried in the weekend papers.

THE BUSH ADMINISTRATION didn't just settle for demonizing, stiffing, and spinning the press. When that senior adviser told Ron Suskind that the White House would create its "own reality," he was speaking more literally than anyone could have imagined. The administration's propaganda machinery encompassed not just the usual government flacks disseminating misleading information but also a hidden and elaborate fake news factory, complete with its own fake "journalists," all of it paid for by taxpayers.

The first revelation of the operation had come early in the election year, on March 14, when Robert Pear, a reporter in the Washington bureau of *The New York Times* who specialized in examining the fine print in the capital's sprawling government bureaucracy, discovered that the Department of Health and Human Services had fielded its own pair of Jayson Blair–like fabricators. Two "reporters" named Karen Ryan and Alberto Garcia had appeared in TV spots distributed to local news stations around the country to promote the administration's new Medicare prescription-drug benefit as the best thing to happen to America's elderly since Social Security. "This is going to be the same Medicare system only with new benefits, more choices, more opportunities for enhanced benefits," enthused Tommy Thompson, the department's secretary, in an "interview" for one of these "reports." He didn't have to worry about being contradicted from any critics of the program; in these "news" segments, everything in the Bush administration was coming up roses. Replete with tag lines like "In Washington, I'm Karen Ryan reporting," the elaborate fictional skits were broadcast whole or in part as actual news by more than fifty stations in forty markets. The departmental budget devoted to this PR campaign, some $124 million, dwarfed that of most actual American news organizations.[24]

A government spokesman defended the fake news with pure Orwell-speak: "Anyone who has questions about this practice needs to do some research on modern public information tools." Ryan, it was explained, was no impostor but an actual "freelance journalist." Once upon a time she had been, but in recent years she had become a public-relations consultant. Her recent assignments included serving as a TV shill for pharmaceutical companies in infomercials for FluMist and Excedrin. Given that drug companies were the principal beneficiaries of the new Medicare law, she was nothing if not consistent in her journalistic patrons. But she was a freelance reporter only in the sense that Mike Ditka would qualify as such when appearing in Levitra ads.

In the same spirit, and even more laughably, the new Department of Homeland Security was revealed to have shelled out $100,000-plus to hire "a Hollywood liaison": Bobbie Faye Ferguson, an actress whose credits included the movie *The Bermuda Triangle* and guest shots on television shows such as *Designing Women* and *The Dukes of Hazzard.* Her job was to "work with moviemakers and scriptwriters" to create Homeland Security infotainment—just the thing, perhaps, were Americans to be attacked by fictional terrorists from Hollywood's summer blockbusters rather than by actual terrorists.[25]

Jon Stewart had a lot of fun with the Ryan-Garcia revelations on his fake-news program, *The Daily Show,* as he made a public show of trying to decide whether to be outraged or flattered by government propaganda imitating his satiric art. One of his own fake correspondents affected fake despair. "They created a whole new category of fake news—infoganda," Rob Corddry said. "We'll never be able to keep up!" But Corddry's joke was not really a joke. The more real journalism fumbled its job, the easier it was for such government infoganda to fill the vacuum.

On the eve of Bush's second inauguration, the most elaborate example yet of administration fake news was uncovered by *USA Today,* the same paper that had discovered Homeland Security's Hollywood liaison. Armstrong Williams, a conservative commentator, talk-show host, and newspaper columnist (for *The Washington Times* and the *Detroit Free Press,* among many others), was unmasked as the front man for a scheme by which $240,000 of taxpayers' money was quietly siphoned through the Department of Education and a private PR firm to Williams so that he would "regularly comment" upon (translation: shill for) the Bush administration's No Child Left Behind program in various media venues during the election year.

But Williams didn't only promote No Child Left Behind while on the administration payroll. Appearing on CNN posing as, of all things, a media ethicist, he had weighed in with his own critique of the CBS "memogate" scandal. During the election campaign, he had also appeared on cable news to trash Kitty Kelley's book lambasting the Bush family, to accuse the media of being Michael Moore's "P.R. machine," and to lambaste Jon Stewart for doing a "puff interview" with John Kerry on *The Daily Show* (which Williams, unsurprisingly, seemed to regard as a real, not a fake, news program). Perhaps the most fascinating Williams TV appearance took place in December 2003, the same month that he was first contracted by the government to receive his payoffs. At a time when no one in television news could get an interview with Dick Cheney, Williams was rewarded with an extended conversation with the vice president that aired on stations owned by Sinclair—the broadcasting company that had banned Ted Koppel's *Nightline* recitation of the fallen and had proposed showing an anti-Kerry documentary under the rubric of "news" just before Election Day. In his chat with Williams, Cheney criticized the press for its coverage of Halliburton and denounced "cheap shot journalism" in which "the press portray themselves as objective observers of the passing scene, when they obviously are not objective."[26] Thus the Williams interview with the vice president, implicitly presented as an example of the kind of objective news Cheney endorsed, was in reality a completely subjective, bought-and-paid-for fake news event for a broadcast company that barely bothered to fake objectivity and whose chief executives were major contributors to the Bush-Cheney campaign. The Soviets couldn't have constructed a more ingenious ploy to bamboozle the citizenry. It was a plot twist worthy of *The Manchurian Candidate*—only *The Manchurian Candidate*, at least, was clearly labeled fiction.

The Williams scandal raised the question of whether there might be more administration-paid agents at loose in the media machine. At the White House, Scott McClellan said he was "not aware" of any other such case and that he hadn't "heard" whether the administration's senior staff had known of the Williams contract—non-denial denials with miles of wiggle room. Williams, meanwhile, told interviewers that he had no doubt that there were others like him being paid for purveying administration propaganda and that "this happens all the time."[27] But he refused to name names—a vow of omertà all too reminiscent of that taken by the low-level operatives first apprehended in the "third-rate burglary" at Watergate.

More news about fake news emerged soon enough, bearing out Williams's statement that "this happens all the time." Two other syndicated newspaper columnists were unmasked as paid enthusiasts for the administration's "marriage" initiatives, with stipends supplied by the Department of Health and Human Services, the same agency that had recruited the fake TV reporters Ryan and Garcia.[28] *The New York Times* found that, all told, at least twenty federal agencies had made and distributed hundreds of fake news segments over the past four years, landing them even in big markets such as New York, Los Angeles, and Chicago.[29]

Everyone was getting in on the act. The Transportation Security Administration gave a PR employee a false name so he could double as a "reporter" in a segment praising airport security as "one of the most remarkable campaigns in aviation history." Lest anyone doubt the administration's commitment to a green agenda, other fake news reports praised initiatives to preserve forests and wetlands. The Pentagon Channel, once an internal Defense Department operation, was now being offered to every cable and satellite operator in the country as a satellite "news" feed from the front, available free to any local news director who logged onto a military-backed Web site. In keeping with the upbeat form letters-to-the-editor sent to newspapers from Iraq, an Army and Air Force Hometown News Service had been established to send local stations videos about all the "good news" from the war. Perhaps most important was an Office of Broadcasting Services, a State Department unit that had once settled for such mundane, above-board tasks as distributing video from news conferences to the press but in early 2002 collaborated with the White House to produce all-out feature segments selling the success of the American efforts in Afghanistan and Iraq.[30]

This propaganda effort was brilliantly conceived. It preyed upon a growing reality of the local TV news business: lower budgets, smaller staffs, less quality control, more and more airtime to fill. Stations were desperate for cheap or free prepackaged material that could relieve the burden of feeding a bottomless news maw. The government segments were cleverly camouflaged by avoiding strident partisanship that would raise alarms about their entirely pro-administration slants. Like genuine news segments distributed by a network's news division to its affiliates, the government news "reports" allowed for the local talent to read scripted lead-ins and voice-overs, so that they would blend right in.

At WHBQ, the Fox affiliate in Memphis, the *Times* found a particularly spectacular example of how well the program worked. For the first anniversary of 9/11, the station had broadcast a touching segment dramatizing how America was helping to liberate the women of Afghanistan. The piece was produced by the State Department and used interviews exclusively conducted, shot, and edited by its contractors to make the department's propagandistic points. The contractors also supplied the narration read by the local Memphis reporter who presented the segment, Tish Clark Dunning. Dunning told the *Times* that she had assumed that the piece was adapted from one originated by network correspondents at either Fox or CNN and had no idea that its actual provenance was the U.S. government.[31]

As these revelations piled up, the Government Accountability Office got on the case, repeatedly finding that the government-made "news" segments amounted to "covert propaganda," which is illegal. But the administration's lawyers circulated a memo challenging the GAO's legal judgment and instructing federal agencies simply to ignore it. So they did. Patricia Harrison, the assistant secretary of state (and former co-chairwoman of the Republican National Committee) who had publicly championed her department's fake-news segments from Afghanistan and Iraq (she preferred to label them "good news" segments), was rewarded with a promotion.[32] In 2005, with Karl Rove's blessing, she became president of the Corporation for Public Broadcasting, an even more powerful platform for producing propaganda. The "good news" that had worked so well on commercial stations such as WHBQ in Memphis could now be expanded to public television.

In 2006, the GAO said that the Bush administration had spent $1.6 billion on advertising and public relations just from 2003 through the second quarter of 2005.[33] Even that figure understated the extent of the propaganda. There was no way to quantify the fictionalizing in every corner of the administration, much of which came to light after the 2004 election. At NASA and NOAA (the National Oceanic and Atmospheric Administration), political appointees rewrote or censored public documents and agency speeches if they conveyed scientific findings about pollution and global warming that contradicted administration environmental policies.[34] One NASA appointee even enforced the addition of the word *theory* to any mention of the Big Bang in NASA materials, in keeping with the Christian right's rejection of evolutionary science.

That particular NASA henchman, a twenty-four-year-old former Bush campaign worker named George Deutsch, resigned after the press discovered that he had invented a Texas A&M bachelor's degree in journalism.[35] An administration propagandist, it seemed, could have credentials just as fake as "reporters" such as Karen Ryan.

But none of these hucksters was as theatrical as Jeff Gannon, who in February 2005 was unmasked after he let loose with a suspect question at a rare Bush press conference shortly after the inauguration. Speaking of the Democrats, Gannon asked the president, "How are you going to work with people who seem to have divorced themselves from reality?" Liberal bloggers, their curiosity aroused by such blatant partisanship from a reporter, soon discovered that Gannon wouldn't have known what reality was if it had slapped him in the face. His name was fake, and he worked for a fake news organization, Talon News, a Web operation with no known audience and staffed mostly by volunteer Republican activists. He also had a picturesque sideline as a two-hundred-dollar-an-hour escort on gay Web sites such as hotmilitarystud.com.

Like another partisan site called GOPUSA, Talon was owned by a Texas delegate to the 2000 Republican Convention. Its "news" was generally indistinguishable from press releases put out by the Republican National Committee and the White House. Talon didn't settle merely for being a passive mouthpiece of GOP spin. Early in the presidential campaign it had falsely confirmed a bogus Drudge Report rumor that a young woman had "taped an interview with one of the major television networks" to talk of an extramarital affair with John Kerry. (Kerry had to publicly deny the smear just as his campaign came out of the gate.) That was the kind of dirty trick only the Watergate criminal G. Gordon Liddy could have dreamed up. Or maybe did. The Talon owner, Bobby Eberle, had posted effusive thanks on the Web to both Liddy and Karl Rove for "their assistance, guidance and friendship."

How a man such as Gannon operating under a pseudonym—his real name was James D. Guckert—could repeatedly have entered the White House under the strictures of post-9/11 security was never convincingly explained. Though Scott McClellan told *Editor and Publisher* that he didn't know Gannon was an alias until just before the story broke, Bruce Bartlett, a White House veteran of the Reagan–Bush I era, said that "if Gannon was using an alias, the White House staff had to be involved in maintaining his cover."[36]

A close reading of the transcripts of televised White House press briefings over the preceding two years revealed that at uncannily crucial moments, "Jeff" was called on by McClellan to field softballs and stanch tough questioning on such topics as Abu Ghraib and Rove's possible involvement in the outing of the CIA officer Valerie Plame Wilson. The effect of his cameos was to turn the briefings into another variation on the canned "Ask the President" town hall meetings of the presidential campaign, at which preselected panelists asked Bush "questions" (sample: "Mr. President, as a child, how can I help you get votes?") before a preselected audience stocked with supporters. (Any stray skeptics were quickly removed.)

The White House was brilliant at making prefab town hall meetings and scripted press conferences alike simulate real, spontaneous give-and-take, at least to channel surfers catching just a video bite or two while clicking past television news. The administration continued the practice after the election with a sixty-stop "presidential road show" in which Bush had "conversations on Social Security" with "ordinary citizens" for the consumption of local and national newscasts. As in the president's phony town hall campaign appearances, the audiences were stacked with prescreened fans. But *The Washington Post* discovered that the preparations were even more elaborate than the finished product suggested; the seeming reality of the event was tweaked as fastidiously as that of a television reality show such as *The Apprentice.* Not only were the panelists recruited from among administration supporters, but they were rehearsed as much as five times the night before, with a White House official playing Bush.[37] Finalists who varied just slightly from the administration's pitch were banished from the cast at the last minute, like contestants on *American Idol.*

This presidential road show was the slickest version yet of a White House propaganda genre whose prototype dated back to Bush's scripted August 2002 "economic forum," where "so-called real Americans" (as Andrew Card called them) were paraded before TV cameras to deflect attention from the proliferating stories of the president's long relationship with Kenneth Lay of Enron. The more that was revealed about the White House's propaganda factory, the more it was apparent that Enron was the patron saint of the administration's fake news as much as of its energy policy. In the words of the documentary *The Smartest Guys in the Room,* Enron, too, was "fixated on its public relations campaigns." It browbeat the press and churned out slick PR videos as if it were a

Hollywood studio. In a typical ruse in 1998, a gaggle of employees rushed onto an empty trading floor at the company's headquarters to put on a fictional show of busy trading for visiting Wall Street analysts being escorted by Lay. "We brought some of our personal stuff, like pictures, to make it look like the area was lived in," a laid-off Enron employee told *The Wall Street Journal* in 2002. "We had to make believe we were on the phone buying and selling," even though "some of the computers didn't even work."

Like Enron's stockholders, American taxpayers paid for the production of the administration's Potemkin villages, even if the message, like that of the Enron show put on for visiting analysts, misrepresented and distorted the bottom line of the house of cards being sold. One PR giant, Ketchum Communications, that flacked for Arthur Andersen, the document-shredding Enron accounting firm destroyed by the scandal, cut the checks for Armstrong Williams and Karen Ryan at the Bush administration's behest. According to a report from congressional Democrats, Ketchum was paid at least $97 million in taxpayers' money for its various governmental services.[38]

It was perhaps inevitable that the White House would export these same propaganda schemes to Iraq, and sure enough, in 2005, an obscure Defense Department contractor, the Lincoln Group, was caught paying off Iraqi journalists to run upbeat news articles (e.g., "The Sands Are Blowing Toward a Democratic Iraq") secretly written by American army personnel and translated into Arabic (at a time when American troops in harm's way were woefully short of Arabic translators of their own). One of the papers publishing the fake news was *Al Mutamar*, the Baghdad daily run by associates of Ahmad Chalabi.[39] This consistency was impressive: as Chalabi, in association with the Rendon Group, helped feed spurious accounts of Saddam's WMDs to American newspapers to gin up the war, so his minions, in association with the Lincoln Group, helped disseminate happy talk to his own country's press to further the illusion that the war was being won even as the insurgency raged unchecked.

The Lincoln Group's various contracts, some of them from the Psychological Operations unit at the Pentagon, were worth more than $130 million, but the origins of the group were as mysterious as the career of the talented Mr. Gannon. Its founders were two thirty-ish hustlers who flaunted their flamboyantly wealthy Washington lifestyle, bragged about connections they didn't have, and hired two lobbying firms to get federal business. One of the men,

Christian Bailey, had had at least four companies since 2002, most of them in-
terlocking, short-lived, and under phantom names. But he had also been involved in Republican fund-raising, which was enough for him to get on the
government's fake-news gravy train. The Pentagon promptly announced an investigation, which months later determined that the Lincoln Group's activities
had violated no law or policy. By then, Rumsfeld had given his own stamp of
approval, applauding the fake news as a "non-traditional means" of providing
"accurate information" to the Iraqi people. He did not explain how placing
camouflaged American propaganda in Iraqi papers could be squared with the
professed American mission of exporting democratic freedoms, including that
of a free and independent press.

IF THERE WAS a single scene that captured the surreal ambience of official
Washington in the Bush years at the moment just before the administration
lost control of public opinion, the press, and its agenda, it would be the White
House Correspondents Association dinner of 2005. Held in the vast ballroom
of the Washington Hilton, the dinner is an annual fête at which journalists
mingle with sources and celebrities and play host to the president, who is then
required to be "funny." Once, these dinners were just typical Washington
rubber-chicken fare, unseen on television and unnoticed beyond the Beltway.
That began to change in 1987, when Michael Kelly, then a reporter for *The Bal-
timore Sun*, invited as a guest Fawn Hall, the glamorous mystery woman in the
Iran-Contra scandal. Over the years, Kelly's amusing prank metastasized into
a pageant of obsequiousness and TV Land glitz, typified by the 2005 roster of
A-list stars from the 1970s (e.g., Goldie Hawn, Mary Tyler Moore) and C-list
publicity hounds from the present (e.g., an axed contestant from *American
Idol*). As the gaggle arrived via red carpet, it was hard to know which was worse:
watching reporters suck up to politicians in power or watching them clamber
to rub shoulders with Joe Pantoliano.

Kelly was at the 2005 banquet only as a ghost. A widely beloved writer and
editor, he had been killed at age forty-six in the early weeks of Operation Iraqi
Freedom, which he strongly supported, while covering it for *The Atlantic
Monthly*. Two years had passed since then, and as it happened, this year's dinner was held on the eve of the second anniversary of George Bush's celebra-

tion of the end of major combat operations on the USS *Abraham Lincoln* less than a month after Kelly's death.

The night's headline act was the First Lady, who in an obvious bit of staged business, got up from her seat on the dais and "interrupted" her husband just as he was launching into a monologue. He returned to his seat, clearing the way for her to do a stand-up routine of her own. The mere sight of Laura Bush playacting at "interrupting" her husband prompted the ballroom full of reporters to leap to their feet and erupt in a roar of sycophancy like partisan hacks at a political convention. When the First Lady proceeded to tell a mildly off-color joke involving her husband, a horse, and masturbation, the audience responded as if Mae West had come back from the dead. The same throng's morning-after rave reviews—reminiscent of those that followed the president's *Top Gun* showboating—acknowledged that the entire exercise was at some level PR but nonetheless bought into the artifice. We were seeing the real Laura Bush, they said. While some observers acknowledged that her script was written by a speechwriter (the genuinely gifted Landon Parvin), very few noted that the routine's most humanizing populist riff, Mrs. Bush's proclaimed affection for the runaway new television hit *Desperate Housewives,* was fiction; her press secretary told *The New York Times*'s Elisabeth Bumiller that the First Lady had yet to watch it.

The press corps' eagerness to facilitate and serve as dress extras in what amounted to an administration promotional video was a metaphor for just how much the reality-based community had been co-opted by Bush's own reality over the past four years. Though the defrocked fake White House correspondent Jeff Gannon was absent from the correspondents' dinner, he did turn up that weekend on Bill Maher's new HBO comedy show, where he told a rehearsed joke of his own in response to a question about his moonlighting as a sex-site escort: "Usually the way it works is people become reporters before they prostitute themselves." It was a more cutting line than perhaps he even knew.

It was also on that weekend—on the exact "Mission Accomplished" anniversary of May 1—that *The Sunday Times* of London published a scoop: the text of what would become known as the "Downing Street memo." The memo was the secret minutes of a July 2002 meeting attended by the British prime minister, Tony Blair, and his top brass, at which Sir Richard Dearlove, the chief of British intelligence, reported on his recent visit with Washington's counterparts. Dearlove, identified in the memo as "C," said that the White House was already determined to go to war, and was working to make sure that "the intelligence and facts" could be "fixed around the policy." The malleable intelligence and facts, of course, pertained to Saddam's WMDs.

In retrospect, this nearly three-year-old memo explained much that had happened thereafter, starting with the White House insistence on overruling Hans Blix and all America's allies (except England) by refusing to allow the UN weapons inspectors to finish their job in Iraq. Yet the same White House press corps that had eagerly disseminated Laura Bush's shtick showed scant interest in the Downing Street memo. In the nineteen daily Scott McClellan briefings that followed, it was the subject of only 2 out of the approximately 940 questions asked, as calculated by Eric Boehlert of *Salon*. No mainstream American paper published its text in full; that was left to *The New York Review of Books* and the Internet.

But the press's post-9/11 docility was coming to an end. In the weeks to come, the Bush presidency would begin its slide into terminal dysfunction. The summer of 2005 brought a perfect storm of catalysts that led to this unraveling: an annoying leak scandal that wouldn't go away, a histrionic antiwar protestor who wouldn't shut up, and a devastating actual storm that dominated the White House's favored propaganda medium of television. In one way or another, all these developments had to do with Iraq. In one way or another, each of them either provoked or shamed the more somnolent brigades of the news media into action. But it was the confluence of all these stories simultaneously that shifted history's gears as they had not been shifted since September 11, 2001.

TEN

"I DON'T THINK ANYBODY ANTICIPATED..."

THE SUMMER OF 2005 arrived with more dire tidings for the administration about the war. Though Dick Cheney said in a Memorial Day interview on CNN that the insurgency in Iraq was in its "last throes," the public wasn't buying it. In June, for the first time, a *Washington Post*/ABC News poll found that a majority of Americans believed that the war in Iraq had not made the United States safer. Whether or not they'd read the Downing Street memo leaked to *The Sunday Times* of London the previous month, a majority also now believed that the administration had "intentionally misled" America into the war. Gallup found that a clear majority (59 percent) wanted to withdraw some or all American troops from Iraq. Most Americans were telling pollsters that the war wasn't "worth it," and the top reasons they cited, said *USA Today*, included "fraudulent claims and no weapons of mass destruction found" and "the belief that Iraq posed no threat to the United States." Even the conservative Republican congressman who had pushed the House cafeteria to rename French fries "freedom fries" (Walter B. Jones of North Carolina), out of anger over France's opposition to the war, was starting to argue for withdrawal.[1]

To try to shore up support, the president gave a new prime-time speech, from Fort Bragg, North Carolina. But with the rhetorical arsenal of WMDs and mushroom clouds now bare, he had little choice but to bring back that oldie but goodie, 9/11, as the specter of doom that awaited America if it didn't stay the course—his course—in Iraq. By the fifth mention of 9/11, it was hard not to think of that legendary *National Lampoon* cover: "If You Don't Buy This Magazine, We'll Kill This Dog."

The military audience was mute, lending the exercise a sepulchral aura of doom. No one was certain whether the troops remained silent because they had been instructed to be so, but whatever the explanation, theirs was the perfect dazed response to what was literally a summer rerun. The president had given almost the identical televised address, albeit with four fewer 9/11 references, at the U.S. Army War College in Pennsylvania in May 2004.

This time fewer TV viewers tuned in than for any prime-time speech in Bush's presidency.[2] He had no one to blame but himself. The color-coded terror alerts, the repeated press conferences announcing imminent Armageddon during election season, the endless exploitation of 9/11 had all taken their numbing toll. Overplaying the fear card, the president had become the boy who cried wolf.

It was probably just as well his audience had dwindled; his speech was a cornucopia of misinformation. He exaggerated the number of coalition partners in Iraq, the number of battle-ready Iraqi troops, and the amount of non-American dollars in the Iraq kitty. He pledged to "prevent Al Qaeda and other foreign terrorists from turning Iraq into what Afghanistan was under the Taliban"—a week after *Newsweek* and *The New York Times* reported on a new CIA assessment that the war was turning Iraq into an even more effective magnet and training ground for Islamic militants than Afghanistan was for Al Qaeda in the 1980s and '90s.[3]

Bush was also shifting, none too subtly, the nature of the mission that had been or would be accomplished in Iraq, defining it down from concrete victory to the inchoate spreading of democracy. Once we were locked into the war, and no WMDs could be found, the original plot line had been dropped with an alacrity that recalled the "Never mind!" with which Gilda Radner's Emily Litella used to end her misinformed *Weekend Update* commentaries on *Saturday Night Live*. But Bush's abrupt switch, from sounding like Patton at the start of the war to parroting Woodrow Wilson now, didn't play; it was tantamount to ambushing an audience at a John Wayne movie with a final reel by Frank Capra.

The fireworks that would complete the demolition of the administration's credibility on the war began right after the Fourth of July 2005. After an eighteen-month hiatus, during which it had been unfolding out of view, the case of who leaked the identity of Joseph Wilson's CIA-agent wife suddenly resurfaced. Patrick Fitzgerald, the special counsel who had taken over the investigation from Ashcroft's Justice Department, succeeded in persuading a federal judge in Washington to send *New York Times* reporter Judith Miller to jail for refusing to name a confidential source that Fitzgerald regarded as essential to his investigation. That one of their own was in the slammer got the press's attention. That Miller had never written a story about Wilson or his wife, Valerie Plame Wilson, as the un-jailed syndicated columnist Robert Novak had, only added to the intrigue. Novak didn't try to resolve the mystery; he refused to explain why or how he had been dealt a get-out-of-jail-free card.

Matt Cooper, a *Time* reporter also in Fitzgerald's sights, avoided Miller's fate by cutting a last-minute deal with his own confidential source, freeing himself to testify before the grand jury. The source was Karl Rove, who had bad-mouthed Wilson and discussed his wife in a July 2003 phone conversation just as the former diplomat was going public about his prewar mission to Niger in search of Saddam's nonexistent uranium transaction. Wilson had always said that Rove was a likely source of the leak of his wife's CIA identity, and so he was, though he ultimately escaped indictment. Trashing adversaries was in Rove's nature, and bad things happened, usually through under-the-radar whispers, to decent people (and their wives) who got in his way. Just as Ann Richards was besieged by rumors that she was a lesbian during Bush's campaign to unseat her as Texas governor in 1994, so John McCain was rumored to be mentally unstable and his wife a drug addict during the 2000 South Carolina primary.[4] The implication that Wilson was a wimp beholden to largesse from his wife, who had suggested him to the CIA for his (nonpaying) Niger mission, was of a thematic piece with the 2004 Bush campaign's takedown of John Kerry. The Democrat's marriage to the wealthy and hard-driving Teresa Heinz Kerry was frequently evoked by the Bush attack troops as a sign that Bush's opponent was a girlie-man.

The difference this time was that Rove got caught, and that put the White House in an excruciating bind. In 2003 both Scott McClellan and Rove had denied that he had had anything to do with leaking Valerie Plame Wilson's identity. The president had vowed to fire anyone involved with the leak. But now Rove was not being fired, and McClellan was stonewalling. The press smelled blood and started badgering the White House press secretary in the White House briefing room, prompting Jon Stewart to observe that the White House press corps had been "secretly replaced . . . with actual reporters."

A cascade of revelations followed, filling in a behind-the-scenes drama that hadn't been visible two years earlier in the frantic administration bobbing and weaving that began with the publication of Wilson's whistle-blowing Op-Ed about the Niger uranium and ended five days later with George Tenet's official recantation of the sixteen words in Bush's State of the Union speech. On July 7, 2003, the day after Wilson's Op-Ed, the president had left for his African trip, and Wilson was clearly a topic for concern as Bush and his entourage departed. Though Ari Fleischer had publicly dismissed Wilson's revelation as "nothing new," a heretofore-unknown State Department memo that began to circulate within the administration that day said otherwise. *The Washington Post* now revealed that the memo, which Colin Powell had been seen holding in his hand as he boarded Air Force One, was a backgrounder on the history of the White House's African uranium claim, and that in its second paragraph, marked with an *S*, Wilson's wife was identified as a CIA officer, the "secret" designation being standard for CIA operatives whose identities are covert.[5] In the three days that followed there were at least four conversations about Wilson and his CIA-agent wife between officials back in Washington and reporters: Libby, Cheney's chief of staff, talked to Miller and Cooper. Rove spoke with Novak and Cooper. Rove's phone conversation with Cooper ended with a mysterious sign off: "I've already said too much."[6]

But even now much of the Washington establishment dismissed the whole case as a lot of fuss over business-as-usual in a town that thrived on leaks. The blasé Beltway attitude about the Plame story was exemplified by Bob Woodward, the scrappy reporter of the Watergate era whose later books were better known for their access to power than their investigation of it. When "all of the facts come out in this case," he told Terry Gross of NPR on July 7, 2005, "it's going to be laughable because the consequences are not that great." The leak case—indeed Valerie Plame Wilson herself—was never mentioned in the four-hundred-plus pages of his latest book on the Bush administration, *Plan of Attack*, even though the case had first exploded more than six months before Woodward completed the book. The Wilsons were nobodies—not players, not part of the tight club to which Woodward and his blue-chip sources belonged.

Yet while Woodward was tone-deaf to the Watergate echoes in the Bush White House's obsessive secrecy, in its detestation of the press, and in its flouting of the law, the parallels were striking to anyone outside the Beltway. After the unmasking of Rove's role, the Bush White House started reading literally from the Nixon script: "I am saying that if anyone was involved in that type of activity which I referred to, they would not be working here," said Ron Ziegler, Nixon's press secretary, when defending the presidential aide Dwight Chapin in 1972, two years before Chapin was convicted of perjury. In his desperation to come up with language to defend Rove, now that the previous denials of Rove's involvement with the leak were inoperative, McClellan said much the same: "Any individual who works here at the White House has the confidence of the president. They wouldn't be working here at the White House if they didn't have the president's confidence."

But this scandal didn't begin, as Watergate had, simply with dirty tricks and spying on the political opposition. It began with the sending of American men and women to war in Iraq on false pretenses. The administration knew how guilty it was. That's why it so quickly trashed any insiders who contradicted its story line about how America got to Iraq, starting with former treasury secretary Paul O'Neill and former counterterrorism czar Richard Clarke. The disproportionality and pettiness of the White House's retribution against Wilson—who was a minor courtier, a Rosencrantz or Guildenstern, compared with the previous insiders who spoke up—revealed just how much he threatened the administration. Uranium had been the sexiest card that Bush and Cheney played in the run-up to the war, and by calling attention to how they overstated the certainty of the nuclear threat, Wilson undermined the legitimacy of the war on which the Bush presidency was staked. The White House pushback against Wilson was a replay of the gangster tactics of the Watergate felon Charles Colson, whose hit men broke into the office of Daniel Ellsberg's psychiatrist, seeking information to smear Ellsberg after the military analyst leaked the Pentagon Papers, the classified history of the Vietnam War, to *The New York Times*. But there was even greater incentive to smear Wilson than there had been with Ellsberg. Nixon compounded the Vietnam fiasco but he didn't start it. The war in Iraq, by contrast, was Bush's invention.

Though there were no plumbers searching for any Wilson psychiatric records, the Bush crusade against the former diplomat was no less intense. A Fitzgerald court filing in the leak case recounted "a strong desire by many, including multiple people in the White House" to further "a plan to discredit, punish or seek revenge against Mr. Wilson."[7]

Following the Watergate template, the Bush administration had first tried to bury the whole Wilson affair—disdaining the importance of the leak of Valerie Plame Wilson's identity much as the Nixon White House had tried to downsize its scandal into a "third-rate burglary." For three months after the leak, there was no investigation at all. When the CIA ordered an investigation, the next stage of denial for the Bush White House, like the Nixon administration, was to try to finesse the scandal by investigating itself. It kept the inquiry safely confined within the Ashcroft Justice Department, with the attorney general receiving regular briefings on its findings. It was at the start of that honeymoon, which lasted another three months, that McClellan declared Rove and Libby innocent of the leak and that Bush said, "I don't know of anybody in my administration who leaked classified information." But as the Nixon Justice Department ultimately had to relinquish its control of the Watergate investigation to the first special prosecutor, Archibald Cox, so Bush's Justice Department had to surrender to Fitzgerald.

Only after the special counsel took over the leak case did investigators start to hustle, seeking Air Force One phone logs and compelling Bush to hire a private lawyer. But by then the conspirators, drunk with the hubris characteristic of the administration, had long been quite sloppy about what they told the authorities. Rove's flat on-camera denial to ABC News of any knowledge of the leak had come, embarrassingly enough, just hours before the Justice Department announced the initial investigation.

The Bush White House had been too arrogant to heed the most basic lesson of Watergate: the cover-up is worse than the crime. Inevitably, and again repeating history, Fitzgerald moved beyond the original alleged illegality, a violation of the Intelligence Identities Protection Act, to prosecute perjury and obstruction of justice by those who had tried to stifle the investigation during those six months before he arrived in Dodge.

The Washington establishment that thought the case was trivial didn't get what it was about and was often distracted by secondary dramas. One of the most inviting of these offshoots was the saga of Judith Miller, who, more than any other reporter, had lent journalistic credence to the administration's prewar WMD rollout with repeated stories whose sourcing was suspect and which the *Times* had overplayed. To the left, her martyrdom in the Plame case was either a cynical attempt to redeem her image and atone for those sins or, worse—according to the blogger Arianna Huffington—an effort to cover up Miller's own culpability as an accomplice in the White House's retributive leaking of Valerie Plame Wilson's name. When Miller finally got the personal waiver she wanted from her source and left prison after eighty-five days of incarceration, it only confirmed her most fervent detractors' theories about her motives. The source, soon to be indicted for obstruction of justice and perjury, was Lewis Libby, the insider's insider, "Cheney's Cheney."

Unlike Robert Novak, Miller was not an accomplice in the leaking of Valerie Plame Wilson's identity, however. But Miller was a Pulitzer Prize–winning diva with an action-packed history and vehement friends and detractors in prominent places. Jail had made her a celebrity. Her credulous WMD reporting lingered like a foul odor around both her and the most influential newspaper in the country. All of this combined to make a combustible package that kept her in the spotlight—so much so that to some critics, Miller loomed so large that she and the *Times* were almost single-handedly responsible for fomenting the invasion of Iraq.

She loomed large to the White House, too. At the same July 8, 2003, hotel breakfast during which Libby told Miller about Valerie Plame Wilson's identity, he also gave her selected information from the still-classified prewar National Intelligence Estimate on Iraq that he said backed up the administration's claims about WMDs. Though the Libby-Miller meeting took place the same day that the front page of *The Washington Post* told of the "senior Bush administration official" who said the African uranium should have been kept out of Bush's State of the Union address,[8] the message the White House sent through Libby to Miller was exactly the reverse. Libby told Miller that the NIE said that

Iraq was "vigorously trying to procure" uranium,[9] a distortion that belied caveats within the document's ninety-odd pages indicating that the claim was "highly dubious."

But this time, at least, Miller was not a patsy for the administration's cherry-picking and hyping of intelligence. Just as she did not write a story about what she had learned about Valerie Plame Wilson during that meeting, so she never wrote about Libby's selective intelligence leak either.

In the end, the leak scandal was not principally about Miller or Novak, useful dupes though they may have been for the White House on occasion. Nor was this story really about Wilson, whom White House surrogates attacked as a partisan and a liar as vehemently as liberals attacked Miller. Each of these secondary characters and their plot lines was, in Alfred Hitchcock's famous parlance, a MacGuffin, which, as defined by the *Oxford English Dictionary,* is "a particular event, object, factor, etc., initially presented as being of great significance to the story, but often having little actual importance for the plot as it develops." For that matter, Wilson's mission to Niger to check out Saddam's supposed attempts to score uranium and even his wife's outing had little more to do with the real story than Janet Leigh's theft of office cash does with the mayhem that ensues at the Bates Motel in *Psycho.*

The leak case was about Iraq, not Niger. The political stakes were high only because the scandal was about the unmasking of an ill-conceived war, not the unmasking of a CIA operative who posed for *Vanity Fair.* The real crime was the sending of American men and women to war on fictitious grounds. The real victims were the American people, not the Wilsons. The real culprits—the big enchilada, in John Ehrlichman's Nixon White House lingo—were not the leakers but those who provoked a war in Iraq for their own motives and in so doing diverted finite resources, human and otherwise, from the fight against those who did attack America on 9/11, and had since regrouped to deadly effect (so far) in Madrid and London. Without Iraq, there never would have been a smear campaign against an obscure diplomat or the bungled cover-up that ensnared Libby and Rove. While the Bush White House's dirty tricks, like Nixon's, were prompted in part by a ruthless desire to crush the political competition at any cost, this administration had upped the ante by playing dirty tricks with war. And those were the chickens now coming home to roost.

Back on July 6, 2003, when Wilson first went public on the *Times* Op-Ed page about his mission to Niger, Novak echoed the Nixon administration's early dismissal of Watergate as a "third-rate burglary"; the uranium matter was just one of those "little elitist issues that don't bother most of the people," he said. But then the American casualty toll in Iraq stood at 169. Now it was over 1,700 and the mission had not been remotely accomplished. That did bother most people.

No debate about the past, of course, could undo the mess that the administration made in Iraq. But the past remained important because it was a road map to the present. Following the uranium in the leak case served the same purpose as following the money had in Watergate: it led to the top of the White House organization chart. The public was beginning to realize that the leaders who had dissembled in the run-up to the war were still in place, still dissembling. Bush and Cheney continued to routinely exaggerate the readiness of Iraqi troops, much as they once inflated Saddam's WMDs, and still engaged in semantic games in which, in Cheney's words, those who attacked America on 9/11 were indistinguishable from insurgents "making a stand in Iraq."

What also made Fitzgerald's investigation compelling as it dragged on was that, in bits and pieces, both it and the renewed investigative journalism surrounding it gradually helped fill in the übernarrative about the march to war. The leak case became a very big window into the genesis of the smoke screen (or, more accurately, mushroom cloud) that the White House used to sell the mission in Iraq.

Up until then, the administration's cover-up of its con job had been impressive. There had been two separate official investigations into the failure of prewar intelligence that with great fanfare and to great acclaim found that American information about Saddam's WMDs, far from being what George Tenet called "slam dunk," had been, as one of the two concluded, "dead wrong." But neither investigation answered the question of how the administration used that wrong intelligence in selling the war, and wittingly or unwittingly, both of these ostensibly thorough inquiries actually protected the White House.

In March 2005, the 601-page report from a special presidential commission led by Laurence Silberman and Charles Robb was hailed as a "sharp critique" by Bush, but contained only a passing mention of Cheney. It made no mention whatsoever of Douglas Feith, the first-term undersecretary of defense for policy, who supervised a rogue intelligence operation in the Pentagon that—in an end run around the CIA, State Department intelligence, and the Defense Intelligence Agency—supplied the vice president with cherry-picked intelligence for his false claims about Iraq. An earlier investigation into prewar intelligence, by the Senate Intelligence Committee, was a scandal in its own right. After the release of its initial findings in July 2004, the committee's Republican chairman, Pat Roberts, promised that a phase two to determine if the White House had misled the public would arrive after the presidential election. More than a year later, it still hadn't. "I don't think there should be any doubt that we have now heard it all regarding prewar intelligence," Senator Roberts concluded upon the release of the Silberman-Robb report. "I think that it would be a monumental waste of time to re-plow this ground any further."[10]

Bush and Cheney repeatedly claimed they'd been exonerated by both commissions. But as the Fitzgerald investigation accelerated, so did the leak of documents saying otherwise. Journalists connected the dots, refuting both the hysterical White House claims about Iraq before the war and its subsequent efforts to scapegoat the CIA or otherwise deflect blame for its misuse of intelligence. It was increasingly obvious that even Joseph Wilson's trip to Africa was at most a footnote to the larger story. Had he never gone to Niger, there were still countless other warning signs, all of them with more official weight than a report from a former ambassador, telling the White House that its steady prewar litany of mushroom clouds and Iraq-Qaeda collaborations was quite possibly bunk. Yet none of these red flags deterred the administration from pounding dubious evidence into Americans' heads.

An investigation in the *Los Angeles Times* found that Bush and his aides kept pumping up their grim warnings about Iraq's mobile biological weapons labs long after U.S. intelligence authorities were told by Germany's Federal Intelligence Service that the principal source for these warnings, an Iraqi defector in German custody code-named Curveball, "never claimed to produce germ weapons and never saw anyone else do so."[11] Murray Waas, writing in the *National Journal,* reported that the President's Daily Brief ten days after 9/11, seen by Bush, Cheney, Rice, Rumsfeld, Wolfowitz, and Powell (among others), said there was no evidence that Iraq had had a role in the attacks and that there was "scant credible evidence" of "significant collaborative ties" between Saddam and Al Qaeda, not least because the dictator considered "theocratic radical Islamist organizations" a threat to his secular regime and wanted, if anything, to infiltrate them with his own spies.[12] (In other words, Saddam's antipathy to Islamic radicals was the same in 2001 as it had been in 1983, when Rumsfeld, then a Reagan administration emissary, embraced the dictator as a secular fascist ally in the American struggle against the theocratic fascist rulers in Iran.) A Defense Intelligence Agency report in February 2002 included documents saying that Ibn al-Shaykh al-Libi, the "top member of Al Qaeda" in American custody and the source of administration claims of Iraq-Qaeda collaboration on WMD training, was likely to be "intentionally misleading the debriefers" with fictional scenarios "he knows will retain their interest."[13] Yet thirteen months later, just ten days before the war, Rice cited that detainee when selling one of his scary fictional scenarios yet one more time, on CBS's *Face the Nation.*

And it wasn't just Wilson who had raised doubts about the purported uranium transaction between Iraq and Niger long before the fateful sixteen words appeared in the 2003 State of the Union address; so had a State Department intelligence analyst. A part of the October 2002 National Intelligence Estimate that Libby did *not* leak to Miller told of the State Department's caveat that "claims of Iraqi pursuit of natural uranium in Africa," by then made public by the British, were "highly dubious," echoing a CIA assessment that "the evidence is weak" and "the Africa story is overblown."[14] The NIE also said that the State Department accepted "the judgment of technical experts at the U.S. Department of Energy" that the aluminum tubes reported by Miller in the September 8, 2002, *Times* and trumpeted on that morning's Sunday talk shows by Cheney, Powell, and Rice were "poorly suited for use in gas centrifuges to be used for uranium enrichment" and were more likely to be used for the conventional weaponry of artillery rockets.[15]

This outpouring of revelations showed that the prewar intelligence was not uniformly dead wrong after all. It was merely the intelligence that the administration chose to overstate, leak to willing journalists, and repeatedly broadcast to the public that consistently proved to be dead wrong.

There was an assembly line for producing and publicizing much of this erroneous evidence about Saddam's capabilities and plans. The first work station was the Policy Counterterrorism Evaluation Group, that rogue Pentagon intelligence operation inside Feith's Office of Special Plans and specifically mandated by Cheney and Libby to mine apocalyptic Iraqi scenarios, especially those involving Iraq-Qaeda "connections." This was the unnamed special unit that had first surfaced in newspaper accounts to little notice in October 2002, but that had somehow escaped the notice of the Silberman-Robb presidential commission on prewar intelligence.

In late 2005 and early 2006, former government officials who had witnessed the Feith operation firsthand finally started speaking out about it. Colonel Lawrence Wilkerson, Powell's chief of staff at the State Department, gave a speech in Washington blasting what he called a Cheney-Rumsfeld "cabal" that produced unprecedented "aberrations, bastardizations, perturbations, changes to the national security decision-making process." He and Powell had spent the night before the Secretary of State's UN presentation trying to throw out as much of the bogus Feith material as they could. "Seldom in my life have I met a dumber man" than Feith, said Wilkerson, seconding the motion of the commander Tommy Franks, who had told Bob Woodward in an interview for *Plan of Attack* that Feith was "the fucking stupidest guy on the face of the earth."

Even more devastating was Paul R. Pillar, the first top CIA official to speak out so critically by name about what he had witnessed. Though he had been national intelligence officer for the Middle East from 2000 to 2005, and in charge of coordinating all intelligence assessments on Iraq, he had not received a request from any administration policy maker for such an assessment "until a year into the war," he wrote in the March/April 2006 *Foreign Affairs*. It was Congress, not the White House, that had requested "the now-infamous October 2002 National Intelligence Estimate (NIE) on Iraq's unconventional weapons programs" (though, Pillar noted, "few members of Congress actually read it").[16]

Pillar was particularly outraged by the administration's hawking of ties between Saddam and Al Qaeda. The "selective use of raw intelligence," he wrote, could be used to link anyone to anyone else "if enough effort is made to find evidence of casual contacts, the mentioning of names in the same breath, or indications of common travels or experiences." Though "the intelligence community never offered any analysis that supported the notion of an alliance between Saddam and Al Qaeda," it was "drawn into a public effort to support that notion." Pillar concluded that "the administration used intelligence not to inform decision-making, but to justify a decision already made."

But the distorted intelligence abetted by the Policy Counterterrorism Evaluation Group was only the first step in the White House process of fomenting its war. The product needed a distributor, and that's where the White House Iraq Group, or WHIG, came in. WHIG had been first disclosed in the summer of 2003, after "Mission Accomplished," by Barton Gellman and Walter Pincus of *The Washington Post*,[17] again to little notice.

The group was convened in August 2002, seven months before the invasion of Iraq, by Andrew Card, the White House chief of staff. Its eight members included Rove, Rice, the spinmeisters Karen Hughes and Mary Matalin—and again Libby. WHIG's mission was to market a war in Iraq, but the official Bush story line had it that no decision had yet been made on the war in August 2002. Dates bracketing the formation of WHIG say otherwise. July 23, 2002—a week or two before WHIG first convened in earnest—was the date of the meeting described in the Downing Street memo, during which the head of British intelligence told his peers that the Bush administration was ensuring that "the intelligence and facts" about Iraq's WMDs "were being fixed around the policy" of going to war. On September 6, 2002—just a few weeks after WHIG first convened—Card alluded to his group's existence by hinting of the plan afoot to market a war against Saddam Hussein: "From a marketing point of view, you don't introduce new products in August." The mushroom clouds and smoking guns came rolling off the assembly line to be showcased on Sunday morning talk shows and in presidential speeches immediately thereafter.

The national security journalist James Bamford, writing in *Rolling Stone*, filled in another part of the story by revisiting the role of the Rendon Group. Rendon had been a contractor for the Pentagon's short-lived Office of Strategic Influence—the office set up to plant phony "news" with foreign media, which had been shut down by Rumsfeld after a hail of criticism following its exposure in *The New York Times* in February 2002. Bamford learned that many of the office's operations were simply diverted to another office, the Information Operations Task Force, "deeper in the Pentagon's bureaucracy" and also connected to Rendon, which had received at least thirty-five contracts with the Defense Department for a total of fifty to one hundred million dollars between 2000 and 2004. Rendon had created the exile organization the Iraqi National Congress after the first Persian Gulf War and had put Ahmad Chalabi, then in London, in charge of it. In at least one case, Rendon abetted the INC in supplying one of the many defectors whose delusional, often coached accounts of

Saddam's WMDs turned up in prewar newspaper stories and whose scenarios continued to be publicized by those in WHIG well after they had been questioned or disproved by U.S. intelligence agencies.[18]

In 2006 a newly surfaced memo recounting a private January 31, 2003, meeting of Bush, Tony Blair, and other top officials indicated just how important this supply of dubious defectors was to the White House propaganda push: the president proposed using one of them to give a public presentation about Saddam's WMDs, if needed to further whip up war fever. At the same meeting, Bush also raised the possibility of flying a U-2 reconnaissance plane painted in UN colors over Iraq to provoke Saddam to fire on Americans and thus fall into breach of UN resolutions.[19]

"Why would the U.S. president and the British prime minister spend any time concocting ways of provoking a material breach if they knew they could prove Saddam had weapons of mass destruction?" asked Philippe Sands, the British professor of international law who first wrote about this new memo in a 2006 edition of his book *Lawless World*.[20] The memo, written by David Manning, the former foreign policy adviser to Blair, was yet another smoking gun confirming that the president knew before the war that his own smoking guns about Iraq WMDs were toy pistols. Another, equally damning document was a one-page summary of the National Intelligence Estimate written specifically for Bush in October 2002 and uncovered by Murray Waas in March 2006 just as the Manning memo was emerging. The summary presented to Bush included the State and Energy Department reservations about the aluminum tubes, proving that the president knew about the uncertainty of that piece of the nuclear WMD evidence months before he plugged it unequivocally in his 2003 State of the Union address.[21] Perhaps most damning of all was the April 2006 revelation by Barton Gellman and Dafna Linzer of *The Washington Post* that the National Intelligence Council, the senior coordinating body for all fifteen U.S. intelligence agencies, had unequivocally branded the Niger story as baseless in a memo also seen by the White House in January as Bush prepared to say the opposite in his State of the Union address.[22]

"WMD—I got it totally wrong," said Judy Miller, co-author of the original *Times* article on the tubes, after she left jail. She retired from the *Times* when the controversy surrounding her, including in the paper's newsroom, refused to abate. Among its other side effects, the Wilson story exposed the gullibility with which she and others in the press had either actively pushed or passively rubber-stamped the White House plot line that any delay in invading Iraq would bring nuclear Armageddon.

But Miller, who had been wrongly accused by the left of leaking Valerie Plame Wilson's identity, had not even been the first to be leaked to. That turned out to be Bob Woodward, who revealed after Miller was out of jail that he had learned of Wilson's CIA connection days ahead of Miller and weeks before Matt Cooper and had kept this news a secret from his own newspaper and the public for more than two years.[23] Miller may have been the diva of Plamegate, but Woodward is the Zelig of the Bush presidency. It was hard to imagine the driven reporter of the Nixon era failing to tell his editors that he had his own personal Deep Throat in a story that was consuming the capital. His public explanation was that he wanted to avoid a subpoena, but that didn't add up: he learned about Valerie Plame Wilson in mid-June 2003, more than six months before Patrick Fitzgerald or subpoenas entered the picture.

Woodward continued to belittle the story he'd left completely out of his book. "I don't know how this is about the buildup to the war, the Valerie Plame Wilson issue," he said on *Larry King Live* on the eve of the Scooter Libby indictment. If one assumes, as Woodward apparently did, against mounting evidence to the contrary, that the White House acted in good faith when purveying its claims of imminent doomsday and pre-9/11 Qaeda-Saddam collaborations, then there's no White House wrongdoing that needs to be covered up. So why would anyone in the administration try to do something nasty to silence a whistle-blower like Joseph Wilson? Where's the story? The West Wing was merely gossiping idly about the guy, Woodward said, in perhaps an unconscious echo of the Karl Rove defense strategy in the leak case.

In *Plan of Attack*, Woodward does write of lobbying to get a dissenting Walter Pincus story about WMDs into the *Post* before the war began. But that story, headlined "U.S. Lacks Specifics on Banned Arms," was too late (three days before the bombing began), watered down, and buried (on page A17). More revealing than that tardy gesture of Woodward's was the outspoken support he received in the controversy over his behavior in the leak case from Mary Matalin, the former Cheney flack who helped shape WHIG's war propaganda. Asked by Howard Kurtz of the *Post* why "an administration not known for being fond of the press put so much effort into cooperating with Woodward," Matalin responded that he does "an extraordinary job" and that "it's in the White House's interest to have a neutral source writing the history of the way Bush makes decisions."[24]

That some of what Woodward wrote was "in the White House's interest" had to be the understatement of the year. Dubious cherry-picked intelligence from the Feith-WHIG conveyor belt ended up in *Plan of Attack* before that information was declassified—including an account of a January 2003 briefing in which Libby told top White House officials of Saddam WMD programs that Powell and Tenet would reject as bogus. No wonder Matalin thought Woodward had done "an extraordinary job." The WHIG gang had spun him silly. Though near the end of *Plan of Attack* Woodward refers to hearing some "troubling" cavils about the prewar intelligence, they were old news and had long since been reported elsewhere by the time the book was published, in April 2004. "In the light of subsequent events, I should have pushed for a front page story, even on the eve of war, presenting more forcefully what our sources were saying," he wrote, as sort of a modified limited mea culpa.

Reporters who did not have Woodward's or Miller's top-level access within the administration not only got the Iraq story right but got it into newspapers early by seeking out what John Walcott, the Knight Ridder Washington bureau chief, called "the blue collar" sources further down the hierarchy.[25] Woodward and Miller's papers had such reporters, too, typified by Walter Pincus and James Risen, but their voices were often lost in the WMD din. In his critique of the *Times* coverage, Dan Okrent, the first public editor appointed by the paper as part of its post–Jayson Blair reforms, wrote that errant WMD reportage was often "inappropriately italicized by lavish front-page display and heavy-breathing headlines" while "several fine articles by David Johnston, James Risen and others that provided perspective or challenged information in the faulty stories were played as quietly as a lullaby." A classic example, Okrent noted, was Risen's "CIA Aides Feel Pressure in Preparing Iraqi Reports," which was "completed several days before the invasion and unaccountably held for a week," not appearing until three days after the war began, when it "was interred on Page B10."[26]

At Knight Ridder, there was a clearer institutional grasp of the big picture. A full six months before the war began, Jonathan S. Landay produced a story headlined "Lack of Hard Evidence of Iraqi Weapons Worries Top U.S. Officials." It was published two days before administration officials fanned out on the Sunday morning talk shows to point ominously at the misguided front-page *Times* story about Saddam's aluminum tubes and almost five months before a Woodward story in *The Washington Post* made reference to similar WMD doubts (deep in a story that began with more of the administration's spurious hyping of its "significant intelligence"). Landay had pursued the story early on, after a low-level source told him, as he put it, "the vice president is lying." Warren P. Strobel, his frequent Knight Ridder collaborator on this reportage, observed in retrospect that "the most surprising thing to us was we had the field to ourselves for so long in terms of writing stuff that was critical or questioning the administration's case for war."[27]

THE WATERLOO for public opinion on the war came, fittingly enough, during Bush's Crawford vacation in August 2005. Cindy Sheehan of Vacaville, California, couldn't have picked a more apt date to begin the vigil that ambushed a president: August 6 was the fourth anniversary of that fateful 2001 day when he responded to an intelligence brief titled "Bin Laden Determined to Attack Inside the United States" by going fishing. On this August 6 of 2005, Bush was no less determined to shrug off bad news. Though fourteen marine reservists had been killed days earlier by a roadside bomb in Haditha, his national radio address that morning made no mention of Iraq. Once again the president was in his bubble, ensuring that he wouldn't see Sheehan coming anymore than he had foreseen any of the other setbacks in his war of choice.

Sheehan was camping out near Bush's ranch because of the loss of her son, Casey. His life and death tragically encapsulated not just the noble intentions of those who volunteered to fight the war but also the arrogance, incompetence, and recklessness of those who gave the marching orders. Specialist Sheehan had been both literally and figuratively an Eagle Scout: a church group leader and an honor student whose desire to serve his country drove him to enlist before 9/11, in 2000. He had died with six other soldiers on a rescue mission in Sadr City on April 4, 2004, at the age of twenty-four, the week after four American security workers had been mutilated in Falluja and two weeks after he arrived in Iraq. That was almost a year after the president had declared the end of "major combat operations."

According to accounts of the battle at the time, the insurgents who slaughtered Specialist Sheehan and his cohort were militiamen loyal to Moktada al-Sadr, the anti-American Shiite cleric. The Americans probably didn't stand a chance. The new Iraqi-trained security forces abandoned their posts almost as soon as al-Sadr's militiamen arrived.[28] Yet in the month before Casey Sheehan's death, Rumsfeld had typically gone out of his way to inflate the size and prowess of these Iraqi security forces, claiming in successive interviews that there were "over 200,000 Iraqis that have been trained and equipped" and that they were "out on the front line taking the brunt of the violence." After Casey Sheehan's death, Sadr only gained in power in the new "democratic" Iraq. Though the American army general Ricardo Sanchez had once promised that his troops would either "kill or capture" him, Sadr survived handsomely, controlling one of the larger blocs in the first National Assembly, playing king-maker in the anointment of the ineffectual prime minister Ibrahim al-Jaafari and contributing sectarian death squads to the new Iraqi police force. It was hard to see what Cindy Sheehan's young son had died for.

The president spurned the mother's request for a meeting. A Bush loyalist, Senator George Allen of Virginia, suggested he reconsider, as "a matter of courtesy and decency." Or, to translate Allen's Washingtonese, as a matter of politics. Only someone as adrift from reality as Bush would need to be told that a vacationing president couldn't win a standoff with a grief-stricken parent commandeering TV cameras and the blogosphere 24/7. But the White House held firm. In a particularly unfortunate gesture, the presidential motorcade, in a rare foray out of the vacation compound, left Sheehan in the dust on its way to a fund-raiser at a fat cat's ranch nearby.[29]

When she dug in and attracted more protestors and media attention, Sheehan could no longer be ignored. That's when the Swift Boating began. As had been the case with Joseph Wilson, Richard Clarke, the impertinent soldier Thomas Wilson, John McCain, and John Kerry, the attack was especially vicious because there was little the White House feared more than a critic who had more battle scars than a president or a draft-ducking vice president who had avoided Vietnam.

True to form, the Swift Boating of Cindy Sheehan surfaced early on Fox News, where she was immediately labeled a "crackpot" by Fred Barnes. The right-wing blogosphere quickly spread tales of her divorce, her angry Republican in-laws, her political flip-flops, her incendiary sloganeering, and her association with known ticket-stub-carrying fans of *Fahrenheit 9/11*. Rush Limbaugh went so far as to declare that Sheehan's "story is nothing more than forged documents—there's nothing about it that's real."

If the subject could be changed to Sheehan's "wacko" politics and the opportunistic left-wing groups that had attached themselves to her like barnacles in Crawford, maybe Americans would forget about her dead son. But if much of the 24/7 media took the bait, much of the public did not. While Sheehan's protest turned into a circus and her public pronouncements began to wear out her welcome, this time the Swift Boating failed, utterly, and that failure was a historical marker in the collapse of political support for the Iraq War in the summer of 2005.

The Swift Boating failed because no defamation of the messenger could erase the original, stubborn fact of Sheehan's grief. She had given powerful voice to the dead and maimed whom the administration had tried for so long to lock out of sight. Though the president continued to avoid meeting with her, he nonetheless blinked. He was forced to make what for him was the ultimate sacrifice: jettisoning chunks of his vacation to defend the war in any bunker he could find in the safe red states of Utah or Idaho. In the first speech of this offensive, Bush felt compelled to take the uncharacteristic step of citing the number of American dead in public (though by day's end the number was already out of date by at least five casualties[30]). For the second speech, the White House recruited its own mom, Tammy Pruett, for the president to showcase as an antidote to Cindy Sheehan. But in a reversion to the president's hide-the-fallen strategy, the chosen mother was not one who had lost a child in Iraq.

In an August 2005 *Newsweek* poll the approval rate for Bush's handling of Iraq plunged to 34 percent—a match for the 32 percent who approved LBJ's handling of Vietnam in early March 1968. The two presidents' overall approval ratings also converged: 41 percent for Johnson then, 42 percent for Bush now. But this wartime Texas president had outdone his predecessor. He had lost not only the country but also his army. A citizenry that was asked to accept tax cuts, not sacrifice, at the war's inception was hardly in the mood to start sacrificing now, with either treasure or blood. Neither bonuses nor fudged standards had solved the volunteer army's manpower shortfall. Recruiters had become so eager for bodies that some were caught trying to fake high school diplomas for potential enlistees. (Soon high school dropouts without a General Educational Development credential would be officially welcomed into the armed forces.) Even "don't ask, don't tell" was up for grabs, as the armed forces started holding on to gay soldiers who did tell, even when they told the press. The Leo Burnett advertising agency was handed $350 million for a new recruitment campaign that, in emulation of Bush's 2005 inaugural address, avoided mentioning Iraq.[31]

The White House no longer had any more control over an expanding political insurgency at home than it did over the one in Iraq. In a special summer congressional election in Ohio, the Democratic candidate, a marine reservist who had served in the war, called the president a "chicken hawk" and received 48 percent of the vote in exactly the kind of bedrock conservative district that had decided the 2004 election for Bush. By the fall, Rick Santorum, a conservative senator who had long slobbered over the president much as Ed McMahon used to over Johnny Carson, had started murmuring his first doubts about the war's "less than optimal" progress. He had just seen a poll showing him down 16 percent in his reelection campaign. He would later skip the president's Veterans Day speech in his home state of Pennsylvania and join all but one of the thirteen other Republican senators up for election in 2006 in a 79-to-19 majority on a Senate resolution begging for an Iraq exit strategy; these incumbents desperately wanted to be able to tell their constituents that they were against the war after they were for it. Not even the president's cable news cadre was holding firm. Bill O'Reilly started knocking Rumsfeld for incompetence, prompting Ann Coulter to chide O'Reilly for being a defeatist. In an emblematic gesture akin to waving a white flag, Robert Novak walked off a CNN set (and out of his TV job) rather than answer questions about his role in smearing Joseph Wilson. On this sinking ship, it was hard to know which rat to root for.

In response, Cheney started escalating his attacks on critics of the administration's prewar smoke screen, labeling them "dishonest and reprehensible" and their "revisionist" history "corrupt and shameless." He sounded but one epithet away from a defibrillator. "We're not going to sit by and let them rewrite history," the vice president said. "We're going to continue throwing their own words back at them." But it was Cheney's and the president's own words that were being thrown back now—not to rewrite history but to reveal it for the first time to an angry country that had learned the hard way that it could no longer afford to be without the truth.

As Democrats such as Russ Feingold, the liberal Minnesota senator, and John Murtha, a Vietnam vet and hawkish congressman from Pennsylvania, floated formulas for getting out of Iraq, Bush held firm. His mantra: "It makes no sense for the commander in chief to put out a timetable" for withdrawal. For other Republicans in Washington, however, the priority was no longer to save Jessica Lynch or Iraqi democracy but to save Santorum and every other endangered candidate. They had a timetable whether the White House liked it or not: the deadline for starting to downsize the American presence in Iraq increasingly looked like Election Day 2006.

BY THE TIME Hurricane Katrina administered the coup de grâce to the Bush presidency in late August 2005, the White House's message machinery was already in an advanced state of disrepair. "In my line of work you got to keep repeating things over and over and over again for the truth to sink in, to kind of catapult the propaganda," the president said with understandable desperation in May 2005 during his sixty-city tour to promote his big post-reelection domestic initiative, the privatizing of Social Security accounts. Support for his plan actually declined as his tour played out, and it was dead on arrival in a Congress his party controlled.

The "good news" the administration offered about the war was now routinely contradicted as soon as it was delivered, if not before. To promote his latest slogan for an Iraq exit strategy—"As the Iraqis stand up, we'll stand down"—Bush bragged about the "30 Iraqi battalions in the lead" in the fighting. But they were only "in the lead" with American support, and his own commanders told Congress that the number of Iraqi battalions capable of fighting unaided had actually declined, from three to one. (Translation: 750 soldiers were now ready to stand up on their own should America's 140,000 troops stand down.) When the president announced the smiting of a man he identified as "the second most wanted Al Qaeda leader in Iraq" and the "top operational commander of Al Qaeda in Baghdad," the rank of the dead insurgent was instantaneously dismissed as inflated, with one blogger documenting thirty-three other "top lieutenants" of Abu Musab al-Zarqawi who had been captured, killed, or identified in the past two and a half years.[32] "He may not even be one of the top 10 or 15 leaders," one Iraq hand told New York's *Daily News*.[33] No wonder the nation shrugged when the president, in yet another stay-the-course speech, talked of ten Qaeda plots that had been foiled on his watch. Americans instinctually knew that these plots were either recycled from past announcements, less scary than advertised, or unsubstantiated.

The White House's desperation could be seen even in its set decoration. In May 2003, the president's imagineers felt the need for only a single elegant banner declaring MISSION ACCOMPLISHED. In November 2005, when the administration trumpeted a belated "National Strategy for Victory in Iraq," the new White House bumper sticker, "Plan for Victory," multiplied by Orwellian mitosis over nearly every square inch of the rather *Queer Eye* yellow-and-blue-patterned stage design for Bush's delivery of the accompanying speech at the U.S. Naval Academy. The "plan" itself proved to be no more real than the stunt turkey the president had wielded in his photo op with the troops two Thanksgivings earlier. Billed by Scott McClellan as "an unclassified version" of the strategy in place since the war's inception, the thirty-five-page manifesto was quickly unmasked as a PR document written sometime in 2005.[34] Lieutenant General Martin Dempsey of the army, who was in charge of training Iraqi troops, told reporters that he had never seen this "Plan for Victory" before its public release.

Most Americans had, in any case, turned the page. Despite the insistently redundant set graphics—and the repetition of the word *victory* fifteen times in Bush's Naval Academy address—Americans believed "Plan for Victory" far less than they once had "Mission Accomplished." A *New York Times*/CBS News poll taken after the speech found that only 25 percent of Americans thought the president had "a clear plan for victory in Iraq." The new 9/11 anniversary failed to register altogether. For the occasion, the Pentagon planned a show to hammer in the false linkage between 9/11 and Iraq once more, this time with a beat, by inviting Clint Black to sing "I Raq and Roll" on the Mall.[35] But by September 11, 2005, memorials to 9/11, like so much else, had been washed away by Hurricane Katrina.

WHEN THE STORM STRUCK in late August, Bush, once more in Crawford, did remind the world of 9/11 after a fashion, unintentionally. He just couldn't stop himself from reenacting his own behavior on the day of the attacks four years earlier. As the levees cracked open in New Orleans, ushering an American city into hell, he chose to fly away from Washington, not toward it, to give a speech in California rather than lead a hands-on government response to Katrina. An attack by wind and water may differ from a terrorist attack, but Bush's character hadn't changed. It was immutable, it was his destiny, and now it was about to be ruthlessly exposed in real time on television before a vacationing nation with lots of free time for tuning in.

The storm, the worst in the country's history, was destined to join the tornado that uprooted Dorothy in *The Wizard of Oz* in the pantheon of American culture. Such was its power that in barely a week, it stripped bare all of the Bush administration's failings: the rampant cronyism, the empty sloganeering of "compassionate conservatism," the reckless lack of planning for all government operations except tax cuts, and the use of spin and photo ops to camouflage failure and substitute for action. The Wizard could never be the Wizard again once Toto parted the curtain and exposed him as Professor Marvel; Bush, too, stood revealed as a blowhard and a snake oil salesman.

Katrina was 9/11 déjà vu with a vengeance, from the president's inattentiveness to the threat before the storm struck to his disappearing act on the day itself to the reckless botching of the reconstruction efforts. His defensive declaration on *Good Morning America* that "I don't think anybody anticipated the breach of the levees" instantly achieved the notoriety of Condoleezza Rice's "I don't think anybody could have predicted that these people would take an airplane and slam it into the World Trade Center." The administration's complete obliviousness to the possibilities for civil disorder, energy failures, and food and water deprivation in a major city under siege lacked only the Rumsfeld tagline of "Stuff happens."

Though history is supposed to occur first as tragedy, then as farce, this time tragedy was being repeated as tragedy. Or so everyone could see except the president. The truth only began to penetrate four days after the storm's arrival, when the White House PR impresario Dan Bartlett suggested that Bush watch a DVD compilation of actual evening news reports.[36] When Bush made his tardy first foray to the site of the storm, there was no bullhorn moment to bail him out. The usual White House efforts to manage the disaster with public relations soon followed, but every stunt he tried before the cameras played like a sick joke: he reminisced about his carousing days in New Orleans, promised a fast rebuilding of Trent Lott's Gulf vacation home (while staying away from less-affluent black storm victims), and congratulated the most conspicuously incompetent official on the scene, FEMA director Michael Brown, with a "Brownie, you're doing a heckuva job." As in the aftermath of 9/11, the press was offered the soulful image of the president looking out the window of Air Force One, but this time the photo backfired and was unsuitable for hawking to Republican donors. Bush came across as detached—a Little Lord Fauntleroy piously exhibiting his compassion from on high while the peons suffered below. When his mother visited evacuees in Houston's Astrodome, her condescension only reinforced that unwanted message of old-school Yankee noblesse oblige. She told a radio interviewer, "So many of the people in the arena here, you know, were underprivileged anyway, so this is working very well for them."[37]

When the first batch of PR strategies failed, a desperate recycling of the White House's greatest hits was cobbled together for round two. Bush called a hasty press opportunity, reconvening the unlikely Sunshine Boys duo of his father and Bill Clinton, who had proven highly popular when speeding relief during the Asian tsunami; he presided over prayers at the Washington National Cathedral, the site of his first effective 9/11 speech; he gave a ludicrously over-hyped prime-time address flecked with speechwriters' "poetry" and framed by a picturesque backdrop. This time the pretty venue was New Orleans's Jackson Square, and in an echo of his *Top Gun* theatrics, Bush was televised taking a laughably stagy stride across the lawn to his lectern. (Message: I am commander in chief, not that vacationing slacker who first surveyed the hurricane damage from my presidential jet.) The president was once again bathed in florid theatrical lighting, reminiscent of his oration before the Statue of Liberty on 9/11's first anniversary. Yet the French Quarter was deserted, and the monument chosen to frame Bush this time, St. Louis Cathedral, was so brightly lighted that it registered on-screen like a two-dimensional Mittel Europa castle painted on a backdrop for a nineteenth-century operetta. Once the speech was over, residents were eager to tell reporters how the White House stage managers immediately pulled the plug on the special generators that supplied the president's visual halo, thereby plunging the abandoned city back into darkness.

The true Katrina narrative was just too powerful to be papered over with White House fictions. Every administration misstep cast a retroactive spotlight on other failures over the past four years. When Laura Bush was sent among the storm's dispossessed, she complained of seeing "a lot of the same footage over and over that isn't necessarily representative of what really happened," sounding just like her husband's defense secretary when he complained that television had exaggerated the post-liberation chaos in Baghdad by showing the same picture of a looter with a vase "over and over." Rumsfeld's game had been not just to scapegoat the press for his failures but to hide the reality that the Pentagon had no plan to secure Iraq. For all Bush's bumper-sticker rhetoric about a Gulf Opportunity Zone and an Urban Homesteading Act, there was no serious administration plan for rebuilding and repopulating New Orleans, either then or in the months to come.

But in this domestic replay of the bungled war, the heartlessness beneath the surface of the president's inaction was more pronounced—perhaps because this time the spectacle could not be kept under wraps on TV and the civilians and landscape on view were American, not Iraqi. There was no safety net of national unity to bolster Bush as it had after 9/11, largely because his intense partisanship had destroyed it. The country's highest-rated TV news anchor, NBC's Brian Williams, started talking about Katrina the way Walter Cronkite once had about Vietnam. Even at Fox News, some talking heads found it impossible to ignore the reality that the administration had been no more successful at securing New Orleans than it had been at pacifying Falluja. One visibly exasperated anchor covering the story on the ground in Louisiana, Shepard Smith, went ballistic while in Bill O'Reilly's usually spin-shellacked "no-spin zone." "The haves of this city, the movers and shakers of this city, evacuated the city either immediately before or immediately after the storm," he told O'Reilly. What he didn't have to say, since it was visible to the entire world, was that it was the poor who were left behind to drown.

Katrina played like a contemporary remake of *Titanic*. New Orleans's first-class passengers made it safely into lifeboats; for those in steerage, it was the horrifying spectacle of every man, woman, and child for himself. The captain in this retelling, Michael Chertoff, the homeland security secretary, was so oblivious to those on the lower decks that he applauded the federal response to the ongoing catastrophe as "really exceptional," while the rest of the world could see otherwise. Both Chertoff (on NPR) and Michael Brown (on *Nightline*) publicly expressed ignorance of the reality that thousands of people were without food and water at the New Orleans convention center—even though every television viewer in the country had been hearing of those twenty-five thousand stranded refugees for at least a day.

The inequality of the suffering also exposed the sham of the relentless Bush photo ops with black schoolchildren trotted out at campaign time to sell his "compassionate conservatism." Incredibly, a "Hurricane Relief" photo gallery, again laden with black faces, was posted on the White House Web site. (In 2004, the Bush-Cheney campaign Web site had a similar page, titled "Compassion" and devoted mainly to photos of the president with black people, Colin Powell included.)[38] But the new "compassion" photos were outweighed by the networks' cinema verité of poor people screaming for their lives. In emulation of the policy on coffins coming home from Iraq, officials at first tried to keep body recovery efforts in New Orleans off-limits to the news media—a plan it had to abandon once it was challenged in court by CNN.

Reeling from the criticism, Bush pleaded to ABC's Diane Sawyer that people not "play politics during this period of time." But just months earlier the president had flown from Crawford to Washington overnight to sign a symbolic bill intervening in the case of Terri Schiavo, a brain-dead hospice patient flogged as a right-to-life cause by the Christian right. He was in no position now to lecture anyone about playing politics with tragedy.

For all the embarrassments, the administration's priority of image over substance remained embedded like a cancer in the Katrina relief process. After the inevitable ceremonial firing of "Brownie," whom Bush now claimed to know as little as he did "Kenny Boy" Lay, the two top deputies still at FEMA were not disaster-relief specialists but experts in PR, which they had practiced as advance men for various Bush campaigns. Rove, tellingly enough, was put officially in charge of the New Orleans reconstruction. *The Salt Lake Tribune* discovered a week after the hurricane that some one thousand firefighters recruited from Utah and elsewhere were not immediately sent to the Gulf Coast but to Atlanta, to be trained as "community relations officers for FEMA" rather than used as emergency workers to rescue the abandoned and dying in New Orleans. When fifty of the firefighters were finally dispatched to Louisiana, their first assignment was "to stand beside President Bush" as he toured the wreckage.[39]

Such imagery did nothing to alleviate the most devastating damage inflicted on the president by Katrina: its erosion of his image as a stalwart protector of the nation's security. The hurricane revealed that four years after 9/11, homeland security was an illusion, in the hands of a large dysfunctional department run by party hacks and incompetents. An agency that Bush had opposed and then reluctantly supported as a political ploy was as big a wreck as New Orleans itself.

The corporate culture of the CEO presidency once more evoked Enron. Michael Brown turned out to be a longtime buddy of Bush's 2000 campaign manager, Joe Allbaugh, who had preceded Brown in the FEMA job. There were other cronies stashed elsewhere throughout the homeland security bureaucracy, which looked like a mirror image of the inept and often corrupt bureaucracy of Iraq reconstruction. The first administration official arrested in the growing Washington scandal surrounding the corrupt lobbyist Jack Abramoff turned out to be an ill-qualified top procurement officer at the White House, whose sway over federal purchasing policy included that for Katrina relief.[40]

The diffident mismanagement of the hurricane's assault sent the entire world a simple and unambiguous message: the United States was unable to fight its current war and protect homeland security at the same time. Maybe, for all the Ashcroft and Ridge theatrics of the past four years and all the accompanying abridgments of civil liberties, the administration was unable to protect homeland security at all. A December 2005 report card issued by the bipartisan leaders of the former 9/11 Commission, Thomas Kean and Lee Hamilton, gave the government an F in categories such as air passenger prescreening, the allocation of homeland security funds according to need rather than pork, and the securing of radio frequencies for emergency workers such as those who were defeated by antiquated communications when the World Trade Center was hit.[41] More than a dozen reports by the Government Accountability Office since 9/11 had found huge failings in almost every shipping security program meant to protect ports such as New Orleans. In the aftermath of Katrina, governors of both parties at the 2006 meeting of the National Governors Association lamented that the war had stripped the National Guard of the equipment and manpower needed to deal with local emergencies, whether hurricanes or terrorism.

As the fictions in the campaign to sell the war in Iraq were gradually exposed after the fact, so the fictions in the administration's official pronouncements about Katrina were undone by a postmortem discovery process. The White House balked at providing documents to a congressional investigation, but the truth came out anyway. One smoking gun was a Homeland Security Department report submitted to the White House in the early hours of August 29–three days before Bush publicly said that he didn't think anyone anticipated the breaching of the levees–saying that "any storm rated category 4 or greater will likely lead to severe flooding and/or levee breaching." That night the White House received from FEMA an eyewitness confirmation of a major levee breach and flooding in New Orleans.[42] Chertoff would blame his department's cluelessness about all this on the "fog of war."

Bush had no explanation at all. On the day the most embarrassing documents about his Katrina response became public, the White House reverted to its default tactic: fomenting the fog of terrorism. The president gave a speech gratuitously detailing what he said was a foiled plot by Al Qaeda to fly a hijacked plane into the US Bank Tower in Los Angeles, the tallest building in the West. But this time the ham-handed tactic failed to upstage the Katrina news. The news media yawned, recognizing that this same foiled plot had been first mentioned by federal officials two years earlier and previously trotted out by the president four months earlier; some counterterrorism officials had never regarded it as a serious operational plan in any case.[43] The newly elected Los Angeles mayor, Antonio Villaraigosa, promptly held his own press conference to say that Bush had shared the supposed new details of this plot with a national cable TV audience but had not bothered to inform him; then he complained of being repeatedly rebuffed in his attempts to meet with the president to discuss homeland security in the nation's second-largest city.

A few weeks later, a teleconference video obtained by the Associated Press showed a passive Bush in Crawford asking no questions in a briefing where he was told that the potential for levee breaches was a "very, very grave concern," and that the Superdome might provide inadequate protection for evacuees.

The video was from August 28, four days before his *Good Morning America* profession of ignorance about the levees. "I hope people don't draw conclusions from the President getting a single briefing," a White House spokesman said. They did. The president who had lived by the manufactured television image found himself pummeled 24/7 by this episode of candid camera.

At least one mystery remained about President Bush's response to Katrina. He still had no explanation of why it had taken almost two days of people being without food, shelter, and water on the Gulf for him to get back to Washington. But his appearance in California the day the levees broke certainly offered clues to his priorities, and the first priority, as always, was saving himself. He had gone west to combat the flood of record-low poll numbers, which was proving no easier to contain than Lake Pontchartrain.

His tack was to give another disingenuous pep talk about Iraq in a military setting. Once again he wrapped himself in the mantle of 9/11, the cataclysm that defined his first term, even at the price of failing to recognize the emerging storm engulfing his second. After dispatching Katrina with a few sentences of sanctimonious boilerplate ("our hearts and prayers are with our fellow citizens"), he likened 9/11 to Pearl Harbor, the war in Iraq to World War II and, implicitly, himself to FDR. Anyone who refused to stay his course was soft on terrorism and guilty of a "pre-September-the-11th mind-set of isolation and retreat."

Yet even as Bush promised "victory," a word that appeared nine times in his script, he was standing at the totemic scene of his failure. The site of his speech was a naval base in San Diego—on the same coastline off which the USS *Abraham Lincoln* had parked for his *Top Gun* victory jig of more than two years earlier. For the return engagement, however, the president did not arrive flying his own plane.

That wasn't the only revision in the old scenario. This time, a reporter at *The Washington Post* discovered, the White House stage managers made sure that the president was positioned so that another hulking aircraft carrier nearby, the USS *Ronald Reagan*, would remain safely out of the television shot.[44] It wouldn't do, after all, to remind anyone now of the president's premature declaration of the end of "major combat operations." That show had long since lost its magic, and it was past time to strike the set.

THE GREATEST STORY
EVER SOLD

A s the war in Iraq entered its fourth year in the spring of 2006, Condoleezza Rice dipped a little toe into reality. "I know we've made tactical errors, thousands of them, I'm sure," she said. "But when you look back in history, what will be judged is did you make the right strategic decisions." And about that she had no doubts. The "important strategic decisions" were—what else?—"right."

By the standards of the Bush administration, where admitting any error is verboten, Rice's statement was a profile in courage—though she continued the White House practice of passing the buck (in this case to the Pentagon and the military) for its own failures. But she had been a political scientist in her academic career, not a historian, and her rose-colored view of history's likely verdict bordered on the delusional. As she spoke, Iraq was teetering on the edge of civil war, its militia were often indistinguishable from death squads, and she and her British counterpart, Jack Straw, were desperately trying to mold Iraq's new "democratic" government to their own interests (i.e., by pushing out the Shiite prime minister Ibrahim al-Jaafari).

The Iraq reconstruction effort, the heart of America's humanitarian stab at nation-building, was grinding to a halt, its projects abandoned or half finished, its incompetent bureaucracy yielding dozens of corruption cases. Among those arrested were employees of Halliburton's KBR division, which had been the subject of a criminal investigation for reputed bill-padding in army contracts predating 9/11 and the war in Iraq but which had nonetheless been awarded no-bid contracts giving it access to the reconstruction billions.

Surely this Marshall Plan run amok was the self-styled CEO administration's grandest reenactment of the Enron ethos yet. Iraq was the ultimate Potemkin village. For all the American taxpayers' money spent on rebuilding the country (some twenty-one billion dollars had been budgeted), its basic services (electricity, water, sewerage) and oil production were all below pre-invasion levels. The 1.5 million public-works jobs that were pledged to get the economy on its feet had ended up numbering only 77,000; unemployment was a staggering 32 percent, while economic growth was a stagnant 5 percent, despite high oil prices.[1] The only major building project to be completed on time and within budget was a $529 million new American embassy[2]—no doubt because it was in the one enclave that American forces had secured, the barricaded Green Zone. (Symbolically enough, it had employed no Iraqi workers at all.) Even the contract for the high priority of building health centers had run out of money, according to the U.S. Army Corps of Engineers, with at most 20 clinics out of a planned 142 to show for $200 million.[3] If, as the secretary of state claimed, Operation Iraqi Freedom was a success, then the patient was dying.

Rice was right about one thing: history will be the judge of the Iraq War. But neither she nor anyone else can predict that verdict. Perhaps future generations will discover that George W. Bush was a visionary who worked a miracle—that by knocking out one thug in the Middle East he set off a domino effect that led to democratic reform in a region gripped by totalitarianism, tribal hatreds, and radical religious fundamentalism. If so, he will be among the luckiest players in the history book, and history tells us that sometimes it does pay to be more lucky than smart.

The other alternative, of course, is that this war of choice could prove to be an enormous victory for Iran and Al Qaeda alike, a commensurate disaster for Israel and the West, and a political boon to other jihadists worldwide (starting with those who consolidated governmental power in U.S.-endorsed elections in Iraq, Palestine, and Egypt). Should that be the case, the Bush presidency could well prove, as its most severe critics have maintained, the worst ever. Its legacy will include the destruction of America's image, credibility, and prestige abroad; record budget deficits produced by unchecked spending and tax cuts; an abused and broken military; a subversion of the Constitution achieved by rigidly ideological judicial appointments, the abridgment of civil liberties, and outright lawbreaking in the White House; an indifference to environmental imperatives, including the energy conservation urgently needed to end America's chronic economic dependence on the congenitally unstable Middle East; and the promotion of America's homegrown religious fundamentalism with both official and political assaults on medical and earth science (including evolution) and the rights of gay Americans. (And that's just the short list.) Even the supposedly beatific Bush achievements will be heavily asterisked. No Child Left Behind education reform did more for the nation's testing industry than for students, who found their curricula narrowed to the two subjects (math and reading) measured by the tests. The administration's AIDS initiative was blunted by being yoked to abstinence programs that flattered Christian right voters in the Republican base but were irrelevant to the rampaging life-or-death tragedy in Africa.

Perhaps there's yet another historical narrative somewhere between these two poles that can be imagined for the Bush presidency, but if so, it should be left for now to a novelist like Philip Roth, whose *Plot Against America,* despite all his denials of any such intention, remains the best early take on the forty-third president. Only fiction can truly deal with a White House that lived and died by fiction. And only a novelist—a new Joseph Heller—could improve on a character like John Ashcroft, who would stand as the most farcical embodiment of the administration's ethos. The attorney general hit the Bush White House trifecta: he was at once incompetent at his job, an irrepressible impresario of vacuous PR stunts, and a foe of the Bill of Rights. After leaving the administration in 2005, he opened a K Street lobbying firm, where he marketed his contacts in the departments of Justice and Homeland Security to, among others, ChoicePoint, a company that brokers credit data (and other personal information) on American citizens. Thus did the government official who recklessly expanded the market for domestic surveillance while in office find a nominally legal way to make a profit on his nominally legal policies as soon as he was out the door. It was the perfect Enron-esque coda to his wartime career.[4]

Once President Bush lost the public after his reelection, ultimately to descend to an approval rating in the thirties even before Katrina, blatant White House fictions were exposed much faster than they ever had been before, as if the press were racing to catch up with the polls. The latently emboldened television news media started routinely practicing the cross-cutting long perfected by Comedy Central's *Daily Show.* In 2004, for instance, when Cheney denied three times in a CNBC interview (with Gloria Borger) that he had ever called a Mohamed Atta–Iraqi intelligence link "pretty well confirmed," it was left to Jon Stewart to nail Cheney's lie by replaying the video of the vice president saying exactly those words on *Meet the Press* in December 2001. Now all the non-fake TV news operations were getting in on the act. When James Risen and Eric Lichtblau of *The New York Times* broke the story of the National Security Agency's warrant-free domestic eavesdropping—a program that undermined the Constitution more effectively than it did terrorists[5]—a damning presidential sound bite was instantaneously ubiquitous. "Any time you hear the United States government talking about wiretap, it requires—a wiretap requires a court order," Bush had said on camera in April 2004, adding for good fictional measure that "nothing has changed, by the way."

In its terminal condition following Hurricane Katrina, the administration seemed to suffer a breakdown like that of HAL, the computer in *2001: A Space Odyssey.* An administration aide was caught on video rehearsing a teleconference in which ten soldiers from the Army's Forty-second Infantry Division in Tikrit and one Iraqi soldier were to be presented as bantering spontaneously with the president about how good security was in Iraq. The White House was so desperate to maintain its crumbling narrative that it often lost track of where the reality that it created ended and the reality recognized by the "reality-based community" and, for that matter, anyone outside the administration's bubble, began. A full year and a half after the first photos from Abu Ghraib, which were now compounded by many more reports of the abuse, torture, and rendition of prisoners at a variety of locations known and unknown, Bush was so out of touch that he still believed he could say, "We do not torture," on camera with a straight face. The administration's similarly doomed effort to deny that Iraq was fracturing into civil war was ridiculed even by Ayad Allawi, the White House's former handpicked prime minister and obedient puppet. "If this is not civil war," he said, "then God knows what civil war is."[6]

On the third anniversary of Shock and Awe, Bob Schieffer of CBS News asked Cheney about his prewar statement that Americans would be "greeted as liberators" in Iraq and his then ten-month-old prediction that the insurgency was in its "last throes." The vice president responded that "statements we've made" were "basically accurate and reflect reality" and that a false perception had been "created because what's newsworthy is the car bomb in Baghdad." But now even Fox News couldn't enforce the administration's reality anymore. When Bob Dole appeared on the network to praise it for its positive coverage of the war—"Iraq: A New Era" was the upbeat Fox rubric—he had to share a split screen with images of a tanker in flames in Iraq. The "Plan for Victory" graphics kept getting larger and larger at Bush stay-the-course speeches until, finally, the humor writer Andy Borowitz peppered the Internet with his satirical news account of a White House plan to have Halliburton build a $13.8 billion PLAN FOR VICTORY sign "as big as the entire land mass of Iraq." Sure, it might crush "the entire Iraqi people," but it would "put an end to all this talk of civil war."

Almost every prominent American supporter of the war outside the Republican hierarchy was bailing out in emulation of the press and public. Liberal hawks had been the first out the door, back in 2004. Now non-neoconservatives, many of whom had been highly skeptical about the war in the first place, ratcheted up the severity of their doubts: William F. Buckley, Jr., deeming the war a failure, expressed a certain pity for Bush's plight in an April TV interview: "If he'd invented the Bill of Rights, it wouldn't get him out of this jam." George Will wrote that "all three components of the 'axis of evil'— Iraq, Iran, and North Korea"—are "more dangerous than they were when that phrase was coined in 2002."[7] Next to flee was the onetime neoconservative Francis Fukuyama, who had turned on the Iraq War before it began and now consigned the neocon movement's foreign ambitions in toto to history's graveyard with a well-timed book-length jeremiad, *America at the Crossroads: Democracy, Power, and the Neoconservative Legacy*.

Those neocons outside the administration who didn't jump ship, such as William Kristol and David Brooks, often scapegoated Rumsfeld for the war's failures much as Rumsfeld and the rest of the administration scapegoated the press. ("We have not had a serious three-year effort to fight a war in Iraq," Kristol observed in February 2006.) If it all could be pinned on the defense secretary, the president might be off the hook. Yet the buck stopped with Bush no less than with any other American president. It was he who made the decision to ignore accurate intelligence about Osama bin Laden when the Qaeda leader was trapped in Tora Bora in late 2001 so that the war effort could be realigned around bogus intelligence about the "gathering threat" of Saddam. This fateful choice, wrote *Newsweek*'s Michael Hirsh, was a strategic blunder to rank with Hitler's decision to invade the Soviet Union in 1941, "at a time when Great Britain was prostrate and America was still out of the war."[8]

But as American involvement in Iraq shifted into its endgame, two questions remained unanswered. Why *did* the administration push, and push so urgently, for a war in Iraq after the summer of 2002? And: Were its original, stated reasons—the threat of WMDs, a connection between Saddam and Al Qaeda—deliberate lies or just honest errors based, as White House defenders would have it, on the same flawed intelligence that was misread by so many others? The second question can't be answered without addressing the first.

There are, of course, many plausible motives for why America would go to war in Iraq. For oil. For Israel. To avenge Saddam's assassination plot against George W. Bush's father. To finish the job left unfinished by that father in the first Persian Gulf war. To exercise American muscle in a slam-dunk mission, a cakewalk, that might intimidate the region's terrorists and hostile states into forever holding their peace. All of these motives were present at the highest reaches of the administration, but which, if any, was the catalyst that ignited the crusade? Writing in *The Assassins' Gate: America in Iraq* in 2005, the journalist George Packer calls Iraq "the 'Rashomon' of wars," concluding that "it still isn't possible to be sure—and this remains the most remarkable thing about the Iraq war." Even a former Bush administration State Department official who was present at the war's creation, Richard Haass, told Packer that he expects to go to his grave "not knowing the answer."

We know for certain that the reasons sold to the public and the world by the administration were decoys. Even if the White House really believed that Saddam was an imminent threat to America, it knew enough to know he was manifestly not remotely the *most* imminent threat, nuclear or otherwise; that would be North Korea's Kim Jong-il. Other nations were far more indisputably havens for radical Islam and terrorists besides, such as Syria, Pakistan, Saudi Arabia, and Iran. If our aim was to take out a murderous dictator simply on humanitarian grounds, why Saddam above all others?

Nor was it remotely plausible, as the White House argued after the war, that a primary motive from the start had been to rebuild post-Saddam Iraq as a shining example of liberal democracy to spark reform throughout the Middle East. Bush was a sworn enemy of such fantasies. Debating with Al Gore in 2000, he said he had opposed the Clinton administration's intervention in Somalia because it "started off as a humanitarian mission, then changed into a nation-building mission, and that's where the mission went wrong. . . . I don't think our troops ought to be used for what's called nation-building." He codified this belief in his stump speech that year: "I'm worried about an opponent who uses nation-building and the military in the same sentence."

Though Bush was fond of stating that 9/11 changed his thinking about everything, he never did change his stance on nation-building in the run-up to the Iraq War; he never talked about building a democracy in Iraq. The reason he didn't talk about it was *not* that he was consciously trying to keep a hidden, hard-to-sell motive secret. The record shows that, for once, Bush's private convictions actually did match his public stance. Neither he nor the administration had any intention of doing any nation-building. The war plan was an easy exercise in regime change, a swift surgical procedure, after which the Iraqis would be left to build their own democracy by spontaneous civic combustion, like Eastern Europeans after the fall of the Soviet Union. The Americans would hang around in small numbers, perhaps, to protect the oil ministry—the only institution they did protect after routing Saddam.

Every single administration action of the time confirms that nation-building was not in the cards. That's why General Jay Garner was picked as the top American official after the fall of Baghdad: The White House wanted a short-term military emissary rather than a full-dress occupation administrator because the job description required only that he manage a quick turnover of power to the Iraqis and an immediate exit for American troops. That's why Rumsfeld and the war cabinet bought a Tommy Franks plan to draw down those troops from 130,000 to 30,000 by the fall of 2003. It's also why the only serious prewar plans for rebuilding Iraq, the State Department "Future of Iraq" project, were shelved by the White House. General Anthony Zinni's "Desert Crossing" plan for Iraq reconstruction,[9] which he bequeathed to Franks, his successor, in 2000, was also shunted aside. Any such bothersome little details were entrusted instead to the Defense Department's Douglas Feith, whose only (non) qualification was that he had been a loyal provider of cherry-picked Iraq intelligence to Cheney and Libby before the war. Just how little Feith would have to do was previewed by Rumsfeld in a speech titled "Beyond Nation Building," delivered at the Intrepid Sea, Air and Space Museum in New York on February 14, 2003, just a month before the war. "Well-intentioned foreigners" who practice nation-building, he said, "come in with international solutions to local problems" and "can create a dependency" that produces "unintended adverse side effects." A "long-term foreign presence in a country can be unnatural," he added, which is why the United States would "leave as soon as possible," should it go to war in Iraq.

That nation-building was a nonstarter is also borne out by the David Manning memo of the Bush-Blair meeting of January 2003. The memo found both leaders anticipating a fast transition to a new Iraqi government, with Bush predicting (and Blair agreeing) that it was "unlikely there would be internecine warfare between the different religious and ethnic groups." On the matter of a post-Saddam government, the memo quoted Rice as saying that "a great deal of work was now in hand." Iraq would be as easy to fix as the Texas Rangers.

Had nation-building been in the White House's plans, surely someone would have bothered to investigate what nation was being rebuilt. Or at least asked the British (or rented *Lawrence of Arabia*) to be reminded of Britain's failure to unite the warring provinces it brought together when creating Iraq out of defeated remnants of the Ottoman Empire at the end of World War I. But ignorance, apparently, was bliss for a president whose lifelong incuriosity about the world beyond his own charmed circle did not change with his arrival in the White House. Writing in *The New York Times Magazine* on the eve of the war in March 2003, Packer described a meeting between Bush and three Iraqis during which "the exiles spent a good portion of the time explaining to the president that there are two kinds of Arabs in Iraq, Sunnis and Shiites." His Iraqi guests concluded that "the very notion of an Iraqi opposition appeared to be new to him."[10] Yes, Bush was incurious, but if he had really been planning on nation-building in Iraq, he would have had to be mentally defective to be *that* incurious.

Even when Jay Garner left Iraq to make way for a new viceroy, L. Paul Bremer III, as the insurgency flared, there was no evidence to suggest that nation-building was on tap. The two heads of "private-sector development" in Iraq were a former Bush campaign finance chair in Connecticut and a venture capitalist who just happened to be Ari Fleischer's brother. Major roles in the Bremer regime were given to twentysomethings with no foreign service experience or knowledge of Arabic simply because they had posted their résumés at the Heritage Foundation,[11] the same conservative think tank where Bremer had chaired a task force, and who might enjoy a postgraduate year in exotic climes. Bremer expressly vetoed any role for Zalmay Khalilzad, the American envoy already dealing with potential Iraqi political leaders, even though the Afghanistan-born Khalilzad was the only high-placed diplomat in the administration who was Muslim, knew the Iraqi principals, and, for that matter, knew the language (or at least one of them).[12] Who needed that level of expertise? (Khalilzad would not be posted to Iraq until the late hour of 2005, to try to perform triage long after Bremer had botched the occupation and gone home.)

Though it has long been a given that the White House was surprised by the insurgency—even if it should not have been—it is less fully recognized that the administration was equally surprised to discover that it would be forced (literally at gunpoint) to build a nation from the ground up, a demanding task for which it was equally unprepared. Maybe a new Iraq could have been built against all odds and despite Iraq's unpromising twentieth-century history, but not without a premeditated plan. The "nation-building" that America finally did undertake was an improvised initiative, heavier on PR than on achievement, to justify the mission retroactively. Only then did the war's diehard defenders disingenuously grandfather it in as a noble calling contemplated by the Bush White House from the start.

So, what really did trigger the war in Iraq? The likely answer to this question, like so much else, can be found in the entrails of the Valerie Plame Wilson leak case. It was not an accident that men as different as Libby and Rove—one a Washington policy intellectual, the other a down-and-dirty political operative—would collide before Patrick Fitzgerald's grand jury. They were very different men playing very different White House roles, but they were bound together by the shared past that the Wilson affair exposed. That past had everything to do with protecting the real "why" of why America went to war.

To track Rove's role, it's necessary to flash back to January 2002. By then the post-9/11 war in Afghanistan had succeeded in its mission to overthrow the Taliban and had done so with a death toll that the American public could accept. In a triumphalist speech to the Republican National Committee, Rove for the first time openly advanced the idea that the war on terror was the path to victory for that November's midterm elections. Candidates "can go to the country on this issue," he said, because voters "trust the Republican Party to do a better job of protecting and strengthening America's military might and thereby protecting America."

But there were unspoken impediments to Rove's plan, of which he was well aware: Afghanistan was slipping off the radar screen of American voters, and the president's most grandiose objective, to capture Osama bin Laden "dead or alive," had capsized in Tora Bora. How do you run as a vainglorious "war president" if the war looks as if it's winding down and the number one evildoer has escaped?

Hardly had Rove given his speech than his fears were confirmed by polls registering the first erosion of the initial near-universal endorsement of the administration's response to 9/11. A *USA Today*/CNN/Gallup survey in March 2002 found that while nine out of ten Americans still backed the war on terrorism at the six-month anniversary of the attacks, support for an expanded, long-term war had fallen to 52 percent. Next to come was the run of bad news: the public revelations that bin Laden had escaped, that Bush had apparently ignored worrisome intelligence about Al Qaeda in August 2001, and that the FBI had blown its chance to press the jailed Zacarias Moussaoui for valuable leads in the weeks before 9/11. By Memorial Day 2002, a *USA Today* poll found that just four out of ten Americans believed that the United States was winning the war on terrorism, a steep drop from the roughly two thirds holding that conviction in January. Rove could see that an untelevised and largely underground war—the "lengthy campaign" that might be "secret even in success," as Bush had formulated it in his measured post-9/11 address to Congress—might not nail election victories without a jolt of shock and awe. It was a propitious moment to wag the dog.

Enter Scooter, stage right. Libby had been joined at the hip with Cheney and Paul Wolfowitz since their service in the Defense Department of the first President Bush's administration, where in its waning days in 1992 they conceived a controversial manifesto preaching the importance of asserting unilateral American military power after the cold war. Well before the next Bush took office, these and other neocons fated to join his camp had become fixated on Iraq, though for reasons having much to do with their own ideas about exerting American force to jump-start a realignment of the Middle East and little or nothing to do with the stateless terrorism of Al Qaeda or with nation-building.[13] Here, ready and waiting on the shelf in-house, were the grounds for a grand new battle that would be showy, not secret, in its success—just the political Viagra that Rove needed for an election year.

But abstract and highly debatable theories on how to assert superpower machismo and alter the political balance in the Middle East would never fly with American voters as a trigger for war or convince them that such a war was relevant to the fight against the enemy of 9/11. And though Americans knew that Saddam was a despot and mass murderer, that in itself was also insufficient to ignite a popular groundswell for regime change. Polls in the summer of 2002 showed steadily declining support among Americans for going to war in Iraq, especially if America were to go it alone.

For Rove and Bush to get what they wanted most, slam-dunk midterm election victories, and for Libby and Cheney to get what they wanted most, a war in Iraq for ideological reasons predating 9/11, their real whys for going to war had to be replaced by more saleable fictional ones. We'd go to war instead because there was a direct connection between Saddam and Al Qaeda and because Saddam was on the verge of attacking America with nuclear weapons.

Both these casus belli were a stretch from the get-go. Not a single one of the thousands of documents found after the fall of the Taliban in Afghanistan substantiated an Iraq-Qaeda alliance. Though there had been contacts between Iraqi officials and Al Qaeda in the mid-1990s, they led nowhere; the last Saddam stab at terrorism against an American target had been his failed assassination attempt on the first President Bush, in 1993.[14] As for the uranium from Niger, it wasn't only Joseph Wilson or the International Atomic Energy Agency's Mohamed ElBaradei who warned off the White House. The CIA asked the French for their evaluation three times before the war—in 2001 and twice in 2002—and in each case the French intelligence chief, Alain Chouet, said it was nonsense. Given that the uranium ore in Niger, as in all former French colonies, was mined by French companies, this was information you could take to the bank.[15]

The facts and intelligence didn't fit the policy, and so, as the Downing Street memo confirmed, they would have to be fixed (and contradictory evidence suppressed) to build a fictional narrative that would speed the march to war. (The Manning memo echoed this language: "Our diplomatic strategy had to be arranged around the military planning.") Not for nothing did Rove and Libby come together in WHIG, whose goal was to turn up the heat on Congress with WMD propaganda, forcing a vote on an Iraq resolution in the politically advantageous weeks before the midterm election.

A war that the United States could initiate on its own deliberate schedule—after it had all its diplomatic, military, and post-invasion ducks in a row—was instead rushed to fruition half-baked to serve Rove's priority over all others. The Rove priority was hardly some idealistic Wilsonian vision of "freedom" in Iraq but the more selfish scheme of consolidating domestic American political power in the hands of a single party: it had long been his aspiration to create a permanent Republican majority in Washington to match the unbroken GOP dominance that was ushered in by William McKinley in 1896 and lasted until the stock market crash of 1929.

This partisan dream, not nation-building, was consistent with the president's own history and Washington ambitions. Bush was a competitor who liked to win the game, even if he was unclear about what to do with his victory beyond catering to the economic interests of his real base, the traditional Republican business constituency. If Bob Woodward's account was true and Bush had vetoed the idea of going to war simultaneously with Al Qaeda and Saddam Hussein immediately after 9/11, his personal political needs were different as the political glow from 9/11 started to fade. Iraq was just the vehicle to ride to victory in the midterms, particularly if it could be folded into the proven brand of 9/11. A cakewalk in Iraq was the easy way, the lazy way, the arrogant way, the telegenic way, the *Top Gun* way to hold on to power. It was of a piece with every other shortcut in Bush's career, and it was a hand-me-down from Dad drenched in oil to boot.

Was this motive so strong that it induced the administration to lie about the intelligence? Certainly this was a White House that was very comfortable with lying.

Two days before the invasion of Iraq in March 2003, Bush had the audacity to say, "Should Saddam Hussein choose confrontation, the American people can know that every measure has been taken to avoid war, and every measure will be taken to win it." His statement recalled Mary McCarthy's explanation to Dick Cavett about why she thought Lillian Hellman was a dishonest writer: "Every word she writes is a lie, including 'and' and 'the.'" The insiders' memoirs of both Richard Clarke and Paul O'Neill showed that every measure had been taken to embrace war with Iraq, not avoid it, and the Manning memo ratified their recollections with its account of Bush's proposal to Blair that Saddam be provoked into war if necessary. As for taking "every measure" to win the war, the war plan said quite the reverse. Anyone who actually proposed a plan for victory was shunted aside—most famously General Eric Shinseki, the army chief of staff who dared suggest in congressional testimony before the invasion that a force of "several hundred thousand soldiers" would be needed to provide "post-hostilities control over a piece of geography" with "the kinds of ethnic tensions that could lead to other problems." The only measures taken to win the war were the cheap and the slipshod, no matter what generals such as Shinseki, Anthony Zinni, or even Colin Powell had to say about it. The war's third anniversary kicked off a march of retired generals notable for their Iraq and Middle East experience calling for Rumsfeld's head. Among them was Marine Lieutenant General Gregory Newbold, the Pentagon's top operations officer from 2000 to October 2002, who revealed that he retired four months before the invasion in part because the administration had used "9/11's tragedy to hijack our security" and fight "an invented war" instead of "the real enemy, Al Qaeda."[16]

Whether the administration's inflated claims about Saddam's WMDs and Iraq-Qaeda ties were outright lies or the subconscious misreading of intelligence by officials with an idée fixe is a distinction without a difference. "I don't think we ever said—at least I know I didn't say that there was a direct connection between September the 11th and Saddam Hussein," Bush said in the spring of 2006. That is technically true, but it is really just truthiness: Bush struck 9/11 like a gong in every fear-instilling speech about Iraq he could. As for WMDs, the White House deliberately designated a mushroom cloud as the headliner in its doomsday litany—even though the evidence for nuclear WMDs, as the top U.S. officials well knew, was the most widely disputed within and beyond the government. If Bush, Cheney, and company were lying to themselves at the same time they were lying to the country, the best that can be said in their defense is that they made the same tragic error of all propagandists who come to ruin: they fell for their own scam.

But that last-ditch defense is hard to make, given that the lying about WMDs continued even after the war and even after the Saddam WMDs were debunked. When Bush said "We found the weapons of mass destruction" to a Polish reporter on May 29, 2003, he already knew that the "mobile biological laboratories" he was referring to were nothing of the kind. As *The Washington Post* reported in 2006, two days before Bush made his claim, a secret Pentagon-sponsored fact-finding mission of nine U.S. and British biological-weapons experts had reported back to Washington that "there was no connection to anything biological" in the trailers, which were jokingly derided by the scientists and engineers who had examined them as "the biggest sand toilets in the world."[17] This was a full year after the Iraqi defector known as Curveball, the main source for vetting these labs, had been branded by the CIA and the Defense Intelligence Agency as a liar. Yet even now these trailers would continue to be hyped for months more to come.

It came as little surprise to anyone when a Patrick Fitzgerald court filing in the spring of 2006 revealed that it was Bush himself who had given specific permission to Libby, via Cheney, to leak cherry-picked intelligence from the National Intelligence Estimate to both Woodward and Miller[18] in a desperate effort to prop up the administration's unraveling WMD claims. The president who had denied knowing "of anybody in my administration who leaked classified information" when the first Valerie Plame Wilson investigation began may have been the biggest leaker of all. The leaks, in time-honored fashion, went to the reporters the White House judged most reliably sympathetic: Woodward, Miller, Novak, in that order of preference and chronology. The motive for Bush's leaking was classic Washington: the president was trying to save his own skin.

WHEN THE WAR'S cheerleaders ran for the exits as Iraq fell apart, they defended their past support in a variety of ways. They expressed deep satisfaction about the removal of a barbarous dictator, as if to imply, as they did more forthrightly before the war, that anyone who opposed invading Iraq was morally disposed to whitewash or countenance Saddam Hussein's unspeakable crimes or was a wimpy pacifist lacking the will to wield American force against terror. Some liberal hawks airily announced that they had never been so silly as to buy the administration's claims about Saddam's WMDs—they had supported the war only to liberate Iraq, not because of any Iraqi threat against America.[19]

If nothing else, this arrogance united such liberal war boosters with the administration in their contempt for the great unwashed American public that bought the false WMD smoking guns in good faith. Fiction about purported WMDs—"the one issue that everyone could agree upon," as Wolfowitz had told *Vanity Fair*—was merely the opiate of the masses. As during Vietnam, condescension was a persistent hallmark of the best and brightest of the hawks. A typical example was Lawrence F. Kaplan, who, writing for *The New Republic* in September 2003, cited a 1999 study to assert that Americans would accept 29,853 deaths to "prevent Iraq from obtaining weapons of mass destruction." Though the failure to find any such weapons was already known by the time Kaplan was writing, six months after the invasion, that inconvenient fact didn't deter him. "The war's bloody aftermath hasn't elicited much of an outcry, either," he wrote, arguing that it was the "civilian elites" and "military elites" who were weak-kneed about the war instead. But it was the public, not the "elites," who turned against the war first—and did so when the casualties were still well below 2,000, not 29,853.

American hawks sometimes showered the same contempt on Iraqis as well: the former had the temerity to imagine that after Saddam fell, present-day Iraq would rally around Ahmad Chalabi, an American tool and neocon favorite who had not been in Iraq since 1958, when he was thirteen. When he faced the Iraqi voters as the head of a new political party in December 2005, he would prove to have literally no constituency: his slate did not win a single seat in the new 275-member Parliament.

Some onetime war boosters atoned for their sins, none more productively than Packer, whose *Assassins' Gate* illuminated his own self-deceptions as well as providing firsthand reportage on the failure of the occupation. Journalists not in Packer's league decided that the best defense was a self-righteous offense. Andrew Sullivan, who had tried to whip up a McCarthy-like witch hunt after 9/11 with the dark and preposterous warning that "the decadent Left in its enclaves on the coasts" threatened to "mount what amounts to a fifth column," now was reduced, not unlike President Bush, to praising his own good heart. "Few journalists have written as passionately as I have against the legalization of torture," he wrote in a letter-to-the-editor defending himself from Paul Krugman's criticism in *The New York Times*. But except in the hermetically sealed amen corner of his own blog, no one will ever count Sullivan among the half-dozen or so journalists who led the way on this horrific story, both in passionate commentary and in the dogged, demanding reporting that painstakingly exposed the abuses. That honor roll is headed by Seymour Hersh, Mark Danner, Dana Priest, Jane Mayer, Tim Golden, and others whose journalism is among the saving graces of an embarrassing era for the American news media.

As the administration's supporters fled, their most frequent farewell was a sentence beginning "If only I had known . . ." as in "If only I had known the White House would do such a lousy job of managing the war, of bungling intelligence, of indulging an obvious incompetent like Rumsfeld." The trouble with this excuse is that there was nothing in the administration's record before 9/11 to suggest that it was capable of anything more than a superficial, PR-focused approach to any project except tax cuts, business deregulation, or pandering to its culturally conservative base. The president who eased through his pre-political life with the help of connections and family retainers was still that same man when he took the country into Iraq.

There were plenty of advance warnings of the crack-up to come for anyone who wanted to pay attention. A government that fudged budget projects and other economic numbers before 9/11 was fated to play just as fast and loose with the facts when projecting the war's costs before the fighting started and enumerating the progress of reconstruction and training Iraqi troops in the war's aftermath. The likelihood that the White House would go into Iraq cowboy-style, with only the vaguest pretense of multilateralism or UN consultation, was also foretold; it was embedded not just in the administration's undisguised contempt for international bodies of all kinds but in its foreign-policy DNA dating back to the Cheney-Rumsfeld-Wolfowitz axis of American unilateralism in the Bush I Defense Department. In the matter of nation-building, it was not only the administration's antipathy to the idea that was a matter of public record; so was its complete lack of skills for the task. As Fred Kaplan asked rhetorically (and presciently) in *Slate* two weeks before the invasion, if the administration "lacks the acumen or persuasive power" to manage its own allies—even Canada—before the war, "then how is it going to handle Iraq's feuding opposition groups, Kurdish separatists, and myriad ethno-religious factions, to say nothing of the turbulence throughout the region?" It was all too predictable that even when the administration was forced into rebuilding Iraq, it would time every pivot point, from the creation of a constitution to the scheduling of elections, to deadlines dictated by Rove's political goals at home (whether a State of the Union speech or a domestic election), rather than to the patience-requiring realities of forging a post-Saddam government. That cynical priority was what had dictated the timing of the rollout of the product in the first place: it wasn't a mushroom cloud that was imminent as the White House pressed for a congressional resolution in the fall of 2002, it was the midterms.

Why so many smart people wanted to lash their reputations to this president's Iraq adventure given all that was known beforehand is as much a case study in psychology as in history. They didn't see what they didn't want to see until it was too late. Sometimes they seemed tone-deaf to the cultural manipulations of the Bush product-rollout apparatus, with its very deliberate and scripted orchestration of cues, especially its ostentatious repetition of nuclear imagery, between Labor Day 2002 and the invasion the following March. Shouldn't it have raised alarms that a war was being rushed on an arbitrary and reckless timetable that was in sync with an American election campaign?

As there was a self-aggrandizing tone to many of the hawks' prose after they turned on the war, so there had been to their cheerleading before the war. The strutting among the boomer journalistic pundits often suggested an overwhelming desire to prove that they could be a part of a greatest generation post-9/11, even if it was other people's children who would have to do the fighting. Their contempt for the war's critics often seems so defensive in retrospect that it's hard not to wonder if the overheated rhetoric was a reflection of their own deep-seated, unmentioned doubts about the Iraq project.

The wider American public who went along for the ride has a better excuse than the smart guys within the Beltway. Americans always love a good story. If a government is going to sell a scary one with brilliant stagecraft and relentless pacing, all the while trading on the emotions of one of the most horrific attacks on Western civilization in modern memory, it's not all that easy to resist. Americans trusted George W. Bush. They were no more expert on Iraq than he was, but they assumed he'd do his homework and get up to speed. That was his job. Even so, polls consistently showed ambivalence about the Iraq War—ambivalence that would finally be worn down by all those mushroom clouds.

The price has been enormous, and not just in American and Iraqi lives. One hideous consequence of the White House's biggest lie—conflating Saddam's regime with the international threat of radical Islam, fusing the war of choice in Iraq with the war of necessity that began on 9/11—is that the public, having turned against one war, automatically rejects the other. When Americans gave up on Iraq in 2005, the percentage who regarded fighting terrorism as a top national priority fell in sync. That's the bottom line of the Bush catastrophe: the administration at once increased the ranks of jihadists by turning Iraq into a new training ground and recruitment magnet while at the same time exhausting America's will and resources to confront that expanded threat.

Worse still, President Bush lost the war of ideas that, in the end, was the most potent American weapon for battling the nihilism of radical Islam. His doctrine of preemptive war, by 2006, had devolved on the ground in America to a rampant isolationism and xenophobia emblemized by a battle over illegal immigrants and the wholesale rejection by citizens and politicians of both parties of an American port-management contract with a rare Arab nation, the United Arab Emirates, that is *not* part of our Middle East problem.

After repeated and pointless Karen Hughes PR "listening tours" in which she tried to win Muslim hearts and minds by posing with little Arab kids as if they were interchangeable with the little black kids in Bush's "compassionate conservative" photo ops back home, even Rumsfeld had had enough. "Our enemies have skillfully adapted to fighting wars in today's media age," the defense secretary said in a 2006 Council on Foreign Relations appearance, complaining that America and its government deserved only a grade of D or D+ on that front and had "barely begun to compete in reaching their audiences." What he couldn't or wouldn't recognize, of course, is that America has reached those audiences all too vividly and counterproductively on his own watch—with the horrors of Abu Ghraib and the whitewashing of the commanders in charge, with planted fake news stories making a mockery of fledgling Iraqi democracy, with grandiose promises to rebuild Iraq's infrastructure that were left unfulfilled by the Americans in the bunker of Baghdad's Green Zone.

What if those thousands of tactical errors belatedly conceded by Rice had not been made? The story might have not turned out all that differently. The "what-if" that matters most is not "what if the Iraqi army had not been disbanded?" but "what if the Bush administration had told the truth?" What if it had not hyped the intelligence and tried to argue the case for regime change in Iraq on its merits, whether geopolitical or humanitarian? What if it had conceded early on that it miscalculated the post-Saddam aftermath in Iraq? What if it had then invited Americans and their elected representatives to have a candid debate about the options, costs, sacrifices, and possible benefits ahead? What if a government that so fervently espoused democracy for the world had had a commensurate faith in democracy at home?

These questions, simple and even naïve as they may be, matter more than all the tactical questions combined. That they are so rarely asked in the wake of this debacle is a measure of just how much the very idea of truth is an afterthought and an irrelevancy in a culture where the best story wins. While the Bush administration's toboggan ride into Iraq was facilitated by an easily cowed press and a timid and often disingenuous political opposition, the news culture that predated both 9/11 and this presidency also played a big role.

It was in the mid 1990s that the American electronic news media jumped the shark. That's when CNN was joined by even more boisterous rival 24/7 cable networks, when the Internet became a mass medium, and when television news operations, by far the main source of news for Americans, were gobbled up by entertainment giants such as Disney, Viacom, and Time Warner. While there had always been a strong entertainment component to TV news, that packaging was now omnipresent, shaping the coverage of stories from Washington scandals to Wall Street bubbles to child abductions to war—and around the clock, not just on the evening news, the morning shows, and the occasional network newsmagazine. In this new mediathon environment, drama counted more than judicious journalism; clear-cut "evildoers" and patriots were prized over ambiguous characters who didn't wear either black or white hats. Once-definable distinctions between truth and fiction were blurred more than ever before, as "reality" was redefined in news and prime-time entertainment alike.

The Bush White House certainly did not invent this culture. It has been years in the making and it is bipartisan. But this administration was the first to take office after it was fully on-line and was brilliant at exploiting it to serve its own selfish reality-remaking ends. The TV maw needs to be fed 24/7, and Bush's producers supplied a nonstop progression of compelling shows to do so. If this White House knew anything, it knew how to roll out a slick product by the yard.

History tells us that politics is cyclical in America, and the Bush cycle may well be in its last throes. But the culture in which it thrived still rides high, waiting to be exploited by another master manipulator from either political party if Americans don't start to take it back.

WHAT THE WHITE HOUSE KNEW AND WHEN IT KNEW IT: TIME LINES OF THE SELLING OF THE WAR

IN THE MONTHS AFTER 9/11, the Bush administration resisted calls for an official investigation into the missteps, intelligence failures, and general haplessness that had led to the attacks. Thanks to the persistence of the victims' families, we now have the 9/11 Commission's definitive history—down to the minute—of how we arrived at that Tuesday in September 2001. We do not yet have an official accounting of what happened after.

The pair of time lines on the following pages is an attempt to map the rollout of the administration's false intelligence claims about Iraq, as typified by that mythical uranium from Africa at the center of the Valerie Plame Wilson case, and to contrast that often-fictional narrative with the contradictory intelligence that the White House failed to divulge to the public as it told and sold its story. As Patrick Fitzgerald's investigation began to prompt revelations about a desperate administration's efforts to salvage its flawed case for war, the gap between these two narrative tracks became more and more visible—and continues to widen with each new revelation of accurate intelligence that the administration either suppressed or ignored.

NOTE ON THE TYPE

Entries in *italics* in the right-hand column chronicle the story that was sold by the Bush administration and other relevant events, news reports, or official statements that were known publicly at the time.

Entries in roman type in the shaded left-hand column chronicle what the administration was learning behind the scenes about intelligence and other war-related matters—and *not* telling the public. The events in this hidden time line were revealed publicly only later; citations note the dates and sources of each revelation.

Footnotes beginning "*See entry . . ." allow the reader to locate the dates in the time lines when the administration received information that contradicted its public statements. In footnotes, roman dates refer to the behind-the-scenes (roman) column; *italic* dates refer to the public (*italic*) column.

TIME LINES

The time lines, seen here as they stood on May 22, 2006, may be accessed online at www.frankrich.com. They will be updated as events warrant, and readers are encouraged to send their own updates and additions for inclusion in the Web version.

SEPTEMBER 15, 2001
During a meeting at Camp David to discuss the war plan, Defense Secretary Rumsfeld and Deputy Defense Secretary Wolfowitz advocate an attack on Iraq, noting the scarcity of "good targets in Afghanistan."
· First reported in Bob Woodward's *Bush at War*, November 2002.

SEPTEMBER 16, 2001
Vice President Dick Cheney speaks with Tim Russert on Meet the Press:

TIM RUSSERT: Saddam Hussein, your old friend, his government had this to say: "The American cowboy is rearing the fruits of crime against humanity." If we determine that Saddam Hussein is also harboring terrorists, and there's a track record there, would we have any reluctance of going after Saddam Hussein?

VICE PRESIDENT CHENEY: No.

MR. RUSSERT: Do we have evidence that he's harboring terrorists?

VICE PRESIDENT CHENEY: There is— in the past, there have been some activities related to terrorism by Saddam Hussein. But at this stage, you know, the focus is over here on Al Qaeda and the most recent events in New York. Saddam Hussein's bottled up, at this point, but clearly, we continue to have a fairly tough policy where the Iraqis are concerned.

MR. RUSSERT: Do we have any evidence linking Saddam Hussein or Iraqis to this operation?

VICE PRESIDENT CHENEY: No.

SEPTEMBER 19, 2001

At a meeting of the Defense Policy Board, Iraqi National Congress leader Ahmad Chalabi and the Mideast scholar Bernard Lewis address the group, arguing for U.S. action against Iraq.

· First reported in *USA Today*,
September 11, 2002.

SEPTEMBER 21, 2001

In the President's Daily Brief (PDB), President Bush is told that there is no evidence of Iraqi participation in 9/11 and "scant credible evidence" of any "significant collaborative ties" between Iraq and Al Qaeda. The president is further told that Saddam regards Al Qaeda and "other theocratic radical Islamist organizations" as threats to his secular regime and that he even considered infiltrating the organization with Iraqi nationals or intelligence operatives. The CIA assessment is also distributed to Vice President Cheney, National Security Advisor Condoleezza Rice and her deputy, Stephen Hadley, Defense Secretary Rumsfeld, Deputy Defense Secretary Wolfowitz, Secretary of State Colin Powell, and others.

· First reported in *National Journal,* November 22, 2005.

SEPTEMBER 28, 2001

According to a poll in The Washington Post, *87 percent say that capturing Osama bin Laden and breaking up his network is a "must do"; 39 percent say overthrowing Saddam, "even if he is not linked to the attacks," is a "must do."*

OCTOBER 15, 2001

"Reporting on a possible uranium yellowcake sales agreement between Niger and Iraq first came to the attention of the U.S. Intelligence Community."

· From the Senate Intelligence Committee's "Report on the U.S. Intelligence Community's Prewar Intelligence Assessments on Iraq," July 7, 2004.

OCTOBER 26, 2001

At a news conference in Prague, the Czech interior minister confirms that an Iraqi intelligence officer, Ahmed Khalil Ibrahim Samir al-Ani, met with the 9/11 ringleader, Mohamed Atta, in Prague in early 2001.

NOVEMBER 20, 2001

"U.S. Embassy Niamey disseminated a cable on a recent meeting between the ambassador and the Director General of Niger's French-led consortium. The Director General said 'there was no possibility' that the government of Niger had diverted any of the 3,000 tons of yellowcake produced in its two uranium mines."

· From the Senate Intelligence Committee's "Report on the U.S. Intelligence Community's Prewar Intelligence Assessments on Iraq," July 7, 2004.

NOVEMBER 21, 2001

President Bush orders Defense Secretary Rumsfeld to "get Tommy Franks looking at what it would take to protect America by removing Saddam Hussein if we have to."

· From Bob Woodward's *Plan of Attack*, April 2004.

NOVEMBER 26, 2001

At a Rose Garden press conference, President Bush emphasizes that "Afghanistan is still just the beginning" and publicly suggests for the first time that Iraq may be the next target in the war on terrorism: "As for Mr. Saddam Hussein, he needs to let inspectors back in his country to show us that he is not developing weapons of mass destruction."

DECEMBER 1, 2001

A Fox News/Opinion Dynamics poll finds that 47 percent believe it is "very likely" that Saddam was "involved" in the 9/11 attacks.

DECEMBER 9, 2001

Appearing on Meet the Press, *Dick Cheney advances the notion of an Iraq-Qaeda connection for the first time:*

VICE PRESIDENT CHENEY: Well, what we now have that's developed since you and I last talked, Tim, of course, was that report that—it's been pretty well confirmed that [Atta] did go to Prague and he did meet with a senior official of the Iraqi intelligence service in Czechoslovakia last April, several months before the attack. Now, what the purpose of that was, what transpired between them, we simply don't know at this point, but that's clearly an avenue that we want to pursue.

MR. RUSSERT: What we do know is they—Iraq is harboring terrorists.

VICE PRESIDENT CHENEY: Correct.

DECEMBER 17, 2001

The results of a CIA-administered polygraph determine that Adnan Ihsan Saeed al-Haideri, a civil engineer who claimed to have helped Saddam's men secretly bury tons of biological, chemical, and nuclear weapons, was lying. Al-Haideri claimed the weapons were buried in subterranean wells, hidden in private villas, and stashed beneath the Saddam Hussein Hospital, the largest medical facility in Baghdad. Days later, Ahmad Chalabi arranges for Judith Miller of *The New York Times* to interview al-Haideri in a Bangkok hotel room under the supervision of the Iraqi National Congress.

· Reported by James Bamford in his book *Pretext for War*, June 2004, and in an article for *Rolling Stone*, December 1, 2005.

DECEMBER 20, 2001

The New York Times *publishes an article by Judith Miller, "Iraqi Tells of Renovations* at Sites for Chemical and Nuclear Arms": "An Iraqi defector who described himself as a civil engineer said he personally worked on renovations of secret facilities for biological, chemical and nuclear weapons in underground wells, private villas and under the Saddam Hussein Hospital in Baghdad as recently as a year ago."

DECEMBER 21, 2001

A Washington Post/ABC News poll finds that after the rapid collapse of the Taliban in Afghanistan, Americans, by a ratio of nearly two to one, believe that the war on terrorism will be a success only with the death or capture of Osama bin Laden and the removal of Saddam Hussein from power. By more than three to one, Americans favor broadening the war to other countries where terrorists are believed to operate, such as Somalia, Sudan, and Yemen. President Bush ends the year with an 86 percent approval rating.

FEBRUARY 2002

"Based on information from the C.I.A. report from the foreign service, on February 12, 2002, the [Defense Intelligence Agency] wrote a finished intelligence product titled 'Niamey signed an agreement to sell 500 tons of uranium a year to Baghdad'.... The piece concluded that 'Iraq probably is searching abroad for natural uranium to assist in its nuclear weapons program.' The product did not include any judgments about the credibility of the reporting."

· From the Senate Intelligence Committee's "Report on the U.S. Intelligence Community's Prewar Intelligence Assessments on Iraq," July 7, 2004.

Joseph P. Wilson IV, a former ambassador to Niger, travels to Niamey and determines the alleged sale to be unfounded.

The Defense Intelligence Agency issues a report that includes documents identifying Ibn al-Shaykh al-Libi, a top member of Al Qaeda in American custody, as a likely fabricator. Among his possible fabrications were claims that Iraq had provided biological and chemical weapons training to Qaeda members. The Defense Intelligence Terrorism Summary concludes that "it is more likely this individual is intentionally misleading the debriefers. Ibn al-Shaykh has been undergoing debriefs for several weeks and may be describing scenarios to the debriefers that he knows will retain their interest."

· The documents are later declassified and made public by Senator Carl Levin (D-Mich.) in November 2005.

MARCH 4, 2002
A high-level intelligence assessment by the Bush administration concluded in early 2002 that the sale of uranium from Niger to Iraq was "unlikely" because of a host of economic, diplomatic, and logistical obstacles, according to a secret State Department memo.

· The memo was declassified in early 2006 through a Freedom of Information Act request filed by Judicial Watch and reported on in *The New York Times*, January 18, 2006.

MARCH 11, 2002
A Washington Post/*ABC News poll finds that while 91 percent support the Afghanistan conflict, the percentage of "strong" support-*

ers has dipped from 79 percent in November to 69 percent in the latest poll. Also, since late November 2001, the proportion who say the war in Afghanistan is going "very well" dropped from 42 percent to 24 percent. An additional 61 percent say the conflict is going "fairly well," up from 51 percent in November.

MARCH 24, 2002

On CNN's Late Edition, Dick Cheney first makes reference to Saddam's nuclear ambitions: "This is a man of great evil, as the President said. And he is actively pursuing nuclear weapons at this time."

APRIL 17, 2002

The Washington Post reports that the Bush administration had concluded that bin Laden had been in Tora Bora in December 2001 but decided not to commit American ground troops then to hunt him, thereby allowing him to escape.

MAY 2002

A fabricator warning is posted in U.S. intelligence databases in reference to a former major in the Iraqi intelligence service, the most important of three CIA sources who claimed to corroborate claims about mobile labs made by the Iraqi defector known as Curveball. The CIA and DIA concluded that he was a liar. (Two of the three sources had ties to Ahmad Chalabi; all three were deemed frauds.)

· First reported in the Los Angeles Times, November 20, 2005.

MAY 19, 2002
"[W]e know [Saddam is] working on nu-clear."—Dick Cheney appearing on NBC's
Meet the Press.

MAY 31, 2002
A USA Today/CNN/Gallup poll finds that Americans are increasingly pessimistic about the war on terrorism after weeks of revelations about missed clues and warnings of likely future attacks. Four in ten Americans believe that the United States and its allies are winning the war on terrorism. In January, when headlines focused on military successes in Afghanistan, two thirds of those polled felt the nation was winning. Now, 35 percent say neither side is winning the war, and 15 percent say the terrorists are winning.

JUNE 1, 2002
In a speech to graduating cadets at West Point, President Bush outlines the case for preemptive war: "If we wait for threats to fully material-ize, we will have waited too long."

JUNE 21, 2002
A CIA report entitled "Iraq and Al Qaeda: Interpreting a Murky Relationship" notes the "many critical gaps" in knowledge of Iraqi links to Al Qaeda due to "limited reporting" and the "questionable reliability of many of our sources." It states that "Reporting is contradictory on hijacker Mohamed Atta's alleged trip to Prague and meeting with an Iraqi intelligence officer, and we have not verified his travels." Regarding reports of Iraq's providing chemical and biological weapons

training, the report states "the level and extent of this assistance is not clear."

· First reported in *Newsweek*,
July 19, 2004.

JUNE 26, 2002

In a letter to the Senate Appropriations Committee, Iraqi National Congress lobbyist Entifadh Qanbar describes the INC's Information Collection Program, which is "designed to collect, analyze, and disseminate" information from Iraq: "Defectors, reports, and raw intelligence are cultivated and analyzed and the results are reported through the INC newspaper [*Al Mutamar*], the Arabic and Western media, and to appropriate governmental, nongovernmental, and international agencies." The memo identifies John Hannah, a senior national-security aide to Vice President Cheney, and William Luti, the deputy undersecretary of defense later in charge of the secret Iraq War–planning outfit, Office of Special Plans, as "U.S. governmental recipients" of these reports.

· First reported in *Newsweek*,
December 15, 2003. Full quote is
from Douglas McCollam, "The List:
How Chalabi Played the Press,"
Columbia Journalism Review,
July/August 2004.

JULY 23, 2002

Senior British officials meet with Prime Minister Tony Blair to discuss Iraq. The minutes of the meeting, known as the Downing Street memo, include the remarks of the head of Britain's MI6 intelligence agency, Sir Richard Dearlove. He reports

on his recent talks in Washington. There was a perceptible shift in attitude. Military action was now seen as inevitable. Bush wanted to remove Saddam, through military action, justified by the conjunction of terrorism and WMD. But the intelligence and facts were being fixed around the policy. The NSC had no patience with the UN route, and no enthusiasm for publishing material on the Iraqi regime's record. There was little discussion in Washington of the aftermath after military action.

Foreign Secretary Jack Straw adds: "It seemed clear that Bush had made up his mind to take military action, even if the timing was not yet decided. But the case was thin. Saddam was not threatening his neighbours, and his WMD capability was less than that of Libya, North Korea or Iran."

· The memo is first revealed in *The Sunday Times* of London on May 1, 2005.

August 2002

Andrew Card forms the White House Iraq Group (WHIG), which begins to meet weekly in the Situation Room. Regular participants include: Karl Rove; communications strategists Karen Hughes, Mary Matalin, and James R. Wilkinson; legislative liaison Nicholas E. Calio; and policy advisers led by Condoleezza Rice and her deputy, Stephen J. Hadley, along with I. Lewis Libby, Cheney's chief of staff.

> · First reported in *The Washington Post*, August 10, 2003.

AUGUST 7, 2002

In a speech to the California Commonwealth Club, Dick Cheney continues to warn of Saddam's pursuit of nuclear weapons: "What we know now, from various sources, is that he has continued to improve the, if you can put it in those terms, the capabilities of his nuclear . . . and he continues to pursue a nuclear weapon."

AUGUST 23, 2002

A Gallup poll finds that a thin majority of Americans still support sending ground troops to Iraq to oust Saddam Hussein, but the number has fallen to pre-9/11 levels, from a high of 74 percent in November to 53 percent. A total of 86 percent say Saddam is supporting terrorist groups planning to attack the U.S.; 53 percent believe he was involved in the 9/11 attacks; 94 percent say Saddam either has weapons of mass destruction or is developing them; 83 percent of those who say he has weapons of mass destruction say he would use them to attack the United States. The poll also finds that the president's job approval rating has fallen to 65 percent—its lowest level since before 9/11.

AUGUST 26, 2002

In a speech to the VFW 103rd National Convention, Dick Cheney returns to the subject of Saddam's nukes: "But we now know that Saddam has resumed his efforts to acquire nuclear weapons."

SEPTEMBER 4, 2002
Meeting with congressional leaders, President Bush announces that he will seek congressional approval before ordering military action against Iraq.

SEPTEMBER 7, 2002
In an interview published in The New York Times, Andrew Card explains the White House's public relations strategy on preemptive war with Iraq: "From a marketing point of view, you don't introduce new products in August."

SEPTEMBER 8, 2002
The lead story in The New York Times, "U.S. Says Hussein Intensifies Quest for A-Bomb Parts," reports that Saddam has sought to acquire thousands of aluminum tubes believed to be intended as components for a centrifuge to enrich uranium for bomb material. The story, co-written by Michael R. Gordon and Judith Miller, cites "Bush administration officials." Dick Cheney, Condoleezza Rice, Donald Rumsfeld, and Colin Powell each appear on Sunday morning news shows to tout the story.
Appearing on Meet the Press, Cheney cites the aluminum tubes in describing Saddam's path to acquiring nuclear weapons:

VICE PRESIDENT CHENEY: Well, in the nuclear weapons arena, you've got sort of three key elements that you need to acquire. You need the technical expertise. You need to have a group of scientists and technicians, engineers, who know how to put together the infrastructure and to build a weapon. He's got that. He had it because of his program that was there previously, which I'll come back and talk about in a minute, but we know he's been working for 20 years trying to acquire this capability. He's got a well-established scientifically, technically competent crew to do it.

Secondly, you need a weapons design. One of the toughest parts about building a nuclear weapon is knowing how to do it. And they've got that. He had it back prior to the Gulf War. We know from things that were uncovered during the course of the inspections back in the early '90s that he did, in fact, have at least two designs for nuclear weapons.

The third thing you need is fissile material, weapons-grade material. Now, in the case of a nuclear weapon, that means either plutonium or highly enriched uranium. And what we've seen recently that has raised our level of concern to the current state of unrest, if you will, if I can put it in those terms, is that he now is trying, through his illicit procurement network, to acquire the equipment he needs to be able to enrich uranium to make the bombs.

TIM RUSSERT: Aluminum tubes.

VICE PRESIDENT CHENEY: Specifically aluminum tubes. There's a story in The New York Times this morning—this is—I don't—and I want to attribute the Times. I don't want to talk about, obviously, specific intelligence sources, but it's now public that, in fact, he has been seeking to acquire, and we have been able to intercept and prevent him from acquiring through this particular channel, the kinds of tubes that are necessary to build a centrifuge. And the centrifuge is required to take low-grade uranium and enhance it into highly enriched uranium, which is what you have to have in order to build a bomb. This is a technology he was working on back, say, before the Gulf War. And one of the reasons it's of concern, Tim, is, you know, we know about a particular shipment. We've intercepted that. We don't know what else— what other avenues he may be taking out there, what he may have already acquired. We do know he's had four years without any inspections at all in Iraq to develop that capability. . . . We know we have a part of the picture. And that part of the picture tells us that he is, in fact, actively and aggressively seeking to acquire nuclear weapons.

Appearing on CNN's Late Edition, Rice tells Wolf Blitzer, "The problem here is that there will always be some uncertainty about how quickly he can acquire nuclear weapons. But we don't want the smoking gun to be a mushroom cloud."

Appearing on CBS's Face the Nation, Rumsfeld echoes Rice:

BOB SCHIEFFER: Well, let me ask you, then, tell me about the seriousness of the problem. We—we read in The New York Times today a story that says that Saddam Hussein is closer to acquiring nuclear weapons. Does he have nuclear weapons? Is there a smoking gun here?

SECRETARY RUMSFELD: The smoking gun is an interesting phrase. It—it implies that what we're doing here is law enforcement; that what we're looking for is a case that we can take into a court of law and prove beyond a reasonable doubt. The problem with that is the way one gains absolute certainty as to whether a dictator like Saddam Hussein has a nuclear weapon is if he uses it, and that's a little late.

Appearing on Fox News Sunday, *Powell tells Tony Snow, "With respect to nuclear weapons, we are quite confident that he continues to try to pursue the technology that would allow him to develop a nuclear weapon. . . . And as we saw in reporting just this morning, he is still trying to acquire, for example, some of the specialized aluminum tubing one needs to develop centrifuges that would give you an enrichment capability."*

On Meet the Press, *Cheney revisits his September 2001 remarks on the likelihood of an Iraq-Qaeda connection:*

VICE PRESIDENT CHENEY: Well, I want to be very careful about how I say this. I'm not here today to make a specific allegation that Iraq was somehow responsible for 9/11. I can't say that. On the other hand, since we did that interview, new information has come to light. And we spent time looking at that relationship between Iraq, on the one hand, and the Al Qaeda organization on the other. And there has been reporting that suggests that there have been a number of contacts over the years. We've seen in connection with the hijackers, of course, Mohamed Atta, who was the lead hijacker, did apparently travel to Prague on a number of occasions. And on at least one occasion, we have reporting that places him in Prague with a senior Iraqi intelligence official a few months before the attack on the World Trade Center. The debates about, you know, was he there or wasn't he there, again, it's the intelligence business. *

---

*See entries for June 21, 2002, and *October 21, 2002.*

MR. RUSSERT: What does the C.I.A. say about that? Is it credible?

VICE PRESIDENT CHENEY: It's credible. But, you know, I think a way to put it would be it's unconfirmed at this point. We've got . . .

MR. RUSSERT: Anything else?

VICE PRESIDENT CHENEY: There is—again, I want to separate out 9/11, from the other relationships between Iraq and the Al Qaeda organization. But there is a pattern of relationships going back many years. . . .*

MR. RUSSERT: But no direct link?

VICE PRESIDENT CHENEY: I can't— I'll leave it right where it's at. I don't want to go beyond that. I've tried to be cautious and restrained in my comments, and I hope that everybody will recognize that.

A New York Times/CBS *poll reports that 68 percent approve of the United States taking military action to try to remove Saddam Hussein from power, though only 27 percent believe the administration has explained the U.S. position regarding Iraq; 62 percent believe the president should seek congressional approval for an attack.*

SEPTEMBER 11, 2002
President Bush commemorates the first anniversary of 9/11 with an elaborately staged speech from Ellis Island.

---

*See entry for September 21, 2001.

SEPTEMBER 12, 2002
President Bush outlines the Iraqi threat in a speech to the UN's General Assembly.

The White House posts to its Web site a document entitled "A Decade of Deception and Defiance," which includes a reference to the Iraqi defector al-Haideri's buried WMD claims and cites Judith Miller's December 2001 New York Times *article.* (The document remains at the White House Web site.)*

*An NBC/*Wall Street Journal *poll finds that 53 percent believe that members of Al Qaeda are based in Iraq.*

SEPTEMBER 14, 2002
In his weekly radio address, President Bush says that Saddam "has illicitly sought to purchase the equipment needed to enrich uranium for a nuclear weapon. Should his regime acquire fissile material, it would be able to build a nuclear weapon within a year."

MID-SEPTEMBER 2002
CIA director George Tenet informs President Bush that both the State and Energy departments have doubts about Saddam's aluminum tubes and that some within the CIA aren't certain that the tubes were meant for nuclear weapons.

· First reported in *National Journal*, March 30, 2006.

At a meeting with Bush, Cheney, and Rice, CIA director Tenet says that a member of Saddam Hussein's inner circle, his foreign minister Naji Sabri, had made a deal to re-

---

*See entry for December 17, 2001.

veal Iraq's military secrets to the CIA and reported that there was "no active weapons of mass destruction program."
· First reported by *60 Minutes*, April 23, 2006.

SEPTEMBER 18, 2002
Testimony at a hearing of the Joint Intelligence Committees on pre-9/11 intelligence failures reveals for the first time that there was specific intelligence about terrorist plans to crash airplanes into the World Trade Center, including a warning in 1998.

SEPTEMBER 20, 2002
"We now have irrefutable evidence that [Saddam] has once again set up and reconstituted his program to take uranium, to enrich it to sufficiently high grade, so that it will function as the base material as a nuclear weapon.... There's no doubt about what he's attempting. And there's no doubt about the fact that the level of effort has escalated in recent months."*—Dick Cheney at a GOP fund-raiser in Casper, Wyoming, as recorded by the Associated Press.

SEPTEMBER 24, 2002
A British dossier provides the first public charge that Iraq sought to buy uranium from an unspecified African country.

SEPTEMBER 24, 2002
CIA director Tenet briefs a closed hearing of the Senate Foreign Relations Committee on Iraq's nuclear program, adding uranium to the aluminum tube story: "The suitability of the tubes for that purpose had

---

*See entry for Mid-September 2002.

been disputed, but this time the argument that Iraq had a nuclear program under way was buttressed by a new and striking fact: the C.I.A. had recently received intelligence showing that, between 1999 and 2001, Iraq had attempted to buy five hundred tons of uranium oxide from Niger, one of the world's largest producers."*

· First reported in *The New Yorker,*
March 31, 2003.

S E P T E M B E R   2 4 ,   2 0 0 2
A CNN/USA Today/Gallup poll finds that 50 percent believe that Al Qaeda is a bigger threat to the United States, while 28 percent say that Iraq is.

S E P T E M B E R   2 5 ,   2 0 0 2
A CBS News poll finds that 51 percent think Saddam was "personally involved" in 9/11; 70 percent say Qaeda members are based in Iraq.

S E P T E M B E R   2 6 ,   2 0 0 2
At a Defense Department briefing, Defense Secretary Rumsfeld discusses collaboration between Iraq and Al Qaeda:

> *We have what we believe to be credible information that Iraq and Al Qaeda have discussed safe haven opportunities in Iraq, reciprocal non-aggression discussions.* We have what we consider to be credible evidence that Al Qaeda leaders have sought contacts in Iraq who could help them acquire weapon of—weapons of*

---

*See entries for November 20, 2001, and March 4, 2002.

*See entry for September 21, 2001.

mass destruction capabilities. We do have—I believe it's one report indicating that Iraq provided unspecified training relating to chemical and/or biological matters for Al Qaeda members.* There is, I'm told, also some other information of varying degrees of reliability that supports that conclusion of their cooperation.

SEPTEMBER 28, 2002

In his weekly radio address, President Bush says the Iraqi regime "has longstanding and continuing ties to terrorist groups, and there are Al Qaeda terrorists inside Iraq."†

OCTOBER 2002

The Pentagon's Northern Gulf Affairs office is renamed the Office of Special Plans, a more generic name meant to obscure its objective of gathering intelligence to build a case and prepare for the invasion of Iraq. The office reverts to its former name in July 2003.

· *Newsday*, August 12, 2003.

OCTOBER 1, 2002

The National Intelligence Communities (NIC) publish a National Intelligence Estimate (NIE) on "Iraq's Continuing Programs for Weapons of Mass Destruction." Due to a formatting problem in an earlier draft version, the dissenting view held by the State Department's Bureau of Intelligence and Research (INR) regarding Iraqi pursuit of African uranium—that

---

*See entry for February 2002 (regarding Ibn al-Shaykh al-Libi).

†See entry for September 21, 2001.

such claims were "highly dubious"—is confined to a text box, separated by some sixty pages from the discussion of the uranium issue.

On the matter of aluminum tubes, the NIE states:

> In INR's view Iraq's efforts to acquire aluminum tubes is central to the argument that Baghdad is reconstituting its nuclear weapons program, but INR is not persuaded that the tubes in question are intended for use as centrifuge rotors. INR accepts the judgment of technical experts at the U.S. Department of Energy (DOE) who have concluded that the tubes Iraq seeks to acquire are poorly suited for use in gas centrifuges to be used for uranium enrichment and finds unpersuasive the arguments advanced by others to make the case that they are intended for that purpose. INR considers it far more likely that the tubes are intended for another purpose, most likely the production of artillery rockets. The very large quantities being sought, the way the tubes were tested by the Iraqis, and the atypical lack of attention to operational security in the procurement efforts are among the factors, in addition to the DOE assessment, that lead INR to conclude that the tubes are not intended for use in Iraq's nuclear weapon program.
>
> · From the Senate Intelligence Committee's "Report on the U.S. Intelligence Community's Prewar Intelligence Assessments on Iraq," July 7, 2004.

A one-page summary of the NIE is prepared for President Bush, handed to him
by CIA director George Tenet, and read
in Tenet's presence. The President's Summary, as it is formally known, states that
while "most agencies judge" that Iraq's
procurement of aluminum tubes was "related to a uranium enrichment effort . . .
INR and DOE believe that the tubes more
likely are intended for conventional
weapons uses."

· First revealed in *National Journal*,
March 2, 2006.

OCTOBER 1, 2002
A Newsweek *poll finds that 24 percent say
removing Saddam would be better for national security; 37 percent say removing bin
Laden/Al Qaeda would be better for security.*

OCTOBER 2, 2002
"On October 2, 2002, the Deputy DCI
testified before the SSCI. Senator Jon Kyl
asked the Deputy DCI whether he had
read the British white paper and whether
he disagreed with anything in the report.
The Deputy DCI testified that 'the one
thing where I think they stretched a little
bit beyond where we would stretch is on
the points about Iraq seeking uranium
from various African locations. We've
looked at those reports and we don't think
they are very credible. It doesn't diminish
our conviction that he's going for nuclear
weapons, but I think they reached a little
bit on that one point. Otherwise I think
it's very solid.'"

· From the Senate Intelligence
Committee's "Report on the U.S.

Intelligence Community's Prewar
Intelligence Assessments on
Iraq," July 7, 2004.

OCTOBER 6, 2002

After recommending that a reference to
the Iraqi pursuit of African uranium be
stricken from a draft of a presidential
speech set for October 7, the CIA faxes a
fuller account of its reasoning: "Three
points: (1) The evidence is weak. One of
the two mines cited by the source as the location of the uranium oxide is flooded.
The other mine cited by the source is under the control of the French authorities.
(2) The procurement is not particularly
significant to Iraq's nuclear ambitions because the Iraqis already have a large stock
of uranium oxide in their inventory. And
(3) we have shared points one and two
with Congress, telling them that the
Africa story is overblown and telling them
this is one of the two issues where we dif-
fered with the British."

· From the Senate Intelligence
Committee's "Report on the U.S. Intelli-
gence Community's Prewar Intelligence
Assessments on Iraq," July 7, 2004.

OCTOBER 7, 2002

*In a televised address from Cincinnati, Presi-
dent Bush says:*

> *Iraq has attempted to purchase high-
> strength aluminum tubes and other equip-
> ment needed for gas centrifuges, which are
> used to enrich uranium for nuclear
> weapons.* *

*See entry for October 1, 2002 (regarding the
President's Summary).

We know that Iraq and Al Qaeda have had high-level contacts that go back a decade. Some Al Qaeda leaders who fled Afghanistan went to Iraq. These include one very senior Al Qaeda leader who received medical treatment in Baghdad this year, and who has been associated with planning for chemical and biological attacks. We've learned that Iraq has trained Al Qaeda members in bomb-making and poisons and deadly gases. *

Facing clear evidence of peril, we cannot wait for the final proof, the smoking gun that could come in the form of a mushroom cloud. . . .

OCTOBER 9, 2002

"On October 9, 2002, an Italian journalist from the magazine *Panorama* provided U.S. Embassy Rome with copies of documents pertaining to the alleged Iraq-Niger uranium transaction. The journalist had acquired the documents from a source who had requested 15,000 Euros in return for their publication, and wanted the embassy to authenticate the documents. Embassy officers provided copies of the documents to the C.I.A.'s [redacted] because the embassy . . . was sending copies of the documents back to State Department headquarters."

· From the Senate Intelligence Committee's "Report on the U.S. Intelligence Community's Prewar Intelligence Assessments on Iraq," July 7, 2004.

---

*See entries for September 21, 2001, and February 2002 (regarding Ibn al-Shaykh al-Libi).

OCTOBER 10, 2002

The House of Representatives votes to pass a resolution on use of force in Iraq.

OCTOBER 11, 2002

The Senate passes the Iraq resolution.
A Pew poll reports that 66 percent believe that Saddam helped the 9/11 terrorists.

OCTOBER 15, 2002

The U.S. embassy in Rome faxes copies of the Niger documents to the State Department, where an INR analyst immediately suspects their legitimacy. The analyst provides copies to other intelligence agencies, which apparently ignore the documents.

· From the Senate Intelligence Committee's "Report on the U.S. Intelligence Community's Prewar Intelligence Assessments on Iraq," July 7, 2004.

OCTOBER 16, 2002

President Bush signs the Iraq resolution, saying, "With this resolution, Congress has now authorized the use of force. I have not ordered the use of force. I hope the use of force will not become necessary."

OCTOBER 21, 2002

The New York Times *reports that Czech President Václav Havel had called the White House in early 2002 to discreetly tell senior administration officials that there was no evidence that 9/11 hijacker Mohamed Atta had met with an Iraqi intelligence officer in Prague—a conclusion shared by the American intelligence community. (Later a*

Czech government spokesman said that Havel did not make the call but reaffirmed that there was no evidence of the Prague meeting.)

DECEMBER 2, 2002
*In remarks to the Air National Guard conference, Vice President Cheney posits a collaboration between Saddam and Al Qaeda: "His regime has had high-level contacts with Al Qaeda going back a decade and has provided training to Al Qaeda terrorists."**

DECEMBER 19, 2002
The official U.S. response to Iraq's declaration of disarmament notes Iraq's failure to account for African uranium, representing the first public accusation by the United States and the first time Niger is specified.†

DECEMBER 21, 2002
CIA director Tenet and his deputy, John McLaughlin, present "The Case" to President Bush, Vice President Cheney, National Security Advisor Rice, and Chief of Staff Card in the Oval Office. Responding to the president's skepticism about the marketability of the case, Tenet exclaims, "It's a slam dunk case!"
· First reported in Bob Woodward's *Plan of Attack*, April 2004.

---

*See entries for September 21, 2001, and February 2002 (regarding Ibn al-Shaykh al-Libi).
†See entries for November 20, 2001, March 4, 2002, October 1, 2002 (regarding the NIE), and October 6, 2002.

DECEMBER 24, 2002
*Niger's prime minister declares publicly that
Iraq has neither purchased nor inquired about
purchasing uranium from Niger since he took
office in 2000.*

JANUARY 2003
In an informal National Intelligence Estimate, intelligence agencies unanimously conclude that Saddam was unlikely to attack the United States unless attacked first. A one-page President's Summary, entitled "Nontraditional Threats to the U.S. Homeland through 2007," is delivered to President Bush, who reads it in the presence of then CIA director George Tenet. Vice President Cheney receives virtually the same intelligence.

· First reported in *National Journal*,
March 2, 2006.

Concerned about the effect on its ties with Niger, the Pentagon requested an authoritative judgment on whether or not Iraq attempted to procure uranium from Niger. The National Intelligence Council (NIC)—the coordinating body for the fifteen agencies that constituted the U.S. intelligence committee—drafted a memo stating unequivocally that the claim was baseless. According to four U.S. officials with firsthand knowledge later interviewed by *The Washington Post*, the NIC memo was delivered to the White House as the administration began to make the Niger claim the centerpiece of its case against Iraq.

· First reported in *The Washington
Post*, April 9, 2006.

JANUARY 10, 2003

A highly classified intelligence assessment, entitled "Questions on Why Iraq Is Procuring Aluminum Tubes and What the IAEA Has Found to Date," states that INR, the Energy Department, and the International Atomic Energy Agency all believed that Iraq was using aluminum tubes for conventional weapons programs. The Senior Executive Memorandum, as it is known, is circulated among high-level administration officials, including Vice President Cheney and Condoleezza Rice.

· First reported in *National Journal*, March 2, 2006.

JANUARY 12, 2003

A Knight Ridder poll finds that half of those surveyed (51 percent) believe that one or more of the 9/11 hijackers were Iraqi citizens; 44 percent said "most" or "some" were Iraqis.

JANUARY 13, 2003

A State Department nuclear analyst sends an e-mail to several intelligence analysts "outlining his reasoning why, 'the uranium purchase agreement probably is a hoax,'" indicating that "one of the documents that purported to be an agreement for a joint military campaign, including both Iraq and Iran, was so ridiculous that it was 'clearly a forgery.'"

· From the Senate Intelligence Committee's "Report on the U.S. Intelligence Community's Prewar Intelligence Assessments on Iraq," July 7, 2004.

JANUARY 16, 2003

The CIA receives copies of the Niger documents.

· From the Senate Intelligence Committee's "Report on the U.S. Intelligence Community's Prewar Intelligence Assessments on Iraq," July 7, 2004.

JANUARY 23, 2003

Condoleezza Rice publishes an Op-Ed in The New York Times, entitled "Why We Know Iraq Is Lying," which states that Iraq's weapons "declaration fails to account for or explain Iraq's efforts to get uranium from abroad."*

*An NBC/*Wall Street Journal *poll finds that 48 percent say Al Qaeda is the greatest threat to the United States; 24 percent say that Iraq is the greater threat.*

JANUARY 26, 2003

In an interview with European press, Secretary of State Powell claims that there is evidence of an Iraq-Qaeda connection:

QUESTION: You referred in your speech to the links between Al Qaeda and Iraq. Now, even some of our secret service chiefs say publicly there is no evidence of that.

SECRETARY POWELL: We do have evidence of it. We are not suggesting that there is

---

*See entries for November 20, 2001, March 4, 2002, October 1, 2002 (regarding the NIE), October 6, 2002, *December 24, 2002,* and January 2003 (regarding the NIC memo).

*a 9/11 link, but we are suggesting—we do
have evidence—of connections over the years
between Iraq and Al Qaeda and other terrorist
organizations.*

*J A N U A R Y   2 8 ,   2 0 0 3
In his State of the Union address, President
Bush completes the administration's portrait
of the Iraqi threat, linking Saddam's search
for uranium with his aluminum tubes for re-
fining the nuclear fuel, his ties to Al Qaeda,
and the specter of another 9/11:*

> *From three Iraqi defectors we know
> that Iraq, in the late 1990s, had several
> mobile biological weapons labs. These
> are designed to produce germ warfare
> agents, and can be moved from place to
> a place to evade inspectors. Saddam
> Hussein has not disclosed these facilities.
> He's given no evidence that he has de-
> stroyed them.* *
>
> *The International Atomic Energy
> Agency confirmed in the 1990s that
> Saddam Hussein had an advanced
> nuclear weapons development program,
> had a design for a nuclear weapon and
> was working on five different methods of
> enriching uranium for a bomb. The
> British government has learned that
> Saddam Hussein recently sought signifi-
> cant quantities of uranium from
> Africa.† Our intelligence sources tell us
> that he has attempted to purchase high-*

---

*See entry for May 2002.
†See entries for November 20, 2001, March 4,
2002, October 1, 2002 (regarding the NIE),
October 6, 2002, *December 24, 2002,* January
2003 (regarding the NIC memo), and January
13, 2003.

strength aluminum tubes suitable for nuclear weapons production.* Saddam Hussein has not credibly explained these activities. He clearly has much to hide.

JANUARY 29, 2003

An ABC poll finds that 42 percent think President Bush presented enough evidence of an Iraqi threat while 56 percent want more; 68 percent believe Iraq provided "direct support" to Al Qaeda.

JANUARY 29, 2003

Secretary of State Powell gives his chief of staff, Colonel Lawrence Wilkerson, a forty-eight-page dossier from the White House containing intelligence on Iraq's WMDs and alleged ties to Al Qaeda gathered by the vice president's office. Powell tells Wilkerson to go to CIA headquarters to begin examining the intelligence in preparation for Powell's speech to the UN Security Council on February 5.

· First reported in *Vanity Fair*, May 2004.

JANUARY 30– FEBRUARY 4, 2003

Over four days and nights, Powell and his staff meet at CIA headquarters to vet the Iraq intelligence. After scrapping the White House dossier and beginning from scratch, Powell and his team wrangle with the vice president's office over which intelligence was sound enough to cite in

---

*See entries for Mid-September 2002, October 1, 2002 (regarding the President's Summary of the NIE), and January 10, 2003.

Powell's speech. The vice president's office presses Powell to include the discredited account of 9/11 hijacker Mohamed Atta's meeting with an Iraqi intelligence officer in Prague. At the final rehearsal of the speech, Powell throws it out. In the early morning of February 5, hours before Powell is to deliver his speech, CIA director Tenet asks to see the text, apparently concerned that Powell had cut too much concerning Iraq's links to Al Qaeda.

· First reported in *Vanity Fair*, May 2004.

January 31, 2003

During a private two-hour meeting among top aides in the Oval Office, President Bush tells British prime minister Tony Blair that while the United States would "put its full weight" behind efforts to secure a second UN resolution before invading Iraq and "would twist arms and even threaten," war was inevitable and had been "penciled in for 10 March" already.

Acknowledging that inspectors had not yet found WMDs, the president raised three possible ways of provoking war with Iraq should the U.S. case prove insufficient: flying a U-2 spy plane, painted in UN colors, over Iraq to draw fire, thereby making Saddam Hussein in breach of Resolution 1441; producing an Iraqi defector to give a public presentation on WMDs; and assassinating Hussein.

The president and prime minister discuss postwar Iraq. Bush expresses doubt that there will be internecine warfare in the aftermath; Condoleezza Rice says that a "planning cell" in the Defense Department had been preparing for postwar Iraq and that "a great deal of work was now in hand."

· As reported by David Manning, then chief foreign policy adviser to Prime Minister Blair, in a memo. The memo was published in an updated edition of Philippe Sands's *Lawless World* (February 2006) and first revealed during the February 2, 2006, broadcast of Britain's *Channel 4 News.*

FEBRUARY 4, 2003

After repeated demands to see American and British evidence of Iraqi attempts to procure uranium from Niger, the International Atomic Energy Agency finally receives the Italian documents and immediately doubts their authenticity.

· From the Senate Intelligence Committee's "Report on the U.S. Intelligence Community's Prewar Intelligence Assessments on Iraq," July 7, 2004.

FEBRUARY 5, 2003

In a final effort to persuade Secretary of State Powell to reinsert the Prague story into his speech, I. Lewis Libby calls Colonel Wilkerson. Wilkerson, already in the Security Council chamber, refuses to take the call. "'Scooter,' said one State Department aide, 'wasn't happy.'"

· First reported in *Vanity Fair,* May 2004.

FEBRUARY 5, 2003

In his speech to the United Nations on the Iraqi threat, Secretary of State Powell discusses Saddam's biological and chemical weapons, his nuclear ambitions, and his ties to Al Qaeda. He makes no reference to attempts to procure uranium.

In his presentation on mobile biological weapons labs, Powell cites the "eyewitness account" of an Iraqi defector that "has been corroborated by other sources":

> *A second source, an Iraqi civil engineer in a position to know the details of the program, confirmed the existence of transportable facilities moving on trailers.*
>
> *A third source, also in a position to know, reported in summer 2002 that Iraq had manufactured mobile production systems mounted on road trailer units and on rail cars.*
>
> *Finally, a fourth source, an Iraqi major, who defected, confirmed that Iraq has mobile biological research laboratories. . . .**

FEBRUARY 6, 2003

Following Secretary of State Powell's presentation, President Bush said, "The Iraqi regime has actively and secretly attempted to obtain equipment needed to produce chemical, biological and nuclear weapons. First-

---

*See entry for May 2002 ("Powell said he was never warned, during three days of intense briefings at C.I.A. headquarters before his U.N. speech, that he was using material that both the D.I.A. and C.I.A. had determined was false." *Los Angeles Times*, November 20, 2005).

hand witnesses have informed us that Iraq has at least seven mobile factories for the production of biological agents, equipment mounted on trucks and rails to evade discovery. Using these factories, Iraq has produced within just months hundreds of pounds of biological poisons."*

A CNN/USA Today/Gallup poll reports that 79 percent think Secretary Powell made a "strong" case for invading Iraq; 66 percent think he made a "strong" case for Iraq's "ties" to Al Qaeda.

FEBRUARY 8, 2003
The UN's Team Bravo conducts the first search of Curveball's former work site, Djerf al Nadaf. "The raid by the American-led biological weapons experts lasted 3½ hours. It was long enough to prove Curveball had lied" about mobile biological and chemical weapons labs.
· First reported in the *Los Angeles Times*, November 20, 2005.

FEBRUARY 21, 2003
A Pew poll finds that 57 percent believe Saddam helped the 9/11 terrorists.

MARCH 6, 2003
During a prime-time press conference on Iraq, President Bush mentions 9/11 eight times.

MARCH 7, 2003
UN weapons inspector Hans Blix reports on progress of inspections, citing more cooperation and asking for more time. He tells the Se-

---

*See entry for May 2002.

curity Council that a series of searches had found "no evidence" of mobile biological production facilities.

IAEA director Mohamed ElBaradei reports that the Niger documents are "not authentic."

MARCH 7, 2003

The public announcement comes after the United States and Britain fail to respond to advance notice of the IAEA's conclusion.

· First reported in *The New Yorker*, October 27, 2003.

MARCH 7, 2003

The United States, Britain, Spain, and Bulgaria put forth a new UN resolution calling for a March 17 deadline for Iraq to disarm.

None of the three evening newscasts mentions the forgeries or uranium intelligence.

MARCH 8, 2003

In an interview with CNN, former ambassador Joseph Wilson discusses the forgeries, noting a front-page story in The Washington Post *and suggesting that the administration acknowledge the intelligence failure: "I think you probably just fess up and try to move on and say there's sufficient other evidence to convict Saddam of being involved in the nuclear arms trade. But Dr. ElBaradei yesterday was pretty clear. He doesn't see that this is happening."*

MARCH 9, 2003

A New York Times *report on the forgeries quotes ElBaradei as suggesting that "there's a lot of people who would be delighted to malign Iraq," adding, "It could range from Iraqi dissidents to all sorts of other sources."*

Appearing on Face the Nation, *Condoleezza Rice discusses Iraq-Qaeda collaboration: "We know from a detainee that—the head of training for Al Qaeda, that they sought help in developing chemical and biological weapons because they weren't doing very well on their own. They sought it in Iraq. They received the help."**

MARCH 11, 2003

A New York Times/CBS poll finds that 45 percent believe Saddam was involved in 9/11.

MARCH 14, 2003

At a White House press briefing, the fifth since the IAEA revelation, a member of the press corps poses the first question about the forgeries.

Senator Jay Rockefeller (D-W.Va.) asks the FBI to investigate the forgeries, writing to FBI director Mueller, "There is a possibility that the fabrication of these documents may be part of a larger deception campaign aimed at manipulating public opinion and foreign policy regarding Iraq."

MARCH 16, 2003

Vice President Cheney appears on Meet the Press: *"We know he's reconstituted these programs since the Gulf War. We know he's out trying once again to produce nuclear weapons and we know that he has a long-standing relationship with various terrorist groups, including the Al Qaeda organization."*

The Washington Post *publishes a story on A17 entitled "U.S. Lacks Specifics on*

---

*See entry for February 2002 (regarding Ibn al-Shaykh al-Libi).

Banned Arms," giving additional reporting credit to "staff writer" Bob Woodward.

MARCH 16, 2003

The Washington Post story arose after "three separate sources" tell Woodward "confidentially that the intelligence on WMD was not as conclusive as the CIA and the administration had suggested." Woodward drafts five paragraphs to this effect for Walter Pincus, which Pincus and the *Post*'s national security editor judged to be "a little strong."

· From Bob Woodward's
Plan of Attack, April 2004.

MARCH 17, 2003

Representative Henry Waxman (D-Calif.) sends a letter to President Bush expressing doubts about the administration's characterization of Iraq's nuclear capability and the threat it poses.

MARCH 19, 2003

The Iraq War begins.

MARCH 23, 2003

The New York Times *reports on CIA claims that the White House pressured the agency to provide intelligence that bolstered its case for war.*

MARCH 24, 2003

The New Yorker *publishes a report by Seymour Hersh on the forged Niger documents.*

MAY 1, 2003

"Mission Accomplished": Riding in a fighter jet emblazoned with the legend GEORGE W.

BUSH, COMMANDER IN CHIEF, President Bush lands on the deck of the aircraft USS Abraham Lincoln and declares the end of "major combat operations" in a speech that evening.

A Gallup poll released today finds that 79 percent of Americans believe the war with Iraq was justified even without conclusive evidence of WMDs.

MAY 6, 2003
New York Times *columnist Nicholas Kristof writes for the first time about a "former U.S. ambassador to Africa" who was dispatched on a CIA mission to Niger and found no evidence of Iraqi attempts to procure uranium.*

MAY 27, 2003
In a field report submitted to Washington, a secret DIA-sponsored fact-finding mission, conducted by nine U.S. and British biological-weapons experts, concludes that "there was no connection to anything biological" in two trailers captured by U.S. and Kurdish troops. Three weeks later, the field report and a 122-page final report are stamped "secret" and shelved.
· First reported in *The Washington Post*, April 12, 2006.

MAY 27, 2003
A Fox News poll finds that 65 percent believe WMDs will be found; 25 percent don't.

MAY 28, 2003
The CIA and DIA publish a white paper declaring that two trucks loaded with lab equipment, found soon after the invasion, were part of Hussein's biological warfare program. The

report dismissed as a "cover story" Iraq's explanation that the equipment generated hydrogen.

MAY 29, 2003

Asked by a Polish interviewer about the failure thus far to find WMDs, President Bush responds:

> *We found the weapons of mass destruction. We found biological laboratories. You remember when Colin Powell stood up in front of the world, and he said, Iraq has got laboratories, mobile labs to build biological weapons. They're illegal. They're against the United Nations resolutions, and we've so far discovered two. And we'll find more weapons as time goes on. But for those who say we haven't found the banned manufacturing devices or banned weapons, they're wrong. We found them.* *

Vanity Fair *contributor Sam Tanenhaus talks with Matt Lauer on* Today *about his story for the July 2003 issue, in which he quotes Deputy Defense Secretary Wolfowitz as saying, "The truth is that for reasons that have a lot to do with the U.S. government bureaucracy we settled on the one issue that everyone could agree on which was weapons of mass destruction as the core reason."†*

---

*See entries for May 2002, February 8, 2003, and May 27, 2003.
†This is the Pentagon's version of the quote, which differs slightly from the way it is worded in the *Vanity Fair* story.

Senator Bob Graham challenges the White House on its prewar intelligence in various conversations with reporters cited by the Associated Press: "If we don't find those weapons, then the fundamental reason that this war was justified will have been undercut. . . . Either our intelligence community didn't know as much as they represented they knew, or the information that they presented had been politicized before it was made available to decision makers. . . . There has been a Nixonian stench to the continued practice of putting the American people in the dark."

Senator John McCain and others begin to talk of hearings on prewar intelligence.

JUNE 2, 2003

Representative Waxman writes a letter to the president inquiring why the uranium charge persisted despite contradictory evidence.

JUNE 3, 2003

*Condoleezza Rice appears on CNBC's Capital Report: "But let's remember what we've already found. Secretary Powell on February 5th talked about a mobile, biological weapons capability. That has now been found and this is a weapons laboratory trailers capable of making a lot of agent that—dry agent, dry biological agent that can kill a lot of people. So we are finding these pieces that were described."**

In a Gallup poll, 56 percent say the war was justified even if no WMDs are found.

---

*See entries for May 2002, February 8, 2003, and May 27, 2003.

JUNE 5, 2003

The Washington Post *reports that many CIA analysts felt pressured by Vice President Cheney and his chief of staff, I. Lewis "Scooter" Libby, who made "multiple trips" to the agency before the war to question analysts about intelligence on WMDs and Iraq's alleged ties to Al Qaeda.*

While visiting Qatar, President Bush downgrades his rhetoric on WMDs, saying, "We recently found two mobile biological-weapons facilities which were capable of producing biological agents."*

JUNE 8, 2003

Appearing on This Week *and* Meet the Press, *Condoleezza Rice addresses the increasing attention to the uranium claims:*

> *At the time that the State of the Union address was prepared, there were also other sources that said that they were, the Iraqis were seeking yellow cake, uranium oxide from Africa. (ABC's* This Week)

> *The president quoted a British paper. We did not know at the time—no one knew at the time, in our circles—maybe someone knew down in the bowels of the agency, but no one in our circles knew that there were doubts and suspicions that this might be a forgery. Of course, it was information that was mistaken. But the—it was a relatively small part of the case about nuclear weapons and nuclear reconstitution. It is also the case that the broad*

---

*See entries for May 2002, February 8, 2003, and May 27, 2003.

*picture about Iraq's programs was a
picture that went very far back in time.**
(NBC's Meet the Press*)*

June 10, 2003

The State Department's Bureau of Intelligence and Research drafts a three-page memo for Undersecretary of State Marc Grossman, who requested a summary of INR's opposition to the White House–endorsed uranium allegation. CIA officer Valerie Plame Wilson is mentioned and identified as Joe Wilson's wife in the second paragraph, which is marked *S* for secret, indicating her covert status.

· First reported in *The Washington Post*, July 21, 2005.

June 11, 2003

The search for WMDs in Iraq so far fruitless, CIA director Tenet hires the former UN weapons inspector David Kay to lead the new Iraq Survey Group.

June 12, 2003

The Washington Post *reports that, according to "senior administration officials and a former government official," the CIA failed to pass on the findings of a "retired U.S. ambassador's" investigation into claims that Iraq was seeking uranium from Niger.*

June 12, 2003

Post reporter Walter Pincus's inquiries regarding the story in early June prompted

---

*See entries for November 20, 2001, March 4, 2002, October 1, 2002 (regarding the NIE), October 6, 2002, *December 24, 2002,* January 2003 (regarding the NIC memo), and January 13, 2003.

internal CIA "fact gathering" on Wilson's mission around the time that the State Department drafted its memo for Undersecretary Grossman.

· First reported in *Time*, August 8, 2005.

Vice President Cheney tells his chief of staff, I. Lewis "Scooter" Libby, that Valerie Plame Wilson worked for the CIA in the Counterproliferation Division.

· First disclosed in the grand jury indictment of Libby, October 28, 2005.

JUNE 12, 2003
A Gallup poll shows 31 percent think that the administration deliberately misled Americans on WMDs.

JUNE 13, 2003
In a New York Times *column, Nicholas Kristof challenges the "senior administration officials and a former government official" cited in the previous day's* Washington Post *story, writing that:*

> *while Director of Central Intelligence George Tenet may not have told Mr. Bush that the Niger documents were forged, lower C.I.A. officials did tell both the vice president's office and National Security Council staff members. Moreover, I hear from another source that the C.I.A.'s operations side and its counterterrorism center undertook their own investigations of the documents, poking around in Italy and Africa, and also concluded that they were false—a judgment that filtered to the top of the C.I.A.*

MID-JUNE 2003

Bob Woodward learns from an as-yet-unnamed administration official that Joe Wilson's wife "worked for the C.I.A. on weapons of mass destruction as a WMD analyst."

· From Woodward's deposition before Special Counsel Patrick Fitzgerald, first disclosed in *The Washington Post*, November 16, 2005.

JUNE 20, 2003

Bob Woodward interviews an administration official for *Plan of Attack*, bringing a list of questions that included the phrase "Joe Wilson's wife." There is no evidence that Woodward asked about her or that the subject came up.

· From Woodward's deposition before Special Counsel Patrick Fitzgerald, first disclosed in *The Washington Post*, November 16, 2005.

JUNE 22, 2003

The Washington Post *reports that the still-classified National Intelligence Estimate "portrayed a far less clear picture about the link between Iraq and al Qaeda than the one presented by the president" in his October 2002 speech in Cincinnati.*

JUNE 23, 2003

An ABC News poll finds 63 percent believe that the war can be justified without WMDs.

JUNE 23, 2003

New York Times reporter Judith Miller meets with I. Lewis "Scooter" Libby, who tells her that Vice President Cheney did not know about Joseph Wilson or his trip and that the CIA never reported it to the vice president's office. Libby also tells Miller that Wilson's wife works in the Weapons Intelligence, Nonproliferation, and Arms Control (WINPAC) division of CIA. Miller writes, "Wife works in bureau?" in her notebook.

· First reported in Miller's account of her grand jury testimony on September 30 and October 12, 2005. The notes from the conversation were discovered in the *Times* newsroom after Miller's September 30 grand jury appearance. Libby had not previously disclosed the meeting to prosecutors or investigators.

Bob Woodward has a phone conversation with Scooter Libby:

I told him I was sending to him an 18-page list of questions I wanted to ask Vice President Cheney. On page 5 of that list there was a question about "yellowcake" and the October 2002 National Intelligence Estimate regarding Iraq's weapons programs. I testified that I believed I had both the 18-page question list and the question list from the June 20 interview with the phrase "Joe Wilson's wife" on my desk during this discussion. I testified that I have no recollection that Wilson or his wife was discussed, and I have no notes of the conversation.

· From Woodward's deposition before Special Counsel Patrick Fitzgerald, first disclosed in *The Washington Post*, November 16, 2005.

JUNE 27, 2003

Woodward meets with Libby in his office:

I testified that on June 27, 2003, I met with Libby at 5:10 p.m. in his office adjacent to the White House. I took the 18-page list of questions with the Page-5 reference to "yellowcake" to this interview and I believe I also had the other question list from June 20, which had the "Joe Wilson's wife" reference. I have four pages of typed notes from this interview, and I testified that there is no reference in them to Wilson or his wife. A portion of the typed notes shows that Libby discussed the October 2002 National Intelligence Estimate on Iraq's alleged weapons of mass destruction, mentioned "yellowcake" and said there was an "effort by the Iraqis to get it from Africa. It goes back to February '02." This was the time of Wilson's trip to Niger.

· From Woodward's deposition before Special Counsel Patrick Fitzgerald, first disclosed in *The Washington Post*, November 16, 2005.

JUNE 30, 2003

In a Today *show interview, Secretary of State Powell says, "We have found the mobile biological weapons labs that I could only show cartoons of that day."**

---

*See entries for May 2002, February 8, 2003, and May 27, 2003 ("Powell said he was never warned, during three days of intense briefings at C.I.A. headquarters before his U.N. speech, that he was using material that both the D.I.A. and C.I.A. had determined was false." *Los Angeles Times*, November 20, 2005).

JULY 6, 2003

Joseph Wilson publishes an Op-Ed in The New York Times *titled, "What I Didn't Find in Africa," identifying himself as the retired ambassador who traveled to Niger and found no evidence of Iraqi attempts to procure uranium. A* Washington Post *story also identifies him by name, and Wilson himself appears on* Meet the Press.

Appearing after Wilson on Meet the Press, *Robert Novak dismisses the uranium story: "[The economy] is the issue that ought to scare President Bush much more than the weapons of mass destruction or uranium from Niger, which I think are little elitist issues that don't bother most of the people, but job loss does."*

On Fox News Sunday, *Tony Snow ignores the Wilson revelation and interviews General Myers:*

SNOW: We have heard rumors that there may be some announcements indicating that they have, in fact, coalition forces, David Kay and others, come across evidence that would vindicate the arguments the president made before the war. True or false?

MYERS: As far as I know, they're—what I know is that they're gathering facts. I have not seen the facts, and we'll have to wait and see. I just don't know.

JULY 6, 2003

Deputy Secretary of State Richard Armitage arranges for the June 10 State Department memo detailing Wilson's trip to Niger and his wife's involvement to be sent to Secretary of State Powell before he leaves for Africa. Carl Ford, assistant secretary of state for intelligence and research, sends the memo to the White House marked "for transmission to Powell."

> · First reported in *The New York Times,* July 16, 2005.

JULY 7, 2003
A British parliamentary report calls into question British intelligence on uranium.

At a press briefing, Ari Fleischer dismisses the Wilson revelation, saying, "Well, there is ʒero, nada, nothing new here. Ambassador Wilson, other than the fact that now people know his name, has said all this before."

JULY 7, 2003
Robert Novak calls Fleischer.

> · Per White House phone logs turned over to Patrick Fitzgerald's grand jury, first reported by Bloomberg News, July 18, 2005.

JULY 7, 2003
The president leaves for Africa in the evening.

JULY 7, 2003
Secretary of State Powell is seen boarding Air Force One with the State Department memo in his hand.

> · First reported in *The Washington Post,* July 21, 2005.

JULY 8, 2003
A Washington Post *report quotes a "senior administration official" as saying, "Knowing all that we know now, the reference to Iraq's attempt to acquire uranium from Africa should not have been included in the State of the Union speech."*

July 8, 2003

Karl Rove speaks with Robert Novak, who tells Rove that Joseph Wilson's wife was a CIA officer named Valerie Plame and that she had recommended Wilson for the Niger investigation. Rove responds, "I heard that, too."

· First reported in *The New York Times*, July 15, 2005.

Judith Miller meets with Scooter Libby a second time, over breakfast at the St. Regis Hotel. Libby tells Miller that the vice president's office requested further intelligence from the CIA regarding Iraqi efforts to procure uranium but that the response "barely made it out of the bowels of the CIA" and that, further, CIA director George Tenet had never heard of Joseph Wilson. The conversation turns to Wilson's wife; Libby tells Miller that she works for the CIA, in the WINPAC division. Miller's notes contain the notation "wife works at Winpac" and the misnomer "Valerie Flame," though Miller later testifies to a grand jury that Libby did not reveal the name and that she does not recall who did.

· From Judith Miller's grand jury testimony, first reported in *The New York Times*, October 16, 2005.

With authorization from the president, through Vice President Cheney, to disclose classified information, Libby reveals portions of the October 2002 National Intelligence Estimate in an effort to counter Wilson's claims and show that Iraq had been "vigorously trying to procure uranium."

· From an April 5, 2006, court filing in *U.S. v. I. Lewis Libby*, first disclosed on the Web site of *The New York Sun*, April 6, 2006.

JULY 10, 2003
At a hearing of the Senate Armed Services committee, Senator Mark Pryor (D-Ark.) asks Defense Secretary Rumsfeld when he knew "that the reports about [Iraq seeking] uranium coming out of Africa were bogus?" Secretary Rumsfeld replied, "Oh, within recent days, since the information started becoming available."*

"One item I showed was cartoons of the mobile biological van. They were cartoons, artist's renderings, because we had never seen one of these things, but we had good sourcing on it, excellent sourcing on it. And we knew what it would look like when we found it, so we made those pictures. And I can assure you I didn't just throw those pictures up without having quite a bit of confidence in the information that I had been provided and that Director Tenet had been provided and was now supporting me in the presentation on, sitting right behind me. And we waited. And it took a couple of months, and it took until after the war, until we found a van and another van that pretty much matched what we said it would look like. And I think that's a pretty good indication that we were not cooking the books."†—Secretary

---

*See entry for *March 7, 2003*.
†See entries for May 2002, February 8, 2003, and May 27, 2003 ("Powell said he was never warned, during three days of intense briefings at C.I.A. headquarters before his U.N. speech, that he was using material that both the D.I.A. and C.I.A. had determined was false." *Los Angeles Times*, November 20, 2005).

of State Colin Powell at State Department
briefing

JULY 11, 2003

In a joint press gaggle with Ari Fleischer
aboard Air Force One, Condoleezza Rice di-
rects blame for the "16 words" at the CIA:

> What we've said subsequently is, know-
> ing what we now know, that some of the
> Niger documents were apparently forged,
> we wouldn't have put this in the Presi-
> dent's speech—but that's knowing what
> we know now.
>
>   All that I can tell you is that if there
> were doubts about the underlying intelli-
> gence in the N.I.E., those doubts were not
> communicated to the President. The only
> thing that was there in the N.I.E. was a
> kind of a standard INR footnote, which
> is kind of 59 pages away from the bulk of
> the N.I.E. That's the only thing that's
> there. And you have footnotes all the time
> in C.I.A.—I mean, in N.I.E.s. So if
> there was a concern about the underlying
> intelligence there, the President was
> unaware of that concern and as was I.*

JULY 11, 2003

In a phone conversation with *Time* reporter Matthew Cooper on "deep background," Karl Rove tells Cooper not to
"get too far out" on Joseph Wilson's
charges about the uranium intelligence.
Without naming her, Rove then tells

---

*See entries for November 20, 2001, March 4,
2002, October 1, 2002 (regarding the NIE),
October 6, 2002, *December 24, 2002,* January
2003 (regarding the NIC memo), and January
13, 2003.

Cooper that Wilson's wife worked at the CIA on issues related to weapons of mass destruction, and that she was responsible for Wilson's trip to Niger, before ending the call saying cryptically, "I've already said too much."

· First reported July 17, 2005, in Cooper's account of his grand jury testimony in *Time*'s July 25 issue.

After the conversation with Cooper, Rove e-mails Deputy National Security Advisor Stephen Hadley, telling him that he "didn't take the bait" when the *Time* reporter suggested that Wilson's revelation was damaging to the president.

· First reported by the Associated Press, July 15, 2005.

JULY 11, 2003

CIA director George Tenet releases a statement in the evening affirming that the "16 words should never have been included in the text written for the President." He goes on to recount all the instances in which the CIA either refrained from including the uranium intelligence in reports to Congress or expressed doubts about it to the British and in the NIE.

An ABC News poll finds that 74 percent support while 25 percent oppose the U.S. troop presence in Iraq; 57 percent say the war was worth fighting while 40 percent say it was not.

JULY 12, 2003

"The President sees this as much ado, that it's beside the point of the central threat that Saddam Hussein presented. . . . Yes, the President has moved on. And I think, frankly, much of the country has moved on, as well."—Ari Fleischer in the daily briefing

July 12, 2003

Scooter Libby tells Matt Cooper that the vice president's office was not responsible for Joseph Wilson's trip to Niger. Cooper asks Libby if he knows anything about Wilson's CIA officer wife having sent her husband on the mission, and Libby says, "Yeah, I've heard that too." Libby does not name her or indicate that her status is covert.

> · First reported July 17, 2005, in Cooper's account of his grand jury testimony in *Time*'s July 25 issue.

Washington Post reporter Walter Pincus is told by an "administration official" that the White House was not putting much stock in the Wilson trip to Africa because it was "set up as a boondoggle by his wife, an analyst with the agency working on weapons of mass destruction."

> · *The Washington Post* first reported on October 12, 2003, that "a Post reporter" had been the recipient of the information about Wilson's wife. Pincus later wrote an account of the conversation, without identifying the source, for the Summer 2005 Nieman Reports, published by the Nieman Foundation for Journalism, at Harvard University.

Judith Miller speaks with Scooter Libby a third time, by phone. Libby resumes his criticism of Joseph Wilson's report on Niger and says that the inclusion of the "16 words" in the president's State of the Union address was the result of "a simple miscommunication between the White House and the C.I.A."

· From Judith Miller's grand jury testimony, first reported in *The New York Times*, October 16, 2005.

JULY 13, 2003

"It turns out that it's technically correct what the president said, that the U.K. does—did say that—and still says that. They haven't changed their mind, the United Kingdom intelligence people."—Donald Rumsfeld on *NBC's* Meet the Press

JULY 14, 2003

Ari Fleischer gives his final press briefing after resigning, saying, "I think this remains an issue about did Iraq seek uranium in Africa, an issue that very well may be true. We don't know if it's true, but nobody but nobody can say it is wrong."

In his syndicated column, Robert Novak names Joseph Wilson's wife, Valerie Plame, as "an Agency operative on weapons of mass destruction," and says that "two senior administration officials" told him that she had recommended her husband for the mission to Niger. There is no mention of the column in that day's White House press briefing.

JULY 16, 2003

In his on-line column for The Nation, *David Corn* first raises the possibility that "two senior administration officials" broke the law when they identified Valerie Plame Wilson to Robert Novak, asking, "Did senior Bush officials blow the cover of a US intelligence officer working covertly in a field of vital importance to national security—and break the *law—in order to strike at a Bush administration critic and intimidate others?"*

JULY 20, 2003
In a New York Times article about the chaos enveloping the search for WMDs in Iraq, Judith Miller refers to 578 "suspect sites" to be searched.

JULY 21, 2003
While visiting Iraq, Paul Wolfowitz tells reporters, "I'm not concerned about weapons of mass destruction," adding that that was now the job of American intelligence agencies. "I'm not saying that getting to the bottom of this WMD issue isn't important. It is important. But it is not of immediate consequence."*

JULY 22, 2003
Telling reporters that he had received two memos from the C.I.A. and a phone call from Director George Tenet in October 2002 that raised concerns about claims that Iraq was seeking uranium from Africa, Deputy National Security Advisor Stephen Hadley takes responsibility for the inclusion of the sixteen words in the president's State of the Union address.

At a White House press briefing, reporters raise the issue of Robert Novak's July 14 column for the first time:

QUESTION: The Robert Novak column last week identified the wife of Ambassador Joseph Wilson as a C.I.A. operative who was working on WMD issues. Novak said that identification is based on information given to him by two administration sources. That col-

---

*See entry for May 29, 2003 (regarding Wolfowitz's interview in Vanity Fair).

umn has now given rise to accusations that the administration deliberatively blew the cover of an undercover C.I.A. operative, and in so doing, violated a federal law that prohibits revealing the identity of undercover C.I.A. operatives. Can you respond to that?

MR. McCLELLAN: Thank you for bringing that up. That is not the way this President or this White House operates. And there is absolutely no information that has come to my attention or that I have seen that suggests that there is any truth to that suggestion. And, certainly, no one in this White House would have given authority to take such a step.

QUESTION: So you're saying—

MR. McCLELLAN: I'm saying that that is not the way that this President or this White House operates, and I've seen no evidence to suggest there's any truth to it.

JULY 30, 2003
The CIA refers the Plame leak to the Justice Department for criminal prosecution.

AUGUST 10, 2003
A report by Barton Gellman and Walter Pincus in The Washington Post examines the administration's exaggeration of the Iraqi threat, from the mischaracterization of aluminum tubes to "the escalation of nuclear rhetoric" in August 2002. Gellman and Pincus also note that "the introduction of the term 'mushroom cloud'" into White House rhetoric "coincided with the formation of a White House Iraq Group, or WHIG, a task force assigned to 'educate the public'" about Iraq's WMDs. The story marks the first known public reference to WHIG.

AUGUST 21, 2003
At a public forum in Seattle, Joseph Wilson names Karl Rove as a likely suspect behind the leaking of his wife's identity, saying, "At the end of the day, it's of keen interest to me to see whether or not we can get Karl Rove frog-marched out of the White House in handcuffs."

SEPTEMBER 14, 2003
Dick Cheney appears on NBC's Meet the Press:

With respect to 9/11, of course, we've had the story that's been public out there. The Czechs alleged that Mohamed Atta, the lead attacker, met in Prague with a senior Iraqi intelligence official five months before the attack, but we've never been able to develop any more of that yet either in terms of confirming it or discrediting it. We just don't know.*

Same on biological weapons—we believe he'd developed the capacity to go mobile with his BW [biological weapons] production capability because, again, in reaction to what we had done to him in '91. We had intelligence reporting before the war that there were at least seven of these mobile labs that he had gone out and acquired. We've, since the war, found two of them. They're in our possession today, mobile biological facilities that can be used to produce anthrax or smallpox or whatever else you wanted to use during the course of developing the capacity for an attack.†

*See entry for June 21, 2002.
†See entries for May 2002, February 8, 2003, and May 27, 2003.

SEPTEMBER 16, 2003
At the White House press briefing, reporters ask about Joseph Wilson's charges against Karl Rove:

QUESTION: Wilson now believes that the person who did this was Karl Rove. He's quoted from a speech last month as saying, "At the end of the day, it's of keen interest to me to see whether or not we can get Karl Rove frog-marched out of the White House in handcuffs."
  Did Karl Rove tell—

MR. McCLELLAN: I haven't heard that. That's just totally ridiculous. But we've already addressed this issue.

QUESTION: But did Karl Rove—

MR. McCLELLAN: If I could find out who anonymous people were—I just said it's totally ridiculous.

QUESTION: But did Karl Rove do it?

MR. McCLELLAN: I said it's totally ridiculous.

SEPTEMBER 22, 2003
In an interview with Fox News anchor Brit Hume, President Bush explains what he believes happened to Saddam's WMDs:

I think he hid them, I think he dispersed them. I think he is so adapted at deceiving the civilized world for a long period of time that it's going to take a while for the troops to unravel. But I firmly believe he had weapons of mass destruction. I know he used them at one time, and I'm confident he had programs that would enable him to have a weapon of mass destruction at his disposal.

A Newsweek *poll finds that 47 percent believe that Saddam was "directly involved" in 9/11.*

SEPTEMBER 25, 2003
The New York Times *reports that an early draft of a report by Iraq Survey Group chief David Kay will likely say that Iraq had no WMDs.*

SEPTEMBER 26, 2003
MSNBC.com reports that George Tenet recently sent the Justice Department a memo urging an investigation into whether the leak of Valerie Plame Wilson's identity was illegal.

SEPTEMBER 28, 2003
"Saddam Hussein—no one has said that there is evidence that Saddam Hussein directed or controlled 9/11, but let's be very clear, he had ties to Al Qaeda, he had Al Qaeda operatives who had operated out of Baghdad."—Condoleezza Rice on NBC's Meet the Press

SEPTEMBER 29, 2003
ABC News producer Andrea Owen and a cameraman approach Karl Rove as he walks toward his car early in the morning:

OWEN: Did you have any knowledge or did you leak the name of the C.I.A. agent to the press?

---

*See entry for September 21, 2001.

ROVE: No.

At which point, Rove shuts his car door.

At the daily press briefing, Scott McClellan again dismisses suggestions that Karl Rove was involved in the leak:

QUESTION: All right, let me just follow up. You said this morning, quote, "The president knows that Karl Rove wasn't involved." How does he know that?

MR. McCLELLAN: Well, I've made it very clear that it was a ridiculous suggestion in the first place. I saw some comments this morning from the person who made that suggestion backing away from that. And I said it is simply not true. So—I mean, it's public knowledge I've said that it's not true.

QUESTION: Well, how—

MR. McCLELLAN: And I have spoken with Karl Rove. I'm not going to get into conversations that the president has with advisers or staff, or anything of that nature. That's not my practice.

QUESTION: But the president has a factual basis for knowing that Karl Rove—

MR. McCLELLAN: Well, I said it publicly. I said that—and so, I've made it very clear.

QUESTION: I'm not asking what you said, I'm asking if the president has a factual basis for saying—for your statement that he knows Karl Rove—

MR. McCLELLAN: *He's aware of what I said, that there is simply no truth to that suggestion. And I have—I have spoken with Karl about it.*

Later in the briefing, McClellan describes the leak as "serious" for the first time:

QUESTION: *But isn't the president concerned when there is a leak of this magnitude that could threaten someone's very life?*

MR. McCLELLAN: *I think I addressed that earlier. Absolutely, the president believes that this is a serious matter when you're talking about the leak of classified information. The leak of classified information, yes, you're absolutely right, can compromise sources and methods. That's why the president takes it very seriously, and we've always taken it very seriously. And if it happened in this case, it's a particularly serious matter and it should be looked into by the Department of Justice.*

At 8:30 P.M., the Justice Department notifies White House counsel Alberto Gonzales that it has opened an investigation into the Plame leak and that Gonzales should direct staff to preserve all documents. Justice grants Gonzales's request to wait until the morning to distribute a memo notifying staff.

SEPTEMBER 29, 2003
Gonzales immediately tells Chief of Staff
Andrew Card about the investigation.
· First disclosed by Gonzales in an
interview with Bob Schieffer
on CBS's *Face the Nation,*
July 24, 2005.

SEPTEMBER 30, 2003
The New York Times *reports on an internal Defense Intelligence Agency assessment determining that most of the intelligence provided by Iraqi defectors who were made available by the Iraqi National Congress was of little or no value. Several defectors supplied by INC leader Ahmad Chalabi had invented or exaggerated their claims to have direct knowledge of Iraq's WMDs.*

Alberto Gonzales informs President Bush of the leak investigation around 7:00 A.M. and reads a memo at the 7:30 senior staff meeting ordering all White House staff to "preserve all materials that might be relevant." He e-mails the memo to all staff and later issues a second, more detailed memo in the evening after receiving a letter from the Justice Department specifying the records that investigators would like to see, including any contacts with Robert Novak or two Newsday *reporters, or anything related to Joseph Wilson.*

"Yes. Let me just say something about leaks in Washington. There are too many leaks of classified information in Washington. There's leaks at the executive branch; there's leaks in the legislative branch. There's just too many leaks. And if there is a leak out of my administration, I want to know who it is. And if the person has violated law, the person will be taken care of."*—President Bush during a Q&A on job creation in Chicago

---

*See entries for July 8, 2003 (regarding Scooter Libby's conversation with Judith Miller), and *April 6, 2006.*

OCTOBER 1, 2003

Scott McClellan continues to defend Rove at the daily briefing:

MR. McCLELLAN: That's a serious issue. And I just made it—I made it clear earlier—you brought up Karl's name—let's be very clear, I said it was a ridiculous suggestion, I said it's simply not true that he was involved in leaking classified information, and nor did he condone that kind of activity. So, I mean, this has been answered. And now we're trying to get into a whole bunch of issues separate and apart from that.

QUESTION: Did your conversation with Rove include whether or not he had tried to highlight that story for reporters?

MR. McCLELLAN: I'm sorry?

QUESTION: Did your conversation with Rove include asking him whether or not he had tried to highlight that—

MR. McCLELLAN: I made it very clear, I have spoken with him—

QUESTION:—that story for reporters, the Novak story?

MR. McCLELLAN: I've spoken with him. I made it very clear that it is not true that he was involved in leaking classified information or that he condoned some of what you're suggesting.

OCTOBER 2, 2003

David Kay issues his interim report: "We have found substantial evidence of an intent of senior-level Iraqi officials, including Sad-

dam, to continue production at some future point in time of weapons of mass destruction." But Kay added: "We have not found at this point actual weapons. It does not mean we've concluded there are no actual weapons. It means at this point in time, and it's a huge country with a lot to do, that we have not yet found weapons."

OCTOBER 6, 2003

*"We're talking about a criminal action, but also hopefully will help set a clear signal we expect other leaks to stop, as well. And so I look forward to finding the truth."**
—President Bush in remarks with Kenyan President Kibaki*

OCTOBER 7, 2003

Bush remarks on leak investigation:

QUESTION: Mr. President, how confident are you the investigation will find the leaker in the C.I.A. case?

THE PRESIDENT: Randy, you tell me, how many sources have you had that's leaked information that you've exposed or have been exposed? Probably none. I mean this town is a—is a town full of people who like to leak information. And I don't know if we're going to find out the senior administration official. Now, this is a large administration, and there's a lot of senior officials. I don't have any idea. I'd like to. I want to know the truth.

*See entries for July 8, 2003 (regarding Scooter Libby's conversation with Judith Miller), and *April 6, 2006.*

That's why I've instructed this staff of mine to cooperate fully with the investigators—full disclosure, everything we know the investigators will find out. I have no idea whether we'll find out who the leaker is—partially because, in all due respect to your profession, you do a very good job of protecting the leakers. But we'll find out.*

Andrew Card sends a memo to White House staff reminding them to comply with the Justice Department's document request: "The President has made clear how important it is to him that everyone should comply with this request."

Scott McClellan defends Rove, Scooter Libby, and Elliott Abrams at the daily briefing:

QUESTION: So you're saying—you're saying categorically those three individuals were not the leakers or did not authorize the leaks; is that what you're saying?

MR. McCLELLAN: That's correct. I've spoken with them.

OCTOBER 10, 2003
Scott McClellan again defends Rove, Libby, and Abrams at the daily press briefing:

QUESTION: Scott, earlier this week you told us that neither Karl Rove, Elliott Abrams, nor Lewis Libby disclosed any classified information with regard to the leak. I

---

*See entries for July 8, 2003 (regarding Scooter Libby's conversation with Judith Miller), and *April 6, 2006.*

wondered if you could tell us more specifically whether any of them told any reporter that Valerie Plame worked for the CIA?

MR. McCLELLAN: Those individuals—I talked—I spoke with those individuals, as I pointed out, and those individuals assured me they were not involved in this. And that's where it stands.

QUESTION: So none of them told any reporter that Valerie Plame worked for the CIA?

MR. McCLELLAN: They assured me that they were not involved in this.

QUESTION: Can I follow up on that?

QUESTION: They were not involved in what?

MR. McCLELLAN: The leaking of classified information.

QUESTION: Did you undertake that on your own volition, or were you instructed to go to these—

MR. McCLELLAN: I spoke to those individuals myself.

OCTOBER 31, 2003
The National Intelligence Council (NIC) distributes a National Intelligence Estimate (NIE) concluding that the insurgency is homegrown and thrives on Iraqi resentment of the U.S. occupation, and warning that the unrest could lead to civil

war. The analysis, produced at the request of U.S. Central Command, is dismissed by the White House and the defense secretary's office as too negative.

· First reported by Knight Ridder, February 28, 2006.

NOVEMBER 1, 2003

"Some of the killers behind these attacks are loyalists of the Saddam regime who seek to regain power and who resent Iraq's new freedoms. Others are foreigners who have traveled to Iraq to spread fear and chaos, and prevent the emergence of a successful democracy in the heart of the Middle East."*—President Bush in his weekly radio address

NOVEMBER 11, 2003

An ABC News poll shows that 44 percent think President Bush was mostly telling the truth about WMDs while 53 percent think he was hiding things or mostly lying.

NOVEMBER 17, 2003

A report in The Weekly Standard *November 24 issue, entitled "Case Closed," publishes excerpts from a secret memo dated October 27, 2003, and obtained by the magazine. The memo, written by Undersecretary of Defense for Policy Douglas Feith to Senators Pat Roberts and Jay Rockefeller of the Senate Intelligence Committee, contains intelligence gathered under the aegis of Feith's Office of Special Plans that purports to show a decade-long relationship between Iraq and Al Qaeda.*

---

*See entry for October 31, 2003.

NOVEMBER 21, 2003
A Los Angeles Times *poll finds that 48 percent still think the "situation in Iraq was worth going to war over."*

DECEMBER 2003
David Kay flies back to CIA headquarters and tells George Tenet that the Iraqi defector known as Curveball was a liar. An Iraq Survey Group investigation turned up Curveball's personnel file, stating that:

> Curveball was last in his engineering class, not first, as he had claimed. He was a low-level trainee engineer, not a project chief or site manager, as the C.I.A. had insisted.
> Most important, records showed Curveball had been fired in 1995, at the very time he said he had begun working on bio-warfare trucks. A former C.I.A. official said Curveball also apparently was jailed for a sex crime and then drove a Baghdad taxi. . . .
> "The Iraqis were all laughing," recalled a former member of the survey group. "They were saying, 'This guy? You've got to be kidding.'"

Kay tells Tenet that he is convinced that Iraq had no mobile labs or other illicit weapons. By Kay's account, he is soon assigned a windowless office without a working telephone.

· First reported in the *Los Angeles Times,* November 20, 2005.

DECEMBER 14, 2003
Saddam Hussein is captured.

DECEMBER 30, 2003
Attorney General John Ashcroft disqualifies himself from any involvement in the Plame investigation. Deputy Attorney General James Comey assumes control of the investigation and immediately appoints U.S. attorney Patrick Fitzgerald as special counsel. The news appears in the New Year's Eve papers.

JANUARY 2004
Ibn al-Shaykh al-Libi, the "top member of Al Qaeda" whose statements became the basis for the administration's assertions that Saddam's regime provided biological and chemical weapons training to Qaeda members, recants his earlier claims.

· Reports of al-Libi's reversal first appeared in the July 5, 2004, issue of *Newsweek. The New York Times* and *The Washington Post* reported the date of his recantation on November 6, 2005.

JANUARY 9, 2004
In an interview published in the Rocky Mountain News, *Dick Cheney again cites long-discredited claims of an Iraqi-Qaeda meeting in Prague:*

VICE PRESIDENT CHENEY: We did have reporting that was public, that came out shortly after the 9/11 attack, provided by the Czech government, suggesting there had been a meeting in Prague between Mohamed Atta, the lead hijacker, and a man named al-Ani [Ahmed Khalil Ibrahim Samir al-Ani], who was an Iraqi intelligence official in Prague, at the embassy there, in April of '01, prior to the 9/11 attacks. It has never been—we've never been able to collect any more information on *that. That was the one that possibly tied the two together to 9/11.**

QUESTION: When I was in Iraq, some of the soldiers said they believed they were fighting because of the September 11 attacks and because they thought Saddam Hussein had ties to Al Qaeda. You've repeatedly cited such links. . . . I wanted to ask you what you'd say to those soldiers, and were those soldiers misled at all?

VICE PRESIDENT CHENEY: . . . With respect to . . . the general relationship. . . . One place you ought to go look is an article that Stephen Hayes did in The Weekly Standard *. . . That goes through and lays out in some detail, based on an assessment that was done by the Department of Defense and forwarded to the Senate Intelligence Committee some weeks ago. That's your best source of information. . . .*

. . .

QUESTION: So you stand by the statements?

VICE PRESIDENT CHENEY: Absolutely. Absolutely.

JANUARY 20, 2004
In his State of the Union address, the president again downgrades his rhetoric on WMDs in the wake of David Kay's failure to find Saddam's stockpiles:

> Already the Kay report identified dozens
> of weapons of mass destruction–related

---

*See entry for June 21, 2002.

program activities and significant amounts of equipment that Iraq concealed from the United Nations. Had we failed to act, the dictator's weapons of mass destruction programs would continue to this day. Had we failed to act, Security Council resolutions on Iraq would have been revealed as empty threats, weakening the United Nations and encouraging defiance by dictators around the world. Iraq's torture chambers would still be filled with victims, terrified and innocent. The killing fields of Iraq, where hundreds of thousands of men and women and children vanished into the sands, would still be known only to the killers. For all who love freedom and peace, the world without Saddam Hussein's regime is a better and safer place.

JANUARY 22, 2004
In an interview with Juan Williams on National Public Radio, Dick Cheney cites evidence of Saddam's mobile biological weapons labs: "In terms of the question what is there now, we know for example that prior to our going in that he had spent time and effort acquiring mobile biological weapons labs, and we're quite confident he did, in fact, have such a program. We've found a couple of semi trailers at this point which we believe were, in fact, part of that program."*

JANUARY 23, 2004
David Kay resigns after concluding that Iraq had no stockpiles of WMDs.

---

*See entries for May 2002, February 8, 2003, May 27, 2003, and December 2003.

Quoted in The New York Times, *Scott Mc-Clellan holds out hope: "Yes, we believe he had them, and yes, we believe they will be found. We believe the truth will come out."*

FEBRUARY 14, 2004

Ibn al-Shaykh al-Libi's reversal regarding his claims that Iraq provided biological and chemical weapons training to members of Al Qaeda is reported in an intelligence document circulated to senior administration officials.

· First reported in *The New York Times,* July 31, 2004.

MAY 2004

The CIA issues a belated notice to its international stations: "Discrepancies surfaced regarding the information provided by . . . Curveball in this stream of reporting, which indicate that he lost his claimed access in 1995. Our assessment, therefore, is that Curveball appears to be fabricating in this stream of reporting."

· From the *Los Angeles Times,* November 20, 2005.

JUNE 3, 2004

The Los Angeles Times *reports that President Bush has consulted with a lawyer, James E. Sharp, regarding the leak investigation.*

JUNE 16, 2004

The 9/11 Commission concludes that the Atta-Ani meeting in Prague never took place.

JUNE 24, 2004

President Bush, accompanied by his lawyer, is interviewed for more than an hour by Special Counsel Patrick Fitzgerald, but not under oath.

JUNE 25, 2004
According to a CNN/USA Today/Gallup poll, 44 percent believe Saddam was "personally involved" in 9/11.

JULY 10, 2004
The Senate Intelligence Committee report on prewar intelligence finds much of it unfounded and leaves reporting on African uranium inconclusive, stating that the CIA has "not published an assessment to clarify or correct its position on whether or not Iraq was trying to purchase uranium from Africa." While it undermines Joseph Wilson's credibility regarding his purported firsthand knowledge of the forgeries and his denial that his wife recommended him for the mission, it fails to vindicate the administration's claims about uranium. Rather, it blames the CIA for incompetence and failing to inform the White House of its misgivings, and further marginalizes State Department dissent on the intelligence. Plans for a phase two, investigating charges that the administration politicized prewar intelligence, are shelved until after the election.

JULY 14, 2004
After faulting the CIA for its incompetence and overly cautious assessments of intelligence, the Bush administration embraces the findings of a British intelligence review, which says that "Britain had credible evidence that Iraq had sought uranium from Niger but inconclusive evidence that Iraq had actually purchased it. The evidence was established independent of documents, subsequently shown to be forgeries, that Iraq had procured uranium from Niger."

SEPTEMBER 16, 2004

The New York Times *reports on a National Intelligence Estimate prepared for President Bush in late July to early August of 2004 that estimates three possible outcomes for Iraq through the end of 2005, with the worst case being civil war and the best case being a tenuous stability.*

SEPTEMBER 21, 2004

In response to a question about the recent National Intelligence Estimate, President Bush says: "The CIA laid out a—several scenarios that said, life could be lousy, life could be okay, life could be better. And they were just guessing as to what the conditions might be like."

MAY 1, 2005

The Sunday Times *of London publishes a secret memo describing a July 23, 2002, meeting among Prime Minister Tony Blair and senior British officials. Known as the Downing Street memo, the document reveals that the head of Britain's MI6 intelligence agency believed that the Bush administration had already decided to go to war and that "military action was now seen as inevitable."* Salon *(on June 9, 2005) reports that in the 19 daily White House press briefings that followed, the memo was the subject of only 2 out of the approximately 940 questions asked by the White House press corps.*

JULY 2, 2005

Lawrence O'Donnell, a former Democratic aide and executive producer for The West Wing, *reveals in* The Huffington Post *that internal* Time *magazine e-mails show that Karl Rove was Matthew Cooper's source.*

JULY 6, 2005

Two years to the day after Joseph Wilson published his Op-Ed accusing the Bush administration of "twisting" prewar intelligence, New York Times *reporter Judith Miller is jailed for refusing to reveal a confidential source to a grand jury investigating the leak of his wife's CIA identity.* Time *reporter Matthew Cooper secures an eleventh-hour waiver from his source to testify.*

JULY 17, 2005

Time *reporter Matthew Cooper publishes an account of his grand jury testimony, revealing that on July 11, 2003, Karl Rove told him that Joseph Wilson's wife worked for the CIA on WMD issues before ending the call saying cryptically, "I've already said too much." Cooper reveals also that on July 12, 2003, he spoke with Scooter Libby, who also told him about Wilson's wife. Neither Rove nor Libby identified her by name or as a covert agent.*

SEPTEMBER 30, 2005

After spending eighty-five days in jail, Judith Miller testifies to Patrick Fitzgerald's grand jury that Scooter Libby was her source.

OCTOBER 12, 2005

After discovering notes from an earlier conversation with Scooter Libby following her first grand jury appearance, Judith Miller testifies again, revealing that she had met with Libby in June—two weeks earlier than the previously disclosed contacts.

OCTOBER 28, 2005

Patrick Fitzgerald announces the indictment of I. Lewis Libby on charges of lying to fed-

eral investigators and obstructing justice in the Plame leak investigation.

FEBRUARY 2, 2006

Excerpts of a memo written by David Manning, Tony Blair's former foreign policy adviser, that detail a January 31, 2003, meeting between Blair, President Bush, and their senior aides in the Oval Office, are revealed in a broadcast of Britain's Channel 4 News. The memo, which appears in an updated edition of Philippe Sand's Lawless World, shows the president already set on invading Iraq and proposing ways to provoke a war, including painting a U-2 spy plane in UN colors to draw Saddam into firing on it and falling into breach of Resolution 1441.

FEBRUARY 9, 2006

National Journal reports on a January 23, 2006, letter from Patrick Fitzgerald to attorneys for Scooter Libby indicating that Libby had "testified in the grand jury that he had contact with reporters in which he disclosed the content of the National Intelligence Estimate ('N.I.E.') . . . in the course of his interaction with reporters in June and July 2003. . . . We also note that it is our understanding that Mr. Libby testified that he was authorized to disclose information about the N.I.E. to the press by his superiors."

MARCH 2, 2006

National Journal reports that on October 1, 2002, CIA director George Tenet handed a one-page digest of the National Intelligence Estimate to President Bush, who read it in Tenet's presence. The summary outlined intelligence community doubts that Iraq's aluminum tubes were intended for WMDs. The

National Journal *story quotes a "senior official" who describes the President's Summary of the NIE as the "one document which illustrates what the president knew and when he knew it," and notes that the administration has refused either to declassify or provide copies of the NIE to congressional intelligence committees.*

APRIL 6, 2006
A story on The New York Sun's *Web site concerning a court filing submitted the previous day by Patrick Fitzgerald reveals that according to Scooter Libby's grand jury testimony, President Bush authorized Libby (through Vice President Cheney) to leak classified information about prewar intelligence.*

ACKNOWLEDGMENTS

THIS IS MY third book for Ann Godoff, a wonderful editor, publisher, and friend who has taught me that book writing can be creative, highly fulfilling, and even (mostly) fun. I would follow her to the moon. I am also extremely grateful to my fearless agent, Esther Newberg, who encouraged this project at every step of the way and made it happen without ever breaking a sweat.

Joel Topcik, my former assistant at *The New York Times* and now an editor at *Broadcasting & Cable,* gallantly served as an essential collaborator: an indefatigable researcher and fact-checker as well as an incisive sounding board. Joel also undertook the daunting task of maintaining the time lines in the appendix. Needless to say, any errors there or elsewhere in this book are my responsibility alone.

For their own thoughts and other help along the way I also thank Joel's predecessor and successor in my office at the *Times,* John Swansburg and Benjamin Toff. Over the Bush years, a number of friends have generously batted around ideas with me and helped shape my own views—especially Alan Brinkley, Michiko Kakutani, Mark Danner, Jerome Groopman, John Gregory Dunne, Joan Didion, Rich Tafel, Richard Plepler, Suzanne Goodson, Richard Holbrooke, Larry Gelbart, and Rocco and Deb Landesman.

For all the journalistic failures of the past few years, there have been many heroes in the so-called mainstream media who have battled considerable obstacles to ferret out the truth from our culture of truthiness—at the *Times* and many other journalistic institutions. Many of them are cited in the preceding pages; without their reportage, I (and the rest of us) would be in the dark. Nor could I have written this book without the support of Arthur Sulzberger, Jr., and Gail Collins of the *Times*, who, in addition to upholding my independence as a columnist, gave me a leave from the paper so I could step back and write in greater scope about the mix of news and culture that I've been able to pursue in my weekly columns for the paper. They and the *Times'* top editors, led by Bill Keller and Jill Abramson, have been steadfast in supporting the paper's credo of reporting without fear or favor.

At Penguin, I have received invaluable editorial and publishing assistance from Bruce Giffords, Jenna Dolan, Jane Cavolina, Adam Goldberger, Maureen Clark, Christine Tanigawa, Amanda Dewey, Tracy Locke, Sarah Hutson, and Liza Darnton. It's been sheer pleasure and sheer professionalism on a very tight schedule. I also owe personal thanks to Fred Conrad, Edward Keating, Jodi Kantor, Stephanie Goodman, and Darel M. Benaim.

Way back when, I was generously encouraged to expand my writing horizons by (in chronological order) Adam Moss, Leon Wieseltier, Maureen Dowd, Joe Lelyveld, and Howell Raines.

In a class of their own are Arthur Gelb, my mentor and shadow editor since he hired me to work at the *Times* in 1980, and his partner in mentorship and all else, Barbara. If there is such a thing as a life force, Arthur has it, and I am blessed to be within his orbit. I am also blessed with an extraordinary family. My sons, Nathaniel and Simon, were both on the threshold of adulthood as our hometown was attacked on 9/11. This book in many ways expresses experiences and conversations that we shared in the aftermath. The same is true of my wife, Alex Witchel, whose human and intellectual contributions to the making of this book are immeasurable. She is the first reader of everything I write and the sharpest editor anyone could hope for. But most of all I love her for our life together when work is done.

Frank Rich
New York
June 2006

NOTES

1. "HOME TO THE HEARTLAND"

1. Fox News Channel, *Hannity & Colmes*, July 16, 2001.

2. CNN, *Larry King Live*, June 10, 2001.

3. Joshua Green, "The Bookie of Virtue," *Washington Monthly*, June 2003.

4. Jean Christensen, "'Pearl Harbor' Premieres with a Bang," Associated Press, May 22, 2001.

5. Elizabeth Shogren and Greg Miller, "All-Out Attack on Bush Energy Plan Is Readied," *Los Angeles Times*, May 16, 2001.

6. John Gregory Dunne, "Virtual Patriotism: Feeling Good About War," *The New Yorker*, November 16, 1998.

7. Gregory L. Vistica, "What Happened in Thanh Phong," *The New York Times*, April 29, 2001 (published at http://www.nytimes.com on April 26, 2001).

8. "Bush Says Media Have Treated Him Fairly After All," Associated Press, August 26, 1999.

9. Robert Bork, "Slouching Toward Bush Won't Save Us from Gomorrah," *The Wall Street Journal*, October 11, 1999.

10. "Bush Flunks Pop Quiz on Foreign Affairs," Associated Press, November 4, 1999.

11. Allison Mitchell, "Bush Planning to See Voters, and to Be Seen," *The New York Times*, September 8, 2000.

12. Ibid.

13. Nicholas Lemann, "The Redemption," *The New Yorker,* January 31, 2000.

14. Nicholas Kristof, "For Bush, Thrill Was in Father's Chase," *The New York Times,* August 29, 2000.

15. David Brooks, "Texas Ranger: Did Running a Baseball Team Help Prepare George W. Bush to Run America?" *The Weekly Standard,* December 13, 1999.

16. Lloyd Grove, "Renegade Reagan Drubs George W.," *The Washington Post,* August 4, 2000.

17. Michael Ennis, "The Cowboy Myth," *Texas Monthly,* October 2004.

18. Lou Cannon, *President Reagan: The Role of a Lifetime* (New York: PublicAffairs, 2000), p. 182.

19. Bill Minutaglio, *First Son: George W. Bush and the Bush Family Dynasty* (New York: Times Books, 1999), p. 208.

20. Dana Milbank, "Dispelling Doubts with the Rangers," *The Washington Post,* July 25, 2000.

21. Anne E. Kornblut, "Day Mixes Holocaust, 'Tonight Show,'" *The Boston Globe,* March 7, 2000.

22. Peggy Noonan, "After Super Tuesday: Saving Private Bush–Again," *The Wall Street Journal,* March 9, 2000.

23. Brent Staples, "The Republican Party's Exercise in Minstrelsy," *The New York Times,* August 2, 2000.

24. Craig Gordon, "Proposed End to Clinton Policing Initiative," *Newsday,* April 10, 2001.

25. Mike Allen, "Budget Is Democrats' Blueprint for Attacks on Bush," *The Washington Post,* April 15, 2001.

26. Jake Tapper, "Smile and Slash," *Salon,* April 14, 2001.

27. Tim Friend, "Stem-Cell Line Availability Unclear," *USA Today,* August 29, 2001.

2. "DEAD OR ALIVE"

1. "White House Chief of Staff Andrew Card told us he was standing with the President outside the classroom when Senior Advisor to the President Karl Rove first informed them that a small, twin-engine plane had crashed into the World Trade Center. The President's reaction was that the accident must have been caused by pilot error." *The 9/11 Commission Report* (http://www.9-11commission.gov/report/911Report.pdf), p. 35.

2. Bill Sammon, "Suddenly, a Time to Lead; 'Difficult Moment for America' Transforms the President," *The Washington Times,* October 7, 2002.

3. Susan Page, "Crisis Presents Defining Challenge for Bush," *USA Today*, September 12, 2001.

4. Mimi Hall, "'Message' Control Arouses Ire," *USA Today*, October 11, 2001.

5. Eric Alterman, "9/11/01: Where Was George?" *The Nation*, October 6, 2003.

6. Paul Farhi, "'D.C. 9/11' Spins Tale of President on Tragic Day," *The Washington Post*, June 19, 2003.

7. Deborah Potter, "Flagging the Problem," *American Journalism Review*, June 2002.

8. Richard L. Berke and Janet Elder, "Poll Finds Support for War and Fear on Economy," *The New York Times*, September 25, 2001.

9. Ann Coulter, "This Is War," *National Review Online*, September 13, 2001.

10. William Kristol et al., "An Open Letter to the President," *The Weekly Standard*, October 1, 2001.

11. Laurie Goodstein, "Falwell's Finger-Pointing Inappropriate, Bush Says," *The New York Times*, September 15, 2001.

12. "A New Presidency," *The Wall Street Journal*, September 19, 2001.

13. Robert Siegel, "Sayyid Qutb's America," National Public Radio, May 6, 2003.

14. Bill Carter and Felicity Barringer, "In Patriotic Time, Dissent Is Muted," *The New York Times*, September 28, 2001.

15. David S. Broder, "Echoes of Lincoln," *The Washington Post*, September 23, 2001.

16. Caryn James, "A Public Flooded with Images from Friend and Foe Alike," *The New York Times*, October 10, 2001.

17. James Bamford, *A Pretext for War: 9/11, Iraq and the Abuse of America's Intelligence Agencies* (New York: Doubleday, 2004), pp. 295–96.

18. James Dao and Eric Schmitt, "Pentagon Readies Efforts to Sway Sentiment Abroad," *The New York Times*, February 19, 2002.

19. Felicity Barringer, "'Reality TV' About G.I.'s on War Duty," *The New York Times*, February 21, 2002.

20. Doug Struck, "Casualties of U.S. Miscalculations; Afghan Victims of CIA Missile Strike Described as Peasants, Not Al Qaeda," *The Washington Post*, February 11, 2002.

21. Howard Kurtz, "War Coverage Takes a Negative Turn; Civilian Deaths, Military Errors Become Focus as Reporters Revisit Bombing Sites," *The Washington Post*, February 17, 2002.

22. Elisabeth Bumiller, "Administration Won't Allow Generic Versions of Drug," *The New York Times*, October 18, 2001.

23. David Johnston, "Ashcroft Plan Would Recast Justice Dept. in a War Mode," *The New York Times,* November 9, 2001.

24. Josh Tyrangiel et al., "And Justice for . . . ; The White House Wants to Try Terrorists in Secret. Is This Really in America's Best Interest?" *Time,* November 26, 2001.

25. David Cole, "How Not to Fight Terrorism," *The Washington Post,* May 5, 2006.

26. Jim McGee, "Ex-FBI Officials Criticize Tactics on Terrorism; Detention of Suspects Not Effective, They Say," *The Washington Post,* November 28, 2001.

27. Mike Allen and Eric Pianin, "President to Address Safety Fears," *The Washington Post,* November 8, 2001.

28. Mike Schneider, "Travel Industry Using President Bush to Help Promote Tourism," Associated Press, November 19, 2001.

29. Dana Milbank, "A Double-Barreled Attack on Daschle," *The Washington Post,* November 9, 2001.

30. Todd S. Purdum, "Democrats Starting to Fault President on the War's Future," *The New York Times,* March 1, 2002.

31. James Bamford, *A Pretext for War: 9/11, Iraq and the Abuse of America's Intelligence Agencies* (New York: Doubleday, 2004), pp. 295–96.

32. Jonathan S. Landay, "Iraq Intelligence: Defector Lied to U.S. About Weapons," *Detroit Free Press,* May 18, 2004.

3. "I DON'T THINK ANYBODY COULD HAVE PREDICTED . . ."

1. Richard L. Berke, "White House Aides Trying to Balance Attention on Terrorism, the Economy and Politics," *The New York Times,* December 26, 2001.

2. Dan Feldstein, "Lay Cancels Date with Congress; Debacle Forces Sharper Focus on Company Audit Committees," *The Houston Chronicle,* February 4, 2002.

3. "Blackout," *Frontline,* June 5, 2001.

4. Richard L. Berke, "Bush Advisor Suggests War as Campaign Theme," *The New York Times,* January 19, 2002.

5. Richard L. Berke, "White House Aides Trying to Balance Attention on Terrorism, the Economy and Politics," *The New York Times,* December 26, 2001.

6. Barton Gellman and Thomas E. Ricks, "U.S. Concludes Bin Laden Escaped at Tora Bora Fight; Failure to Send Troops in Pursuit Termed Major Error," *The Washington Post,* April 17, 2002.

7. Mike Allen, "GOP Takes in $33 Million at Fundraiser; Dinner Shatters Record; Sept. 11 Photo to Be Sold," *The Washington Post,* May 15, 2002.

8. James Risen and David Johnston, "Agent Complaints Lead F.B.I. Director to Ask for Inquiry," *The New York Times,* May 24, 2002.

9. Mimi Hall, "Poll: USA Less Optimistic on War," *USA Today,* May 31, 2002.

10. Vernon Loeb, "Cheney to Lead Anti-Terrorism Plan Team," *The Washington Post,* May 9, 2001.

11. Barton Gellman, "A Strategy's Cautious Evolution; Before September 11, the Bush Anti-Terror Effort Was Mostly Ambition," *The Washington Post,* January 20, 2002.

12. Andrew C. Revkin, "With White House Approval, E.P.A. Pollution Report Omits Global Warming Section," *The New York Times,* September 15, 2002.

13. Rick Weiss, "HHS Seeks Science Advice to Match Bush Views," *The Washington Post,* September 17, 2002.

14. Jeff Gerth and Don Van Natta, Jr., "In Tough Times, a Company Finds Profits in Terror War," *The New York Times,* July 13, 2002.

15. Floyd Norris, "Corporate Conduct: News Analysis; Hard Talk, Softer Plans," *The New York Times,* July 10, 2002.

16. Patrick McGeehan, "Goldman Chief Urges Reforms in Corporations," *The New York Times,* June 6, 2002.

17. Elisabeth Bumiller and Edmund L. Andrews, "Economic Outlook Is Positive, Bush Tells Texas Forum," *The New York Times,* August 14, 2002.

18. Eric Lichtblau and Charles Piller, "War on Terrorism Highlights FBI's Computer Woes," *Los Angeles Times,* July 28, 2002.

19. Jeanne Cummings, "States Mend Homeland Security Blanket–Local Governments Set Plans Amid Miscommunication with Washington, Lack of Funds," *The Wall Street Journal,* August 13, 2002.

20. Blake Morrison, "Air Marshal Program in Disarray, Insiders Say," *USA Today,* August 15, 2002.

21. Eric Schmitt, "Ashcroft Proposes Rules for Foreign Visitors," *The New York Times,* June 6, 2002.

22. Ed Henry, "Heard on the Hill: Got Plumbers?" *Roll Call,* June 13, 2002.

4. "YOU DON'T INTRODUCE NEW PRODUCTS IN AUGUST"

1. Elisabeth Bumiller, "Bush Aides Set Strategy to Sell Policy on Iraq," *The New York Times,* September 7, 2002.

2. Elisabeth Bumiller, "Keepers of Bush Image Lift Stagecraft to New Heights," *The New York Times,* May 15, 2003.

3. Ibid.

4. Elisabeth Bumiller, "Bush Aides Set Strategy to Sell Policy on Iraq," *The New York Times,* September 7, 2002.

5. Ibid.

6. Ibid.

7. Michael R. Gordon and Judith Miller, "U.S. Says Hussein Intensifies Quest for A-Bomb Parts," *The New York Times,* September 8, 2002.

8. Bob Drogin, "No Leaders of Al Qaeda Found at Guantánamo," *Los Angeles Times,* August 18, 2002.

9. Peter Finn, "Al Qaeda Deputies Harbored by Iran; Pair Are Plotting Attacks, Sources Say," *The Washington Post,* August 28, 2002.

10. Colum Lynch, "War on Al Qaeda Funds Stalled," *The Washington Post,* August 29, 2002.

11. Adam Clymer, "Congress Acts to Authorize War in Gulf," *The New York Times,* January 13, 1991.

12. Alison Mitchell and Carl Hulse, "Congress Authorizes Bush to Use Force Against Iraq, Creating a Broad Mandate," *The New York Times,* October 11, 2002.

13. Brent Scowcroft, "Don't Attack Saddam," *The Wall Street Journal,* August 15, 2002.

14. James A. Baker III, "The Right Way to Change a Regime," *The New York Times,* August 25, 2002.

15. Peggy Noonan, "Time to Put the Emotions Aside," *The Wall Street Journal,* September 11, 2002.

16. CBS News, *Face the Nation,* August 4, 2002.

17. Todd S. Purdum and Patrick E. Tyler, "Top Republicans Break with Bush on Iraq Strategy," *The New York Times,* August 16, 2002.

18. William Kristol, "The Axis of Appeasement," *The Weekly Standard,* August 26–September 2, 2002.

19. Gary Hart and Warren B. Rudman, co-chairs, *America—Still Unprepared, Still in Danger* (New York: Council on Foreign Relations Press, October 2002).

20. NBC News, *NBC Nightly News,* September 7, 2002.

21. The next day a Czech government spokesman partially contradicted the *Times* report, denying that Havel had said this directly to the White House but reaffirming Havel's certainty that there was no factual basis to the Atta-Iraqi connection.

22. Dana Priest and Dan Eggen, "9/11 Probers Say Agencies Failed to Heed Attack Signs," *The Washington Post,* September 19, 2002.

23. Newt Gingrich, "His Heart and Mind," *The Wall Street Journal*, November 27, 2002.

24. From a "Live Online" chat with Woodward at washingtonpost.com, November 19, 2002.

25. Bob Woodward, *Bush at War* (New York: Simon & Schuster, 2002), p. 84.

26. Steven R. Weisman, "Iran Is Going Ahead with Nuclear Plant, Despite U.S. Concerns," *The New York Times*, December 25, 2002.

27. Condoleezza Rice, "Why We Know Iraq Is Lying," *The New York Times*, January 23, 2003.

28. Richard L. Berke and Janet Elder, "Poll Finds Support for War and Fear on Economy," *The New York Times*, September 25, 2001.

29. "CNN/*USA Today*/Gallup: Support for U.S. Ground Troops Invading Iraq at 50% Before Powell Speech; 57% After Speech," *The Hotline*, February 6, 2003.

30. Tom Zeller, "How Americans Link Iraq and Sept. 11," *The New York Times*, March 2, 2003.

31. Michael Crowley, "Bush Eats the Press," *New York Observer*, March 17, 2003.

32. Ibid.

33. Hans Blix, *Disarming Iraq* (New York: Pantheon, 2004).

5. "MISSION ACCOMPLISHED"

1. Lisa de Moraes, "They Gave a War and ABC Hardly Showed Up," *The Washington Post*, March 21, 2003.

2. David Charter, "Movie Men Add Special Effects to Media War," *The Times* of London, March 11, 2003.

3. Bill Carter, "CBS News and White House Differ on Rebutting Hussein," *The New York Times*, February 27, 2003.

4. Matthew Rose and Greg Jaffe, "Here's How a Pentagon Aide Manages to Spin the War," *The Wall Street Journal*, March 21, 2003.

5. Emily Nelson, "Battle for Viewers Colors TV Pictures from Iraq," *The Wall Street Journal*, April 4, 2003.

6. Patrick E. Tyler and Steven Lee Myers, "Allies Strike in Baghdad and Press into Basra," *The New York Times*, April 7, 2003.

7. Sean Aday, "The G-Rated War; The Media Have Covered Up the Casualties—and We've Got the Data to Prove It," Gadflyer.com, April 29, 2004.

8. "Embedded Reporters: What Are Americans Getting?" Project for Excellence in Journalism, April 3, 2003 (http://www.journalism.org).

9. Greg Mitchell, "15 Stories They've Already Bungled," *Editor and Publisher*, March 27, 2003.

10. "The Dyspepsia of Peter Jennings," editorial, *New York Post*, March 23, 2003.

11. Scott Gold, "'I Just Want to Know'; Tired of Waiting for Answers, a Texas Father Tracks Down Iraqi Tape of Dead U.S. Troops," *Los Angeles Times*, April 3, 2003.

12. Sean Aday of George Washington University's School of Media and Public Affairs was a collaborator on this project in addition to the previously cited study of the Iraq War battle coverage.

13. Guy Gugliotta, "Iraq War Could Put Ancient Treasures at Risk," *The Washington Post*, March 3, 2003.

14. Paul Martin, "Troops Were Told to Guard Treasures," *The Washington Times*, April 20, 2003.

15. Guy Gugliotta, "Looted Iraqi Relics Slow to Resurface; Some Famous Pieces Unlikely to Reappear," *The Washington Post*, November 8, 2005.

16. Tom Shales, "Aboard the *Lincoln*, a White House Spectacular," *The Washington Post*, May 2, 2003.

17. Amy Goldstein and Karen DeYoung, "Bush to Say Major Combat Has Ended," *The Washington Post*, May 1, 2003.

18. David E. Sanger, "In Full Flight Regalia, the President Enjoys a 'Top Gun' Moment," *The New York Times*, May 2, 2003.

19. Elisabeth Bumiller, "Keepers of Bush Image Lift Stagecraft to New Heights," *The New York Times*, May 15, 2003.

20. Anna Gorman, "All Hands at Last in Reach of Loving Arms; The *Lincoln* Returns from Extended Mission," *Los Angeles Times*, May 3, 2003.

21. Eric Boehlert, "How the GOP Struck Gold with Its Permanent 'War on Terrorism,'" Salon.com, May 8, 2003.

6. "WE FOUND THE WEAPONS OF MASS DESTRUCTION"

1. Quoted from the Pentagon transcript of the interview, dated May 9, 2003. The language differs slightly in the *Vanity Fair* article.

2. Massimo Calabresi and Timothy J. Burger, "Who Lost the WMD?" *Time*, July 7, 2003.

3. Douglas Jehl, "Agency Disputes C.I.A. View on Trailers as Weapons Labs," *The New York Times*, June 26, 2003.

4. Seymour M. Hersh, "Who Lied to Whom?" *The New Yorker*, March 31, 2003.

5. Walter Pincus, "Report Cast Doubt on Iraq–Al Qaeda Connection," *The Washington Post*, June 22, 2003.

6. Lloyd Grove, "The Reliable Source," *The Washington Post*, July 19, 2003.

7. Judith Miller, "A Chronicle of Confusion in the U.S. Hunt for Hussein's Chemical and Germ Weapons," *The New York Times*, July 20, 2003.

8. Eric Schmitt, "Wolfowitz Sees Challenges, and Vindication, in Iraq," *The New York Times*, July 22, 2003.

9. Amy Waldman, "U.S. 'Still at War,' General Declares; G.I. Dies; 20 Hurt," *The New York Times*, July 4, 2003.

10. "The Frog March of History; The Official Sport of Washington," *The Note*, ABCNews .com, September 29, 2003 (http://www.abcnews.go.com/sections/politics/TheNote/ TheNote_Sep29.html).

11. Richard W. Stevenson and Eric Lichtblau, "President Orders Full Cooperation in Leaking of Name," *The New York Times*, October 1, 2003.

12. CBS News, *Face the Nation*, July 24, 2005.

13. Richard Morin and Dan Balz, "Public Says $87 Billion Too Much," *The Washington Post*, September 14, 2003.

14. Charles J. Hanley, "'Good' News and 'Bad' Battle It Out in Baghdad," Associated Press, October 17, 2003.

15. Jon Anderson, "Full Text of Stripes' Interview with Lt. Gen. Ricardo Sanchez," *Stars and Stripes*, October 15, 2003.

16. Dana Milbank, "Curtains Ordered for Media Coverage of Returning Coffins," *The Washington Post*, October 21, 2003.

17. "Truth, War and Consequences," *Frontline*, October 9, 2003 (a transcript of the program is available at http://www.pbs.org/wgbh/pages/frontline/shows/truth/).

18. Eric Schmitt and Thom Shanker, "A C.I.A. Rival; Pentagon Sets Up Intelligence Unit," *The New York Times*, October 24, 2002.

19. Warren P. Strobel and Jonathan S. Landay, Knight Ridder Newspapers, "Pentagon, CIA Feud over Spy Reports on Iraq," *The Biloxi (Miss.) Sun Herald*, October 25, 2002.

20. Ledyard King, "Same Letter to the Editor Praising Army in Iraq Pops Up Across Nation," Gannett News Service, October 10, 2003.

21. Kevin Freking, "Clark's Jabs Rain on Bush over Iraq; Candidate Caustic About Way of War," *Arkansas Democrat-Gazette*, October 29, 2003.

22. Mike Allen, "Inside Bush's Top-Secret Trip," *The Washington Post*, November 28, 2003.

23. Mike Allen, "The Bird Was Perfect but Not for Dinner," *The Washington Post*, December 4, 2003.

24. Al Kamen, "One Show Turkey and a Lot of Fowl," *The Washington Post*, December 10, 2003.

25. Monica Davey, "Man in the News; 'An Independent Prosecutor'—Patrick J. Fitzgerald," *The New York Times*, December 31, 2003.

7. "SLAM DUNK"

1. Ron Suskind, *The Price of Loyalty: George W. Bush, the White House, and the Education of Paul O'Neill* (New York: Simon & Schuster, 2004), p. 86.

2. John F. Dickerson, "Confessions of a White House Insider," *Time*, January 19, 2004.

3. Rachel Donadio, "Richard Clarke's Unsecret Agent," *New York Observer*, April 5, 2004.

4. Judith Miller, "Former Terrorism Official Faults White House on 9/11," *The New York Times*, March 22, 2004.

5. Scot J. Paltrow, "Government Accounts of 9/11 Reveal Gaps, Inconsistencies," *The Wall Street Journal*, March 22, 2004.

6. Patrick Healy, "Kerry Requests Book on Iraq by Ex-Bush Official," *The Boston Globe*, March 22, 2004.

7. Dana Milbank, "Clarke Stays Cool as Partisanship Heats Up," *The Washington Post*, March 25, 2004.

8. David E. Sanger, "Grisly Deaths Don't Dent an Upbeat Bush Message Stressing Iraq Successes," *The New York Times*, April 2, 2004.

9. Bill Carter and Jacques Steinberg, "Issues of Taste; To Portray the Horror, News Media Agonize," *The New York Times*, April 1, 2004.

10. *CNN Late Edition*, March 14, 2004.

11. Melani McAlister, *Epic Encounters: Culture, Media and U.S. Interests in the Middle East, 1945–2000* (Berkeley and Los Angeles: University of California Press, 2001), p. 208.

12. Jerry Seper, "Survivor Groups Hit for Use of 9/11," *The Washington Times*, May 25, 2004.

13. The release is available at http:news.soc.mil/releases/04APR/040430-01.htm.

14. David Bauder, "CBS News Says It Held Prison Abuse Story," Associated Press, May 3, 2004.

15. A transcript and audio clips are available at Media Matters for America, http://mediamatters.org/items/200405050003.

16. Russ Rizzo, "Affiliate Won't Air 'Nightline,'" *News & Record* (Greensboro, N.C.), April 30, 2004.

17. By the spring of 2006, the number of press casualties in Iraq would nearly double, surpassing both World War II and Vietnam in this grim statistic.

18. Mike Allen, "Cheney Praises Fox News Channel; Vice President Calls Network 'More Accurate' Than Others," *The Washington Post*, April 30, 2004.

19. http://www.thesmokinggun.com/archive/0322061cheney1.html.

20. Peter W. Galbraith, "The Mess," *The New York Review of Books*, March 9, 2006.

21. Robert Collier, "Family Demands the Truth; New Inquiry May Expose Events That Led to Pat Tillman's Death," *San Francisco Chronicle*, September 25, 2005.

22. Josh White, "Tillman's Parents Are Critical of Army," *The Washington Post*, May 23, 2005.

23. Monica Davey and Eric Schmitt, "Army Ordered to Look Again at Battle Death," *The New York Times*, March 5, 2006.

8. "REPORTING FOR DUTY"

1. *CBS Evening News*, March 19, 2004.

2. "Another Look at the Infamous Speech; Being Fair to Howard Dean," *World News Tonight with Peter Jennings*, ABC, January 28, 2004.

3. Steven Thomma, "Massachusetts Senator Announces Bid for 2004 Presidency," Knight Ridder Washington Bureau, September 3, 2003.

4. Matea Gold, "Spotlight Follows Kerry on Day Off," *Los Angeles Times*, March 13, 2004.

5. Michael Dobbs, "Records Counter a Critic of Kerry," *The Washington Post*, August 19, 2004.

6. Kate Zernike and Jim Rutenberg, "Friendly Fire: The Birth of an Attack on Kerry," *The New York Times*, August 20, 2004.

7. Her best-known role is as a scheming teenager in *The World of Henry Orient*, starring Peter Sellers, in 1964. See http://www.imdb.com for Spaeth's complete credits.

8. Kate Zernike and Jim Rutenberg, "Friendly Fire: The Birth of an Attack on Kerry," *The New York Times*, August 20, 2004.

9. Jim Rutenberg and Kate Zernike, "Veterans' Group Had G.O.P. Lawyer," *The New York Times*, August 25, 2004.

10. Elizabeth Jensen, "Conservative TV Group to Air Anti-Kerry Film," *Los Angeles Times*, October 9, 2004.

11. Elizabeth Jensen, "Sinclair Retreats on Kerry Film," *Los Angeles Times*, October 20, 2004.

12. Elisabeth Bumiller, "The President and the Gun: To the Avenger Go the Spoils," *The New York Times*, June 21, 2004.

13. Walter V. Robinson, "1-Year Gap in Bush's Guard Duty; No Record of Airman at Drills in 1972–73," *The Boston Globe*, May 23, 2000.

14. Mike Peters, "Comics, Controversy and Cash: Did You See Bush at Alabama Guard Stint? If So, 'Doonesbury' Creator Will Pay," *The Dallas Morning News*, February 24, 2004.

15. Michael Isikoff and Mark Hosenball, "Terror Watch: The Story That Didn't Run," *Newsweek*, September 22, 2004.

16. Richard T. Cooper, "General Casts War in Religious Terms," *Los Angeles Times*, October 16, 2003.

17. David D. Kirkpatrick, "A Senator's Call to 'Win This Culture War,'" *The New York Times*, September 1, 2004. The quote about the president's "moral clarity" comes from the DVD itself.

18. John F. Dickerson and Karen Tumulty, "Raising the Volume; It's Only March, but It Feels Like September on the Campaign Trail," *Time*, March 22, 2004.

19. Richard W. Stevenson and Eric Lichtblau, "As Ashcroft Warns of Qaeda Plan to Attack U.S., Some Question the Threat and Its Timing," *The New York Times*, May 27, 2004.

20. Ashcroft's "dirty bomb" plot had long since evaporated by the time Padilla was formally charged with lesser crimes in November 2005. See "Terror Suspect Padilla Charged," CNN.com, November 22, 2005.

21. Randall C. Archibold, "Cheney, Invoking the Specter of a Nuclear Attack, Questions Kerry's Strength," *The New York Times*, October 20, 2004.

22. Susan Page, "Poll: Sending Troops to Iraq a Mistake," *USA Today*, June 24, 2004.

23. Dexter Filkins, "General Says Less Coercion of Captives Yields Better Data," *The New York Times*, September 7, 2004.

24. Laurie Goodstein and William Yardley, "President Benefits from Efforts to Build a Coalition of Religious Voters," *The New York Times*, November 5, 2004.

25. Gary Langer, "A Question of Values," *The New York Times*, November 6, 2004.

26. Jeff Jarvis, "The Shocking Truth About the FCC: Censorship by Tyranny of the Few," Buzzmachine.com, November 15, 2004 (http://www.buzzmachine.com/archives/2004_11_15.html).

9. "WHEN WE ACT, WE CREATE OUR OWN REALITY"

1. Doug Halonen, "FCC Is Now 'Pvt. Ryan's' Battleground; Wildmon Lobby Floods Agency with Objections to Language," *Television Week*, November 15, 2004.

2. Laura Parker, "Abuse Trial Focuses Tightly on Graner's Actions," *USA Today*, January 17, 2005.

3. R. Jeffrey Smith and Dan Eggen, "Gonzales Helped Set the Course for Detainees," *The Washington Post*, January 5, 2005.

4. Deb Riechmann, "Bush Travels to California to Address Troops," Associated Press, December 7, 2004.

5. Scott Gold, "Ft. Bliss Training Was Poor, Members of Guard Unit Say," *Los Angeles Times*, December 23, 2004.

6. Robert F. Worth, "Army Punishes 23 for Refusing Convoy Order," *The New York Times*, December 7, 2004.

7. Marni McEntee, "Troops Add Improvised Armor to Humvees," *Stars and Stripes*, February 4, 2004.

8. Joseph A. Reaves, "Valley Firm Disputes Rumsfeld, Is Ready to Supply Army Armor," *The Arizona Republic*, December 10, 2004.

9. Michael Moss, "Safer Vehicles for Soldiers: A Tale of Delays and Glitches," *The New York Times*, June 26, 2005.

10. Michael Moss, "Pentagon Study Links Fatalities to Body Armor," *The New York Times*, January 7, 2006.

11. Roxanne Roberts, "On Inaugural Night, ISO an After-Party with a Pulse," *The Washington Post*, January 22, 2004.

12. Edward Wong, "Pivot Points in the Middle East," *The New York Times*, November 14, 2004.

13. Dexter Filkins and James Glanz, "Rebels Routed in Falluja; Fighting Spreads Elsewhere," *The New York Times*, November 15, 2004.

14. Paul Farhi, "Don't Mind Me. I'm Just Doing My Job," *The Washington Post*, January 30, 2005.

15. James Glanz, William J. Broad, and David E. Sanger, "Huge Cache of Explosives Vanished from Site in Iraq," *The New York Times*, October 25, 2004.

16. Mark Mazzetti, "Soldiers Describe Looting of Explosives," *Los Angeles Times*, November 4, 2004.

17. According to Matthew Bogdanos, the Marine Reserve colonel who led the U.S. hunt for the antiquities looted from the Iraqi museum, that looting, too, contributed di-

rectly to arming terrorists, who bartered the stolen art for munitions. "In my opinion, as a cash source for the terrorists, it ranks just below kidnappings for ransom and on a par with forced donations from local residents and merchants," he wrote. See "The Terrorist in the Art Gallery," *The New York Times,* December 10, 2005.

18. Katharine Q. Seelye, "Newsweek Apologies for Report of Koran Insult," *The New York Times,* May 16, 2005.

19. R. Jeffrey Smith, "Documents Helped Sow Abuse, Army Report Finds; Top Officials Did Not Make Interrogation Policies Clear," *The Washington Post,* August 30, 2004.

20. Mark Danner, *Torture and Truth: America, Abu Ghraib, and the War on Terror* (New York: The New York Review of Books, 2004), p. 176.

21. Neil A. Lewis and Eric Schmitt, "Inquiry Finds Abuses at Guantánamo Bay," *The New York Times,* May 1, 2005.

22. Robin Wright and Al Kamen, "U.S. Outreach to Islamic World Gets Slow Start, Minus Leaders; Effort Involves No Muslims; Hughes Will Not Arrive Until Fall," *The Washington Post,* April 18, 2004.

23. Eric Schmitt, "Military Details Koran Incidents at Base in Cuba," *The New York Times,* June 4, 2005.

24. Robert Pear, "U.S. Videos, for TV News, Come Under Scrutiny," *The New York Times,* March 15, 2004.

25. Mimi Hall, "Homeland Security Guides the Stars," *USA Today,* March 8, 2005.

26. Mike Allen, "Chemical, Nuclear Arms Still 'Major Threat,' Cheney Says; Vice President Decries 'Cheap Shot' Journalism," *The Washington Post,* December 17, 2003.

27. David Corn, "Armstrong Williams: I Am Not Alone," TheNation.com, January 10, 2005.

28. Jim Drinkard and Mark Memmott, "HHS Says It Paid Columnist for Help," *USA Today,* January 28, 2005.

29. David Barstow and Robin Stein, "Under Bush, a New Age of Prepackaged News," *The New York Times,* March 13, 2005.

30. Ibid.

31. Ibid.

32. Ibid.

33. Christopher Lee, "Update: Prepackaged News," *The New York Times,* February 14, 2006.

34. Juliet Eilperin, "U.S. Pressure Weakens G-8 Climate Plan; Global-Warming Science Assailed," *The Washington Post,* June 17, 2005.

35. Andrew C. Revkin, "A Young Bush Appointee Resigns His Post at NASA," *The New York Times,* February 8, 2006.

36. Posted to the Letters section of Romenesko, a media news site at Poynter.org.

37. Jim VandeHei and Peter Baker, "Social Security: On with the Show; President's 'Conversations' on Issue Are Carefully Orchestrated, Rehearsed," *The Washington Post,* March 12, 2005.

38. "Federal Public Relations Spending," U.S. House of Representatives, Committee on Government Reform—Minority Staff, January 2005 (http://www.house.gov/georgemiller/pr_report_final.pdf).

39. Mark Mazzetti and Borzou Daragahi, "U.S. Military Covertly Pays to Run Stories in Iraqi Press," *Los Angeles Times,* November 30, 2005.

10. "I DON'T THINK ANYBODY ANTICIPATED . . ."

1. Valerie Bauerlein, "Jones Sails a Contrarian Course, Scolds Bush, Bucks GOP Leaders," Associated Press, May 17, 2005.

2. *NBC Nightly News with Brian Williams,* June 29, 2005.

3. Douglas Jehl, "Iraq May Be Prime Place for Training of Militants, C.I.A. Report Concludes," *The New York Times,* June 22, 2005. (*Newsweek*'s account was posted on its Web site on June 19, 2005.)

4. Joshua Green, "Karl Rove in a Corner," *The Atlantic Monthly,* November 2004.

5. Walter Pincus and Jim VandeHei, "Plame's Identity Marked as Secret; Memo Central to Probe of Leak Was Written by State Dept. Analyst," *The Washington Post,* July 21, 2004.

6. Matthew Cooper, "What I Told the Grand Jury," *Time,* July 25, 2005.

7. "Government's Response to Defendant's Third Motion to Compel Discovery," *U.S. v. I. Lewis Libby,* April 5, 2006.

8. Walter Pincus, "White House Backs Off Claim on Iraqi Buy," *The Washington Post,* July 8, 2003.

9. "Government's Response to Defendant's Third Motion to Compel Discovery," *U.S. v. I. Lewis Libby,* April 5, 2006.

10. Katherine Shrader, "Intelligence Agencies Said 'Dead Wrong' on Prewar Iraq Intelligence," Associated Press, March 31, 2005.

11. Bob Drogin and John Goetz, "The Curveball Saga; How U.S. Fell Under the Spell of 'Curveball,'" *Los Angeles Times,* November 20, 2005.

12. Murray Waas, "Key Bush Intelligence Briefing Kept from Hill Panel," *National Journal,* November 22, 2005.

13. Nicole Gaouette, "Prewar Claims Set Off Bells," *Los Angeles Times*, November 7, 2005.

14. "Report on the U.S. Intelligence Community's Prewar Intelligence Assessments on Iraq," Select Committee on Intelligence, U.S. Senate, July 7, 2004.

15. Murray Waas, "What Bush Was Told About Iraq," *National Journal*, March 2, 2006.

16. Paul R. Pillar, "Intelligence, Policy, and the War in Iraq," *Foreign Affairs*, March/April 2006.

17. Barton Gellman and Walter Pincus, "Depiction of Threat Outgrew Supporting Evidence," *The Washington Post*, August 10, 2003.

18. James Bamford, "The Man Who Sold the War," *Rolling Stone*, November 17, 2005.

19. John Daniszewski, "Book Casts Doubt on Case for War," *Los Angeles Times*, February 11, 2006.

20. Ibid.

21. Murray Waas, "What Bush Was Told About Iraq," *National Journal*, March 2, 2006.

22. Barton Gellman and Dafna Linzer, "A 'Concerted Effort' to Discredit Bush Critic; Prosecutor Describes Cheney, Libby as Key Voices Pitching Iraq-Niger Story," *The Washington Post*, April 9, 2006.

23. Jim VandeHei and Carol Leonnig, "Woodward Was Told of Plame More Than Two Years Ago," *The Washington Post*, November 16, 2005.

24. Howard Kurtz, "The Man with the Inside Scoop; For Bob Woodward, Proximity to Power Cuts Both Ways," *The Washington Post*, November 28, 2005.

25. Michael Massing, "Now They Tell Us," *The New York Review of Books*, February 26, 2004.

26. Daniel Okrent, "Weapons of Mass Destruction? Or Mass Distraction?" *The New York Times*, May 30, 2004.

27. See Kristina Borjesson, ed., *Feet to the Fire: The Media After 9/11, Top Journalists Speak Out* (Amherst, N.Y.: Prometheus Books, 2005).

28. John F. Burns, Jeffrey Gettleman, and Christine Hauser, "7 U.S. Soldiers Die in Iraq as a Shiite Militia Rises Up," *The New York Times*, April 5, 2004.

29. Angela K. Brown, "Bush Passes War Protesters en Route to Fundraiser," Associated Press, August 12, 2005.

30. Mike Allen and Sam Coates, "Bush Says U.S. Will Stay and Finish Task," *The Washington Post*, August 23, 2005.

31. Jason George, "Recruit Ads Urge Parents to Let Kids Go–into Army; TV Campaign

Hopes to Win Over Skeptical Moms and Dads in Time of War," *Chicago Tribune*, August 13, 2005.

32. http://blogenlust.net/.

33. James Gordon Meek, "W. Dead Wrong on Terror Big, Sez Pro," *Daily News*, September 30, 2005.

34. Scott Shane, "Bush's Speech on Iraq War Echoes Voice of an Analyst," *The New York Times*, December 4, 2005.

35. Johanna Neuman, "Pentagon's 'Freedom Walk' Is a March Along America's Divide; The Rally Marking 9/11 Also Will Honor Troops, a Linkage That Some Find Unsettling or Worse," *Los Angeles Times*, September 11, 2005.

36. Evan Thomas, "How Bush Blew It," *Newsweek*, September 19, 2005.

37. Doug Simpson, "Flood Waters Recede as New Orleans Braces for What Lurks Beneath," Associated Press, September 6, 2005.

38. Lawrence Weschler, "He's the Picture of Racial Compassion," *Los Angeles Times*, May 13, 2004.

39. Lisa Rosetta, "Frustrated: Fire Crews to Hand Out Fliers for FEMA," *The Salt Lake Tribune*, September 6, 2005.

40. R. Jeffrey Smith and Susan Schmidt, "Bush Official Arrested in Corruption Probe," *The Washington Post*, September 20, 2005.

41. "Final Report on 9/11 Commission Recommendations," 9/11 Public Discourse Project, December 5, 2005.

42. Eric Lipton, "White House Was Told Hurricane Posed Danger," *The New York Times*, January 24, 2006.

43. Peter Wallsten and Josh Meyer, "Bush Gives New Details About Old Report of L.A. Terror Plot," *Los Angeles Times*, February 10, 2006.

44. Peter Baker and Josh White, "Bush Calls Iraq War Moral Equivalent of Allies' WWII Fight Against the Axis," *The Washington Post*, August 31, 2005.

EPILOGUE: THE GREATEST STORY EVER SOLD

1. Thomas Frank, "Costs to Rebuild Shifting to Iraqis; $21 Billion U.S. Effort to End Short of Goals," *USA Today*, March 24, 2006; Nina Kamp, Michael O'Hanlon, and Amy Unikewicz, "Op-Chart; The State of Iraq: An Update," *The New York Times*, March 19, 2006.

2. Barbara Slavin, "Giant U.S. Embassy Rising in Baghdad," *USA Today*, April 19, 2006.

3. Ellen Knickmeyer, "U.S. Plan to Build Iraq Clinics Falters; Contractor Will Try to Finish 20 of 142 Sites," *The Washington Post*, April 3, 2006.

4. Andrew Zajac, "Lobbyist Ashcroft Pulls in $269,000; Clients Capitalize on Policies He Promoted," *Chicago Tribune*, January 10, 2006.

5. Lowell Bergman, Eric Lichtblau, Scott Shane, and Don Van Natta, Jr., "Spy Agency Data After Sept. 11 Led FBI to Dead Ends," *The New York Times*, January 17, 2006. This article was a follow-up to the original James Risen–Eric Lichtblau story on NSA surveillance.

6. David E. Sanger and Thom Shanker, "On Anniversary, Bush and Cheney See Iraq Success," *The New York Times*, March 20, 2006.

7. George F. Will, "Rhetoric of Unreality; Where Is Iraq After Nearly 3 Years of War?" *The Washington Post*, March 2, 2006.

8. Michael Hirsh, "Clumsy Leadership," MSNBC.com, February 22, 2006.

9. George Packer, *The Assassins' Gate: America in Iraq* (New York: Farrar, Straus and Giroux, 2005), p. 119.

10. George Packer, "Dreaming of Democracy," *The New York Times Magazine*, March 2, 2003.

11. Ariana Eunjung Cha, "In Iraq, the Job Opportunity of a Lifetime; Managing a $13 Billion Budget with No Experience," *The Washington Post*, May 23, 2004.

12. Michael R. Gordon and General Bernard E. Trainor, *Cobra II: The Inside Story of the Invasion and Occupation of Iraq* (New York: Pantheon Books, 2006), pp. 475–76.

13. The definitive account of this history is James Mann, *Rise of the Vulcans: The History of Bush's War Cabinet* (New York: Viking, 2004).

14. Peter Bergen, "Enemy of Our Enemy," *The New York Times*, March 28, 2006.

15. Bob Drogin and Tom Hamburger, "Niger Uranium Rumors Wouldn't Die," *Los Angeles Times*, February 17, 2006.

16. Lt. Gen. Gregory Newbold, "Why I Think Rumsfeld Must Go," Time.com, April 9, 2006.

17. Joby Warrick, "Lacking Biolabs, Trailers Carried Case for War; Administration Pushed Notion of Banned Iraqi Weapons Despite Evidence to Contrary," *The Washington Post*, April 12, 2006.

18. Murray Waas, "Libby Says Bush Authorized Leaks," *National Journal*, April 6, 2006.

19. See "Liberal Hawks Reconsider the Iraq War," *Slate*, January 12–16, 2004.

INDEX

ABOUT THE AUTHOR

Frank Rich became a *New York Times* Op-Ed columnist in 1994 after serving for thirteen years as the newspaper's chief drama critic. He has written about culture and politics for many other publications and was on the staffs of *Time,* the *New York Post,* and *New Times* magazine after starting his career as a founding editor of *The Richmond Mercury,* a weekly newspaper, in the early 1970s. He is the author of *Ghost Light,* a childhood memoir; *Hot Seat: Theater Criticism for* The New York Times, *1980–1993;* and *The Theatre Art of Boris Aronson,* co-authored with Lisa Aronson. A native of Washington, D.C., he lives in Manhattan with his wife, the author Alex Witchel, who is a reporter for *The New York Times.*